Folklore as an Historical Science

George Laurence Gomme

PREFACE

If I have essayed to do in this book what should have been done by one of the masters of the science of folklore—Mr. Frazer, Mr. Lang, Mr. Hartland, Mr. Clodd, Sir John Rhys, and others—I hope it will not be put down to any feelings of self-sufficiency on my part. I have greatly dared because no one of them has accomplished, and I have so acted because I feel the necessity of some guidance in these matters, and more particularly at the present stage of inquiry into the early history of man.

I have thought I could give somewhat of that guidance because of my comprehension of its need, for the comprehension of a need is sometimes half-way towards supplying the need. My profound belief in the value of folklore as perhaps the only means of discovering the earliest stages of the psychological, religious, social, and political history of modern man has also entered into my reason for the attempt.

Many years ago I suggested the necessity for guidance, and I sketched out a few of the points involved (*Folklore Journal*, ii. 285, 347; iii. 1-16) in what was afterwards called by a friendly critic a sort of grammar of folklore. The science of folklore has advanced far since 1885 however, and not only new problems but new ranges of thought have gathered round it. Still, the claims of folklore as a definite section of historical material remain not only unrecognised but unstated, and as long as this is so the lesser writers on folklore will go on working in wrong directions and producing much mischief, and the historian will judge of folklore by the criteria presented by these writers—will judge wrongly and will neglect folklore accordingly.

I hope this book may tend to correct this state of things to some extent. It is not easy to write on such a subject in a limited space, and it is difficult to avoid being somewhat severely technical at points. These demerits will, I am sure, be forgiven when considered by the light of the human interest involved.

All studies of this kind must begin from the standpoint of a definite culture area, and I have chosen our own country for the purpose of this inquiry. This will make the illustrations more interesting to the English reader; but it must be borne in mind that the same process could be repeated for other areas if my estimate of the position is even tolerably accurate. For the purpose of this estimate it was necessary, in the first place, to show how pure history was intimately related to folklore at many stages, and yet how this relationship had been ignored by both historian and folklorist. The research for this purpose had necessarily to deal with much detail, and to introduce fresh elements of research. There is thus produced a somewhat unequal treatment; for when illustrations have to be worked out at length, because they appear for the first time, the mind is apt to wander from the main point at issue and to become lost in the subordinate issue arising from the working out of the chosen illustration. This, I fear, is inevitable in folklore research, and I can only hope I have overcome some of the difficulties caused thereby in a fairly satisfactory manner.

The next stage takes us to a consideration of materials and methods, in order to show the means and definitions which are necessary if folklore research is to be conducted on scientific lines. Not only is it necessary to ascertain the proper position of each item of folklore in the culture area in which it is found, but it is also necessary to ascertain its scientific relationship to other items found in the same area; and I have protested against the too easy attempt to proceed upon the comparative method. Before we can compare we must be certain that we are comparing like quantities.

These chapters are preliminary. After this stage we proceed to the principal issues, and the first of these deals with the psychological conditions. It was only necessary to treat of this subject shortly, because the illustrations of it do not need analysis. They are self-contained, and supply their own evidence as to the place they occupy.

The anthropological conditions involve very different treatment. The great fact necessary to bear in mind is that the people of a modern culture area have an anthropological as well as a national or political history, and that it is only the anthropological history which can explain the meaning and existence of folklore. This subject found me compelled to go rather more deeply than I had thought would be necessary into first principles, but I hope I have not altogether failed to prove that to properly understand the province of folklore it is necessary to know something of anthropological research and

4

its results. In point of fact, without this consideration of folklore, there is not much value to be obtained from it. It is not because it consists of traditions, superstitions, customs, beliefs, observances, and what not, that folklore is of value to science. It is because the various constituents are survivals of something much more essential to mankind than fragments of life which for all practical purposes of progress might well disappear from the world. As survivals, folklore belongs to anthropological data, and if, as I contend, we can go so far back into survivals as totemism, we must understand generally what position totemism occupies among human institutions, and to understand this we must fall back to human origins.

The next divisions are more subordinate. Sociological conditions must be studied apart from their anthropological aspect, because in the higher races the social group is knit together far more strongly and with far greater purpose than among the lower races. The social force takes the foremost place among the influences towards the higher development, and it is necessary not only to study this but to be sure of the terms we use. Tribe, clan, family, and other terms have been loosely used in anthropology, just as state, city, village, and now village-community, are loosely used in history. The great fact to understand is that the social group of the higher races was based on blood kinship at the time when they set out to take their place in modern civilisation, and that we cannot understand survivals in folklore unless we test them by their position as part of a tribal organisation. The point has never been taken before, and yet I do not see how it can be dismissed.

The consideration of European conditions is chiefly concerned with the all-important fact of an intrusive religion, that of Christianity, from without, destroying the native religions with which it came into contact, conditions which would of course apply only to the folklore of European countries.

Finally, I have discussed ethnological conditions in order to show that certain fundamental differences in folklore can be and ought to be explained as the results of different race origins. We are now getting rid of the notion that all Europe is peopled by the descendants of the so-called Aryans. There is too much evidence to show that the still older races lived on after they were conquered by Celt, Teuton, Scandinavian, or Slav, and there is no reason why folklore should not share with language, archæology, and physical type the inheritance from this earliest race.

In this manner I have surveyed the several conditions attachable to the study of folklore and the various departments of science with which it is inseparably associated. Folklore cannot be studied alone. Alone it is of little worth. As part of the inheritance from bygone ages it cannot separate itself from the conditions of bygone ages. Those who would study it carefully, and with purpose, must consider it in the light which is shed by it and upon it from all that is contributory to the history of man.

During my exposition I have ventured upon many criticisms of masters in the various departments of knowledge into which I have penetrated; but in all cases with great respect. Criticism, such as I have indulged in, is nothing more than a respectful difference of opinion on the particular points under discussion, and which need every light which can be thrown upon them, even by the humblest student.

I am particularly obliged to Mr. Lang, Mr. Hartland, Dr. Haddon, and Dr. Rivers, for kindly reading my chapter on Anthropological Conditions, and for much valuable and kind help therein; and especially I owe Mr. Lang most grateful thanks, for he took an immense deal of trouble and gave me the advantage of his searching criticism, always in the direction of an endeavour to perfect my faulty evidence. I shall not readily part with his letters and MS. on this subject, for they show alike his generosity and his brilliance.

To my old friend Mr. Fairman Ordish I am once more indebted for help in reading my sheets, and I am also glad to acknowledge the fact that two of my sons, Allan Gomme and Wycombe Gomme, have read my proofs and helped me much, not only by their criticism, but by their knowledge.

24 Dorset Square, N.W.

FOLKLORE AS AN HISTORICAL SCIENCE

Chapter I

HISTORY AND FOLKLORE

It may be stated as a general rule that history and folklore are not considered as complementary studies. Historians deny the validity of folklore as evidence of history, and folklorists ignore the essence of history which exists in folklore. Of late years it is true that Dr. Frazer, Prof. Ridgeway, Mr. Warde Fowler, Miss Harrison, Mr. Lang, and others have broken through this antagonism and shown that the two studies stand together; but this is only in certain special directions, and no movement is apparent that the brilliant results of special inquiries are to bring about a general consideration of the mutual help which the two studies afford, if in their respective spheres the evidence is treated with caution and knowledge, and if the evidence from each is brought to bear upon the necessities of each.

The necessities of history are obvious. There are considerable gaps in historical knowledge, and the further back we desire to penetrate the scantier must be the material at the historian's disposal. In any case there can be only two considerable sources of historical knowledge, namely, foreign and native. Looking at the subject from the points presented by the early history of our own country, there are the Greek and Latin writers to whom Britain was a source of interest as the most distant part of the then known world, and the native historians, who, witnessing the terribly changing events which followed the break-up of the Roman dominion over Britain, recorded their views of the changes and their causes, and in course of time recorded also some of the events of Celtic history and of Anglo-Saxon history. Then for later periods, no country of the Western world possesses such magnificent materials for history as our own. In the vast quantity of public and private documents which are gradually being made accessible to the student there exists material for the illustration and elucidation of almost every side and every period of national life, and no branch of historical research is more fruitful of results than the comparison of the records of the professed historian with the documents which have not come from the historian's hands.

All this, however, does not give us the complete story. Necessarily there are great and important gaps. Contemporary writers make themselves the judges of what is important to record; documents preserved in public or private archives relate only to such events as need or command the written record or instrument, or to those which have interested some of the actors and their families. Hence in both departments of history, the historical narrative and the original record, it will be found on careful examination that much is needed to make the picture of life complete. It is the detail of everyday thought and action that is missing—all that is so well known, the obvious as it passes before every chronicler, the ceremony, the faith, and the action which do not apparently affect the movements of civilisation, but which make up the personal, religious and political life of the people. It is always well to bear in mind that the historical records preserved from the past must necessarily be incomplete. An accident preserves one, and an accident destroys another. An incident strikes one historian, and is of no interest to another. And it may well be that the lost document, the unrecorded incident, is of far more value to later ages than what has been preserved. This condition of historical research is always present to the scientific student, though it is not always brought to bear upon the results of historical scholarship.[1] But the scope of the historian is gradually but surely widening. It is no longer possible to shut the door to geography, ethnography, economics, sociology, archæology, and the attendant studies if the historian desires to work his subject out to the full.[2] It is even getting to be admitted that an appeal must be made to folklore, though the extent and the method are not understood. After all that can be obtained from other realms of knowledge, it is seen that there is a large gap left still—a gap in the heart of things, a gap waiting to be filled by all that can be learned about the thought, ideas, beliefs, conceptions, and aspirations of the people which have been translated for them, but not by them, in the laws, institutions, and religion which find their way so easily into history.

The necessities of folklore are far greater than and of a different kind from those of history. Edmund Spenser wrote three centuries ago "by these old customs the descent of nations can only be proved where other monuments of writings are not remayning,"[3] and yet the descent of nations is still being proved without the aid of folklore. It is certain that the appeal will not be made to its fullest extent unless the folklorist makes it clear that it will be answered in a fashion which commands attention. It appears to me that the preliminary conditions for such an appeal must be ascertained from the folklore side. History has not only justified its existence, but during the long period of years during which it has been a specific branch of learning it has shown its capacity for proceeding on strictly scientific and ever-widening lines. Folklore has neither had a long period for its study nor a completely satisfactory record of scientific work. It is, therefore, essential that folklore should establish its right to a place among the historical sciences. At present that right is not admitted. It is objected to by scholars who will not admit that history can proceed from anything but a dated and certified document, and by a few who do not admit that history has anything to do with affairs that do not emanate from the prominent political or military personages of each period. It is silently, if not contemptuously ignored by almost every historical inquirer whose attention has not been specially directed to the evidence contained in traditional material. Thus between the difficulties arising from the interpretation of texts which, originating in oral tradition, have by reason of their early record become literature, and the difficulties arising from the objections of historians to accept any evidence that is not strictly historical in the form they assume to be historical, traditional material has not been extensively used as history. It has also been wrongly defined by historians. Thus, to give a pertinent example, so good a scholar as Mr. W. H. Stevenson, in his admirable edition of Asser's *Life of King Alfred*, lays to the crimes of tradition an error which is due to other causes. Indeed, he states the cause of the error correctly, but does not see that he is contradicting himself in so doing. It is worth quoting this case. It has to do with the identification of "Cynuit," a place where the Danes obtained a victory over the English forces, and Kenwith Castle in Devonshire has been claimed as the site of the struggle and "a place known as Bloody Corner in Northam is traditionally regarded as the scene of a duel between two of the chieftains in 877, and a monument recording the battle has been erected."[4] Mr. Stevenson's comment upon this is: "We have in this an instructive example of the worthlessness of 'tradition' which is here, as so frequently happens elsewhere, the outcome of the dreams of local antiquaries, whose identifications become gradually impressed upon the memory of the inhabitants;" and he then proceeds to show that this particular tradition was produced by the suggestion of Mr. R. S. Vidal in 1804. Of course, the answer of the folklorist to this charge against the value of tradition is that the example is not a case of tradition[5] at all. On the contrary, it is a case of false history, started by the local antiquary, adopted by the scholars of the day, perpetuated by the government in its ordnance survey of the district, and kept alive in the minds of the people not by tradition but by a duly certified monument erected for the express purpose of commemorating the invented incident. There is then no tradition in any one of the stages through which the episode has passed. It is all history and false history. Historians cannot shake off their responsibilities by looking upon the local antiquary as the responsible author of tradition. They cannot but admit that the local antiquary belongs to the historical school, even though he is not a fully equipped member of his craft, and because he blunders they must not class him as a folklorist. They must bring better evidence than this to show the worthlessness of tradition. In the meantime it is the constant definition of tradition as worthless, the relegation of worthless history "to the realms of folklore,"[6] which does so much harm to the study of folklore as a science.[7] Because the historian misnames an historical error as tradition, or fails to discover, at the moment he requires it, the fact which lies hidden in tradition, he must not dismiss the whole realm of tradition as useless for historical purposes.

Let us freely admit that the historian is not altogether to blame for his neglect and for his ignorance of tradition as historical material. He has nothing very definite to work upon. Even the great work of Grimm is open to the criticism that it does not *prove* the antiquity of popular custom and belief—it merely states the proposition, and then relies for proof upon the accumulation of an enormous number of examples and the almost entire impossibility of suggesting any other origin than that of antiquity for such a mass of non-Christian material. Then the great work of Grimm, ethnographical in its methods, has never been followed up by similar work for other countries. The philosophy of folklore has taken up almost all the time of our scholars and students, and the contribution it makes to the history of the civilised races has not been made out by folklorists themselves. It does not appear to me to be difficult to make out such a claim if only

11

scientific methods are adopted, and the solution of definite problems is attempted;[8] and if too the difficulties in the way of proof are freely admitted, and where they become insuperable, the attempt at proof is frankly abandoned. I believe that every single item of folklore, every folk-tale, every tradition, every custom and superstition, has its origin in some definite fact in the history of man; but I am ready to concede that the definite fact is not always traceable, that it sometimes goes so far back as to defy recognition, that it sometimes relates to events which have no place in the after-history of peoples who have taken a position on the earth's surface, and which, in the prehistory stage, belong to humanity rather than to peoples. Folklore, too, is governed by its own laws and rules which are not the laws and rules of history. These concessions, however, do not mean the introduction of the term "impossible" to our studies. They mean rather a plea for the steady and systematic study of our material, on the ground that it has much to yield to the historian of man, and to the historians of races, of peoples, of nations, and of countries.

Carved wooden figure of the pedlar in Swaffham Church.

Carved wooden figure of the pedlar's dog in Swaffham Church. **CARVED WOODEN FIGURES IN SWAFFHAM CHURCH, NORFOLK**

We cannot, however, show that this is so without facing many difficulties created for the most part by folklorists themselves. In the first place it is necessary to overtake some of the earlier conclusions of the great masters of our science. The first rush, after the discovery of the mine, led to the vortex created by the school of comparative mythologists, who limited their comparison to the myths of Aryan-speaking people, who absolutely ignored the evidence of custom, rite, and belief, and who could see nothing beyond interpretations of the sun, dawn, and sky gods in the parallel stories they were the first to discover and value. We need not ignore all this work, nor need we be ungrateful to the pioneers who executed it. It was necessary that their view should be stated, and it is satisfactory that it was stated at a time early in the existence of our science, because it is possible to clear it all away, or as much of it as is necessary, without undue interference with the material of which it is composed.

The school of comparative mythologists did not, however, entirely control the early progress of the study of folklore. There was always a school who believed in the foundation of myth being derived from the facts of life. Thus Dr. Tylor, in a remarkable study of historical traditions and myths of observation,[9] long ago noted that many of the traditions current among mankind were historical in origin. Writing nearly forty years ago, he had to submit to the influence, then at its height, of Adalbert Kuhn and Max Müller, and he conceded that there were many traditions which were fictional myths. I think this concession must now be much more narrowly scrutinised, and preparation made for the conclusion that every genuine myth is a myth of observation, the observation by men in a primitive state of culture, of a fact which had struck home to their minds. The question is, to what part of human history does the central fact appertain? Here is undoubtedly a most difficult problem. What the student has to do is to admit the difficulty, and to state, if necessary, that the fact preserved by tradition is not in all cases possible to discover with our present knowledge. This is a perfectly tenable position. Human imagination cannot invent anything that is outside of fact. It may, and of course too frequently does, misinterpret facts. In attempting to explain and account for such facts with insufficient knowledge, it gets far away from the truth, but this misinterpretation of fact must not be confused with the fact itself. In a word, it must be borne in mind by the student of tradition that every tradition which has assumed the form of saga, myth, or story contains two perfectly independent elements—the fact upon which it is founded, and the interpretation of the fact which its founders have attempted.

There is further than this. The other branch of traditional material, namely that relating to custom, belief, and rite, rests upon a solid basis of historic fact; customs which are strange and irrational to this age are not in consequence to be considered the mere worthless following of practices which owe their origin to accident or freak; beliefs which do not belong to the established religion are not in consequence to be considered as mere superstition; rites which were not established by authority are not in consequence to be classed as mere specimens of popular ignorance. But the difficulties in the way of getting all this accepted by the historian are many, and, again, not a few of them are the creation of the folklorist himself. Not only has he neglected to classify and arrange the scattered items of custom, belief, and rite, and to ascertain the degree of association which the scattered items have with each other, but he has set about the far more difficult and complex task of comparative study without having previously prepared his material.

The historian and the folklorist are thus brought face to face with what is expected from both, in order that each may work alongside of the other, using each other's materials and conclusions at the right moment and in the right places. The folklorist has the most to do to get his results ready, and to explain and secure his position. He has been wandering about in a somewhat inconsequential fashion, bent upon finding a *mythos* where he should have sought for a *persona* or a *locus*, engaged in an extensive quest after parallels when he should have been preparing his own material for the process of comparative science, seeking for origins amidst human error when he should have turned to human experience. He has to change all this waywardness for systematic study, and this will lead him in the first place to disengage from the results hitherto obtained those which may be accepted and which may form the starting-point for future work. But his greatest task will be the reconsideration of former results and the rewriting of much that has been written on the wrong lines, and when this is done we shall have the historian and folklorist meeting together in the spirit which Edmund Spenser so finely and truly described three centuries ago in his treatment of Irish history: "I do herein rely upon those bards or Irish chronicles ... but unto them besides I add mine own reading and out of them both together with comparison of times likewise of manners and customs, affinity of words and manner, properties of natures and uses, resemblances of rites and ceremonies, monuments of churches and tombs and many other like circumstances I do gather a likelihood of truth, not certainly affirming anything, but by conferring of times language monuments and such like I do hunt out a probability of things which I leave to your judgment to believe or refuse."[10]

I shall of course not be able to undertake either of these tasks. I shall attempt, however, to indicate their scope and importance; and as a preliminary to the consideration of the definite departments into which the subject falls, it is advisable, I think, to test the relationship of tradition to history by means of one or two illustrations. It may be that the illustrations I shall give are not accepted by all students, that some better illustration is forthcoming by further research. This is one of the drawbacks from which tradition suffers, and must suffer, until our studies are much further advanced than they are at present. But I am glad to accept this possibility of error as part of the case for the study of tradition, because the error of one student cannot be held to disqualify the whole subject. It only amounts to saying that the particular fact which seems to me to be discoverable in the examples dealt with has to be surrendered in favour of another particular fact. My conclusions may be dismissed, but that which is not dismissible is the discoverable fact, and it is only when the true fact is discovered in each traditional item that previous inferences may be neglected or ignored and inquiry cease.[11]

I

The evidence of historic events which enter into tradition relates principally to the earliest periods, but much of it relates to periods well within the domain of history and yet reveals facts which history has either hopelessly neglected or misinterpreted. We shall find that these facts, though frequently relating to minor events, often have reference to matters of the highest national importance, and perhaps nowhere more definitely is this the case than in the legends connected with particular localities. Of one such tradition I will state what a somewhat detailed examination tells in this direction. It will, I think, serve as a good example of the kind of research that is required in each case, and it will illustrate in a rather special manner the value of these traditions to history.

The *locus* of the legend centres round London Bridge. The earliest written version of this legend is quoted from the MSS. of Sir Roger Twysden,

15

who obtained it from "Sir William Dugdale, of Blyth Hall, in Warwickshire, in a letter dated 29th January, 1652-3." Sir William says of it that "it was the tradition of the inhabitants as it was told me there," and Sir Roger Twysden adds of it that: "I have since learnt from others to be most true." This, therefore, is a very respectable origin for the legend, and I will transcribe it from Sir William Dugdale's letter which begins "the story of the Pedlar of Swaffham-market is in substance this":—

"That dreaming one night if he went to London he should certainly meet with a man on London Bridge which would tell him good news he was so perplext in his mind that till he set upon his journey he could have no rest; to London therefore he hasts and walk'd upon the Bridge for some hours where being espyed by a shopkeeper and asked what he wanted he answered you may well ask me that question for truly (quoth he) I am come hither upon a very vain errand and so told the story of his dream which occasioned the journey. Whereupon the shopkeeper reply'd alas good friend should I have heeded dreams I might have proved myself as very a fool as thou hast, for 'tis not long since that I dreamt that at a place called Swaffham Market in Norfolk dwells one John Chapman a pedlar who hath a tree in his backside under which is buried a pot of money. Now therefore if I should have made a journey thither to day for such hidden treasure judge you whether I should not have been counted a fool. To whom the pedlar cunningly said yes verily I will therefore return home and follow my business not heeding such dreams hence forward. But when he came home being satisfied that his dream was fulfilled he took occasion to dig in that place and accordingly found a large pot of money which he prudently conceal'd putting the pot amongst the rest of his brass. After a time it happen'd that one who came to his house and beholding the pot observed an inscription upon it which being in Latin he interpreted it that under that there was an other twice as good. Of this inscription the Pedlar was before ignorant or at least minded it not but when he heard the meaning of it he said 'tis very true in the shop where I bought this pot stood another under it which was twice as big; but considering that it might tend to his further profit to dig deeper in the same place where he found that he fell again to work and discover'd such a pot as was intimated by the inscription full of old coins: notwithstanding all which he so conceal'd his wealth that the neighbours took no notice of it."[12]

Blomefield thought it "somewhat surprising to find such considerable persons as Sir William Dugdale and Sir Roger Twysden to patronise or credit such a monkish legend and tradition savouring so much of the cloister, and that the townsmen and neighbourhood should also believe it," but I think we shall have reason to congratulate ourselves that so good a folk-tale was preserved for us of this age.

The next and, it appears, an independent version, is given in the *Diary of Abraham de la Pryme*, under the date November 10th, 1699:—

"Constant tradition says that there lived in former times, in Soffham (Swaffham), *alias* Sopham, in Norfolk, a certain pedlar, who dreamed that if he went to London bridge, and stood there, he should hear very joyfull newse, which he at first sleighted, but afterwards, his dream being dubled and trebled upon him, he resolv'd to try the issue of it, and accordingly went to London, and stood on the bridge there two or three days, looking about him, but heard nothing that might yield him any comfort. At last it happen'd that a shopkeeper there, hard by, haveing noted his fruitless standing, seeing that he neither sold any wares nor asked any almes, went to him and most earnestly begged to know what he wanted there, or what his business was; to which the pedlar honestly answer'd, that he had dream'd that if he came to London and stood there upon the bridg, he should hear good newse; at which the shopkeeper laught heartily, asking him if he was such a fool as to take a journey on such a silly errand, adding, 'I'll tell thee, country fellow, last night I dream'd that I was at Sopham, in Norfolk, a place utterly unknown to me, where methought behind a pedlar's house in a certain orchard, and under a great oak tree, if I digged I should find a vast treasure! Now think you,' says he, 'that I am such a fool to take such a long jorney upon me upon the instigation of a silly dream? No, no, I'm wiser. Therefore, good fellow, learn witt of me, and get you home, and mind your business.' The pedlar, observeing his words, what he had sayd he had dream'd and knowing they concenterd in him, glad of such joyfull newse went speedily home, and digged and found a prodigious great treasure, with which he grew exceeding rich, and Soffham church being for the most part fal'n down he set on workmen and reedifyd it most sumptuously, at his own charges; and to this day there is his statue therein, cut in stone, with his pack at his back, and his dogg at his heels; and his memory is also preserved by the same form or picture in most of the old glass windows, taverns, and ale-houses of that town unto this day."[13]

Now this version from Abraham de la Pryme was certainly obtained from local sources, and it shows the general popularity of the legend, together with the faithfulness of the traditional version.[14] But other evidence of the traditional force of the story is to be found. Observing that De la Pryme's *Diary* was not printed until 1870, though certainly the MS. had been lent to antiquaries, it is curious that the following almost identical account is told in the *St. James's Chronicle* of November 28th, 1786:—[15]

"A Pedlar who lived many Years ago at Swaffham, in Norfolk, dreamt, that if he came up to London, and stood upon the Bridge, he should hear very joyful News; which he at first slighted, but afterwards his Dream being doubled and trebled unto him, he resolved to try the Issue of it; and accordingly to London he came, and stood on the Bridge for two or three Days, but heard nothing which might give him Comfort that the Profits of his Journey would be equal to his Pains. At last it so happened, that a Shopkeeper there, having noted his fruitless standing, seeing that he neither sold any Wares, or asked any Alms, went to him, and enquired his Business; to which the Pedlar made Answer, that being a Countryman, he had dreamt a Dream, that if he came up to London, he should hear good News: 'And art thou (said the Shopkeeper) such a Fool, to take a Journey on such a foolish Errand? Why I tell thee this—last Night I dreamt, that I was at Swaffham, in Norfolk, a Place utterly unknown to me, where, methought, behind a Pedlar's House, in a certain Orchard, under a great Oak Tree, if I digged there, I should find a mighty Mass of Treasure. Now think you, that I am so unwise, as to take so long a Journey upon me, only by the Instigation of a foolish Dream! No, no, far be such Folly from me; therefore, honest Countryman, I advise thee to make haste Home again, and do not spend thy precious Time in the Expectation of the Event of an idle Dream.' The Pedlar, who noted well his Words, glad of such joyful News, went speedily Home, and digged under the Oak, where he found a very large Heap of Money; with Part of which, the Church being then lately fallen down, he very sumptuously rebuilt it; having his Statue cut therein, in Stone, with his Pack on his Back and his Dog at his Heels, which is to be seen at this Day. And his Memory is also preserved by the same Form, or Picture, on most of the Glass Windows of

18

the Taverns and Ale-houses in that Town."

The differences in these versions are sufficient to show independent origin. The identities are sufficient to illustrate, in a rather remarkable manner, how closely the words of the tradition were always followed. It appears from the last words of the contributor to the *St. James's Chronicle*, who signed himself "Z," that he heard it by word of mouth about the time of his writing it down,[16] so that there is more than a hundred years between him and the Dugdale version, which was also recorded from "constant tradition."

In Glyde's *Norfolk Garland* (p. 69), is an account of this legend, but with a variant of one incident. The box containing the treasure had a Latin inscription on the lid, which John Chapman could not decipher. He put the lid in his window, and very soon he heard some youths turn the Latin sentence into English:—

"Under me doth lie Another much richer than I."

And he went to work digging deeper than before, and found a much richer treasure than the former. Another version of this rhyme is found in *Transactions of the Cambridge Antiquarian Society* (iii. 318) as follows:—

"Where this stood Is another as good."

And both these versions are given by Blomefield.

Now if there were no other places besides Swaffham in Norfolk to which this legend is applied the interest in it would, of course, not be very great. But there are many other places, and we will first note those in Britain. The best is from Upsall, in Yorkshire, as follows:—

"Many years ago there resided, in the village of Upsall, a man who dreamed three nights successively that if he went to London Bridge he would hear of something greatly to his advantage. He went, travelling the whole distance from Upsall to London on foot; arrived there, he took his station on the bridge, where he waited until his patience was nearly exhausted, and the idea that he had acted a very foolish part began to rise in his mind. At length he was accosted by a Quaker, who kindly inquired what he was waiting there so long for? After some hesitation, he told his dreams. The Quaker laughed at his simplicity, and told him that *he* had had last night a very curious dream himself, which was, that if he went and dug under a certain bush in Upsall Castle, in Yorkshire, he would find a pot of gold; but he did not know where Upsall was, and inquired of the countryman if he knew, who, seeing some advantage in secrecy, pleaded ignorance of the locality, and then, thinking his business in London was completed, returned immediately home, dug beneath the bush, and there he found a pot filled with gold, and on the cover an inscription in a language which he did not understand. The pot and cover were, however, preserved at the village inn, where one day a bearded stranger like a Jew, made his appearance, saw the pot, and read the inscription on the cover, the plain English of which was—

"'Look lower, where this stood Is another twice as good.'

The man of Upsall hearing this resumed his spade, returned to the bush, dug deeper, and found another pot filled with gold, far more valuable than the first. Encouraged by this discovery, he dug deeper still, and found another yet more valuable.

"This is the constant tradition of the neighbourhood, and the identical bush yet exists (or did in 1860) beneath which the treasure was found; a burtree, or elder, *Sambucus nigra*, near the north-west corner of the ruins of the old castle."[17]

It would be tedious to go through other English versions,[18] but I must point out that it is connected with a London district. This is shown not by the actual presence of the legend, which has died out in London, but by its representation in the parish church of Lambeth. The legend so strongly current at Swaffham, in Norfolk, is represented in the church in the shape of a carving in wood of a figure to represent the pedlar, and below him the figure of what is locally called a dog.[19] A comparison of this carving with the representation of the pedlar's window formerly existing in Lambeth Church, but which was sacrilegiously removed in 1884 by the late vicar of the parish, shows much the same general characteristics, and search among the parish books shows it to relate to a pedlar known by the name of Dog Smith, who left property still known by the name of the "Pedlar's Acre" to the parish.[20] All this suggests that we have here the last relics of the pedlar legend located in London.

The Pedlar of Lambeth and his dog, figured in the window (now destroyed) of Lambeth Church (from Allen's "History of Lambeth"). **THE PEDLAR**

OF LAMBETH AND HIS DOG
FIGURED IN THE WINDOW (NOW DESTROYED) OF LAMBETH CHURCH

The next stage in the history of this legend shows it to belong to the world's collection of folk-tales. There is, however, a preliminary fact of great significance to note, namely that two non-British versions refer to London Bridge. Thus a Breton tale refers to London Bridge, and the interest of this story is sufficiently great to quote it here from its recorder straight from the Breton folk:—

"Long ago, when the timbers of the most ancient of the vessels of Brest were not yet acorns, there were two men in a farmhouse in the Côtes du Nord disputing, and they were disputing about London Bridge. One said it was the most beautiful sight in the world, while the other very truly said, 'No! the grace of the good God was more beautiful still.' And as the dispute went on, 'Let us,' said one of them, 'settle it once and for all, and in this way: let us now this moment go out along the high-road and let us ask the first three men we meet as to which is the most beautiful—London Bridge or the grace of the good God? And which ever way they decide, he who holds the beaten opinion shall lose to the other all his possessions, farm and cattle and horses, everything.' So each being confident he was right, they went out: and the first man they met declared that though the grace of the good God was beautiful, London Bridge was more beautiful still; and the second the same, and the third. And the man whose opinion was beaten, a rich farmer, gave up all he had and was a beggar.

"'Now,' said he to himself when the other, taking his horse by the bridle, had left him—'now let me go and see this London Bridge which is so wonderfully beautiful;' and, being very manful and stout, he set out at once to walk, and walking on and on was there by nightfall. But, good Christian that he was, he could see in it nothing to shake his belief that the grace of the good God was more beautiful still.

"Soon the bridge was silent, and the last to cross it had gone home; and he, notwithstanding his losses, tired out and sleepy, lay down and fell into a doze there; and, while he was dozing, there came by two men, and one of them, standing quite close by him, said to the other, 'The night is fine, the wind gentle, the stars clear! On such a night whoever were to collect the dew would be able to heal the blind.' 'It is true,' answered the other; 'but none know of it.' And they passed on, quietly as they had come. Thereupon up rose the beggared farmer, and with basin and cup set about collecting the dew; and in a very short time performed with it the most wonderful cures; finally curing the daughter of a neighbouring Emperor who had been blind from her birth, and whom her grateful father gave to him at once in marriage, since directly she set eyes on him she loved him."[21]

The pedlar of Lambeth and his dog as drawn in 1786 for Ducarel's "History of Lambeth". **THE PEDLAR OF LAMBETH FROM DUCAREL'S "HISTORY OF LAMBETH," 1786**

The second non-British variant, which also attaches to London Bridge, is to be found in the *Heimskringla*,[22] and I will quote William Morris's translation:—

"West in Valland was a man infirm so that he was a cripple and went on knees and knuckles. On a day he was abroad on the way and was asleep there. That dreamed he that a man came to him glorious of aspect and asked whither he was bound and the man named some town or other. So the glorious man spoke to him: Fare then to Olaf's church the one that is in London and thou wilt be whole. Thereafter he awoke, and fared to seek Olaf's church and at last he came to London bridge and there asked the folk of the city if they knew to tell him where was Olaf's church. But they answered and said that there were many more churches there than they might wot to what man they were hallowed. But a little thereafter came a man to him who asked whither he was bound and the cripple told him. And sithence said that man: We twain shall fare both to the church of Olaf for I know the way thither. Therewith they fared over the bridge and went along the street which led to Olaf's church. But when they came to the lich gate then strode that one over the threshold of the gate but the cripple rolled in over it and straightway rose up a whole man. But when he looked around him his fellow farer was vanished."

I shall have to refer again to these Breton and Norse versions, because of their retention of London Bridge as the locale of the story, in common with all the versions which have been found in Britain. In the meantime it is to be noted that the remaining non-British variants are told of other bridges and other places. Holland, Denmark, Italy, Cairo, have their representative variants;[23] and it thus presents to the student of tradition an excellent example for inquiry as to the value to history of legends world-wide in their distribution attaching themselves to historical localities.

There are some obvious features about this group of traditions, which at once lead to interesting questions. There is first the fact that all the British variants of the treasure stories centre round London Bridge; secondly, there is the extension beyond Britain to the Breton variant and the Norse variant, both non-British legends, of which the *locus* is London Bridge. From these two facts it is clear that London Bridge had some special influence at a period of its history which dates before the separation of the Breton folk from their Celtic brethren in Britain, for the Bretons would not after their separation acquire a London Bridge tradition; and again at a period of its history when Norse legend and saga were fashioning. In the one case the myth-makers must have been Celts of the fourth century, and the only bridge known to these Celts must have been that belonging to Roman Lundinium; in the other case the myth-makers were Norsemen, and the bridge known to them was the later bridge so frequently referred to in the chronicle accounts of the Danish and Norse invasions of England.

It is not difficult, by a joint appeal to history and folklore, to trace out from this very definite starting-point the events which brought about this particular specialisation of the world-spread treasure myths.

Obviously the first point to note is that London Bridge loomed out greatly in the minds and understanding of people at two distinct periods of its history.[24] That the first period relates to its building is suggested by the date supplied by the evidence of the Breton version. The people who wondered at its building, or the results of its building, were certainly not the builders themselves, and we thus see a distinction in culture between the bridge builders and the wonder builders. This condition is exactly provided for by

23

the building of the earliest London Bridge. It was a work of the Romans of Lundinium,[25] and the people who stood in wonder at this great enterprise were not the Roman engineers and builders, accustomed to such undertakings all over the then known world, and they must therefore have been the surrounding non-Roman people, who were the Celtic tribesmen. Now the culture-antagonism between the Romans of Lundinium and the Celts of Britain is, I believe, a factor of great importance,[26] though almost universally neglected by our historians, because they do not study the facts of early history on anthropological lines. Not only is it discoverable, as I think, from the facts of history, but the facts of tradition confirm the facts of history at all points. Thus I think it is important, if we can, to obtain independent testimony of the attitude of the surrounding people to the builders of London Bridge. We can do this by reference to the peasant beliefs concerning bridges, as, for instance, in Ireland, where on passing over a bridge they invariably pulled off their hats and prayed for the soul of the builder of the bridge,[27] and to the fact that the Romans themselves looked upon bridge-building as a sacred function, and would no doubt use this part of their work to the fullest extent, in order to impress the barbarism opposed to them.[28] The extent of this impression may probably be contained in the old and widely spread nursery rhyme of "London Bridge is Broken Down," an examination of which has led Mrs. Gomme to conclude that it contains reference to an ancient belief that the building of the bridge was accompanied by human sacrifice.[29] This conclusion is confirmed by the preservation in Wales of a bridge-sacrifice tradition. It relates to the "Devil's Bridge" near Beddgelert. "Many of the ignorant people of the neighbourhood believe that this structure was formed by supernatural agency. The devil proposed to the neighbouring inhabitants that he would build them a bridge across the pass, on condition that he should have the first who went over it for his trouble. The bargain was made, and the bridge appeared in its place, but the people cheated the devil by dragging a dog to the spot and whipping him over the bridge."[30] This is a distinct trace of a substituted animal sacrifice for an original human sacrifice. But this is a practice which sends us back to the most primitive times, and in particular we are referred to an exact parallel in India, where, on the governing English determining to build a bridge of engineering proportions and strength over the Hoogley River at Calcutta, the native Hindu tribesmen immediately believed that the first requirement would be a human sacrifice for the foundation.[31] The traditions attaching to London Bridge are therefore identical with the current beliefs concerning the Hoogley Bridge, and the culture-relationship of the bridge-builders to the surrounding people in both cases is that of an advanced civilisation to tribesmen. Now if these conditions of modern India are repetitions of the conditions of ancient Britain in the days of Lundinium, and of this there can be but little doubt, there is no difficulty in understanding to what part of history these traditions have led us. We are again in the days when London Bridge was a marvel—a marvel which sent travelling through the Celtic homes of Britain a new application of the treasure myth which they had inherited from remote ancestors. The marvel lived on through the ages when London was in the unique position of being an undestroyed city in Saxon times, times which witnessed the destruction of all other cities of Roman foundation,[32] and the sending forth of the Celtic refugees to Brittany.[33] The accumulation during a long-continuing period of conceptions of treasure being found by way of the bridge leading to London, would become the direct force for keeping the tradition alive; and while the facts of history show us the important position of London during the period which witnessed the departure of the Celtic Bretons to their continental home,[34] the facts of tradition show us the Celtic tribesmen deeming it a way to wealth through the magic potency of dreamland. The Celtic tribesmen stood outside Roman Lundinium. Its life was not their life, and their conversion of its position into a mythic treasure house or a mythic road to treasure, and their association of it with the bloody rites of the foundation sacrifice, are in strict accord with the historical relationship of the tribal life of Celtic Britain to the city life of Roman Lundinium.

I may be permitted perhaps to emphasise this significant accordance of history and tradition when working together. I have already alluded to the fact that I have worked out the history of London independently, and upon lines quite different from the present study. I have therefore a wider grasp of the two currents of history and folklore in this particular case than could in the ordinary way fall either to the historian or to the folklorist. That I can find in both just the complementary facts which help to realise the whole situation, to fill in the gaps of history which nowhere directly tells of the relationship of Roman Lundinium to the British Celts, to extend the outlook of folklore which nowhere recognises that there was a great Roman city of Lundinium which would dominate the minds of those not trained to city life, is a fortunate circumstance which neither historian nor folklorist is likely to repeat frequently, and I am entitled, I think, to claim the utmost from it. I can at least claim that it answers all the facts in a way that has not yet been accomplished. Thus Sir John Rhys has discussed the treasure legend and he can only account for it as part of the mythical trappings of Arthur into which "London Bridge is introduced," because London Bridge "formerly loomed very large in the popular imagination as one of the chief wonders of London." Sir John Rhys refers for confirmation of this to the "notion cherished as to London and London Bridge by the country people of Wales even within my own memory," and then goes on to say that "the fashion of selecting London Bridge as the opening scene of a treasure legend had been set perhaps by a widely spread English story," that of the Pedlar of Swaffham.[35] All this is very unsatisfactory. Modern notions of this sort would not set the fashion two centuries ago, nor extend it to Brittany. Nor is the suggestion in accord with other evidence as to the extension of tradition. What has happened is that the Arthur cycle has appropriated two London Bridge traditions and has worked them up into the Arthur form, the traditions themselves belonging to the far older period to which I have here referred them—a period when the burial of treasure was a necessary corollary to the events which were happening.[36] Buried treasure legends are found all over the country. They belong to the period of conquest and fighting. They are the evidence which tradition yields of the unrest of the times which caused them to arise. They are the fragments of history which tradition has preserved, while history has coldly passed them by.[37]

With this in the background as the *corpus* of a legend-covered London Bridge, we come to the second period.

London Bridge to the Norsemen of the tenth and eleventh centuries was a place of fierce fighting and struggle, a place of victory and death. The saga takes pains to describe this wondrous bridge[38] before it describes the great fight there and its capture by King Olaf, a fight which produced a war-rhyme which, in Laing's version, begins with the same words as the English nursery rhyme, "London Bridge is broken down!"[39] and which

26

Morris renders as a tribute to King Olaf, "thou brakest down London Bridge." There is little wonder, then, that the men of King Olaf took back with them to saga-land a great memory of this bridge and this fight, transferred to it their own variant of the world-wide treasure legend, and made a legend not of money treasure, but of regained health to a crippled warrior. The corresponding non-British version of Brittany helps us to understand that the cure of disease was originally associated with the gains of treasure, and in the Norse version the treasure incident is altogether dropped, but in its place is the recovery of health, a treasure more in accord with the sterner needs and recollections of a great fight. The Norse story is helpful to us as showing how London Bridge could enter into the legends of a people, and remain with them even after that people was no longer living in Britain, and it becomes therefore a valuable addition to the evidence for the more ancient transference from Britain to Brittany of the original legend.

Altogether the piecing together of the items of historical value in this legend is most complete. We have not only recovered for history hitherto lost conceptions of the place held by Roman Lundinium among the Celtic tribesmen, but we have recovered also evidence of the true culture-position of the Celtic tribesmen towards their Roman conquerors. The examination of this legend may have been long and tedious, but the result is, I think, commensurate. It illustrates the power of tradition to set historical data in their proper environment, to restore the proportion which they bear to unrecorded history, and if the student will but follow the evidence carefully, I think he will find these results.

We will take a step forward, and turn from local to personal attachments of tradition. There is a whole class of traditions attached to personages about whose historical existence there can be but little doubt, and just because of the accretion of tradition round them their historical existence has oftentimes been denied. The most famous example in our history is of course King Arthur, and so great an authority as Sir John Rhys is obliged to resort to a special argument to account for the problems he is faced with. He argues, and argues strongly, for an historic Arthur—an Arthur who was the British successor of the Roman emperor after Britain had ceased to be a part of the Roman Empire.[40] But because of the myths which have grown round him, he suggests that there must also have been "a Brythonic divinity named Arthur," and we are thus introduced to a dual study of history and myth which does not appear to me to take us very far, and which, in fact, just separates history from myth, instead of showing where they join hands. This dual conception of myth is indeed a rather favourite resort of those scholars who cannot appreciate the evidence that proves a character in a mythic tradition to be an actual historical personage. It is the basis of the famous Sigfried-Arminius controversy. It does duty in many less important cases,[41] and most frequently in connection with northern mythology, where the line between mythic and historical events gathering round a hero is generally so finely drawn as to be almost imperceptible. But it is so obviously a piece of special pleading on self-created lines that other explanation is needed. And another explanation is to be obtained if only students will rely upon the evidence of tradition itself instead of appealing to every fancy derived from sources which have nothing to do with tradition.

The history of King Arthur has been the subject of inquiry too frequently for it to be possible in these pages to discuss the dual theory as it has been applied to him, but I will attempt to show that it is quite unnecessary thus to explain the history of King Arthur by turning to the history of another of our great heroic figures, one of the greatest to my mind, who, like Arthur, has secured not only a fair share of special tradition belonging to himself personally, but a larger share than others of that corpus of tradition which has descended from our earliest unknown ancestors, and become attached to the historical hero of later times—I mean, Hereward, the last of the Saxon defenders of his land against William the Norman.[42] The analysis of the Hereward legend affords a good example of the process by which tradition is preserved by historical fact, and in its turn helps to unravel the real history which lies at the source. Instead, therefore, of attempting to travel over the voluminous literature which is the outcome of the King Arthur story, I will use for the same purpose the shorter story of Hereward the Englishman.

We start with the fact that Hereward is unknown to history until his great stand in the Island of Ely against the might of William, the conqueror of England. And yet to the banners of this "unknown" chieftain there flocked the discontented heroism of England, men ranking from the noble to the peasant, and including such great figures as Morcar, Edwine, and Waltheof. I

28

always think, too, that the little band of Berkshire men, who started across the country to join Hereward in the fens, and were intercepted and cut to pieces by a Norman troop,[43] give us more than a passing glimpse at the estimation in which Hereward was held by his countrymen. Such a man commanding so much, in face of so much, could not have been the unknown person which history makes him.

How then can we ascertain why he was held in such estimation? History being quite silent, tradition steps into the gap. It is the tradition recorded in post-Herewardian times, be it noted. In this great body of tradition, contained in a Latin MS. of the twelfth century, he journeys to Scotland, where he slew a bear and saved the people whom it had oppressed; from thence to Cornwall, where he fought and slew a great champion, the lover of the princess; from thence to Ireland, where he assisted the King in war, and back again to Cornwall to rescue again the princess from a distasteful wooer, and, finally, to Flanders. Even in the camp of the Norman, which he visits in traditional fashion, he has an adventure with witches which takes us to the worship of wells. Much of his adventure is but the application of well-known traditional events,[44] and it is important to note that the geography of the supposed travels belongs to the very home of tradition, the unknown territories of the Celts, Ireland, Cornwall, and Scotland.

Now all this tradition is certainly not true of Hereward. But what it does is to certify to his greatness in the eyes of his countrymen, to show that his countrymen were anxious to explain why he was so great in A.D. 1070, and why before that date he was unknown to them. This is an important point to have gained. It shows the vacuum which was occupied by tradition because contemporary, or nearly contemporary, thought required it to be filled up. The popular mind abhors a vacuum as much as the material world of nature does. It will fill it with its own conceptions, if it cannot fill it with recognised facts. Hereward must have been a famous man when he took his stand in the fens of Ely. That his biographers explain his fame by the application of ancient traditions is only saying that his countrymen reckoned his fame as of the very highest; ordinary current events of the day would not suit their ideas of the fitness of things. Hereward was as Alfred had been, as Arthur had been, and so he must have his share of the national tradition, even as these heroes had. To say less of him was to have put him below the

29

others. And history in this case could not help, for it was in the hands of Hereward's enemies, and they were careful to say nothing or very little of English heroes at this period. The great battle of Hastings had been lost, but of all the English men who had fought and died there we only know of three names beyond those of the king and his house. Leofric the abbot of Peterborough, Godric the sheriff of Berkshire, and Asgar the sheriff of London, have become known by accident, as it were. All others are unnamed and unhonoured. Therefore, when the great deeds of Hereward came to be chronicled, it was not enough to say he was at Hastings; the deeds of old must be chronicled of him as they had been chronicled of others.

This accretion of popular tradition to account for the fame of Hereward when he took command at Ely, though it proclaims in the strongest terms that Hereward was famous in the eyes of his countrymen, displaces history therefore. Putting the case in this way, we may proceed to examine what recorded history exactly has to say of Hereward, and then by noting what it has left unsaid, we may perhaps be able to fill the gap by a reasonable deduction from the facts. In Domesday there are clearly two Herewards, one having lands in Lincolnshire in the time of King Edward and *not* at the date of the survey, the other having lands in Warwickshire in the time of King Edward and *also* at the date of the survey. Here we have two widely different counties and two widely different conditions, and it is right with all the evidence to conclude that they relate to different personages. The Lincolnshire Hereward is the hero of the fens. He held of the abbot of Peterborough, and Ulfcytil, who was appointed in 1062, was the abbot in question. This brings us to only four years before the battle of Hastings, and another entry in Domesday, thanks to the scholarship of Mr. Round, proves that Hereward was deprived of his Lincolnshire lands not before but after the great fights at Hastings and in the fens. Therefore the story shapes itself somewhat in this fashion. Hereward was in England in 1062. He was then a man of the abbot of Peterborough; that is to say, a tenant bound to perform military service to his lord. His lord, the abbot, was at Hastings with his tenants, and fought there. That Hereward of all the abbot's tenants should have followed his lord to Hastings is more than likely; the strange thing would be that he should not have done so. That going thither nameless among the many, he should gain experience under Harold, though no fame has come to him through the historians from a field where Saxon fame was buried; that his own genius should make him use his experience when need arose; that among the English all survivors from that field who were still unwilling to bow the knee to William would be reckoned as heroes by their depressed countrymen; that on this account alone he would be given rank above Morcar, who had kept away from Hastings—are the conclusions to be drawn legitimately from the silence as well as the actual records of history, compared with the story told by tradition. History and tradition are in accord, not in conflict; the gaps of history are filled by tradition—that tradition which was suitable and worthy of so great a hero, namely the ancient tradition told of all heroes. Reopening these gaps and putting in its right place the tradition which had hitherto prevented them from being seen, we are able to appeal to history to yield up the true story of one of the greatest of English heroes, a story which shows him to have been at Hastings by the side of Harold, to have won fame there, to have continued the fight for English liberty as leader of the English patriots, and to have earned a place in the unsung English epic.

But his place in English tradition helps us to understand the value and position of tradition in such cases. The traditions clustering round the name of Hereward do not compel us to interpret them as Hereward facts. The historian, however, need not on this account fear for Hereward. He should rather value the traditions as evidence of the greatness of the English hero among the conquered English. They applied to him the legends of their oldest heroes. All that was delightful to them in tradition was attached to their present hero. He was worthy of a place among their greatest. And thus the fact of added tradition brings out the estimate of the worth of the hero to those among whom he lived and for whom he fought.

The traditions themselves belong to far other times, and the facts contained in them must be interpreted from the oldest ideas of our race. It is only by thus disengaging the traditions which have grown round the historical person that the correct interpretation of the position can be attempted, and when that is done we are left, not with a mass of uncertain and misleading testimony about a national hero, but with certain definite historical facts belonging to Hereward, and certain traditions attached to Hereward, certifying to his great place in the popular estimation, telling of facts which do not, it is true, belong to Hereward, but which, in a special sense, belong to the people who were reverencing Hereward.

If I have made it clear from these examples that the explanation of historic fact and mythic tradition in combination does not lead either to the discrediting of history or to the creation of new mythic realms, I need not dwell much longer on this class of illustrations of the relationship between history and tradition. Over and over again, in the local records, are examples to be found where history is in close contact with tradition, and I am far more inclined to question the evidence which proves the falseness of any authenticated tradition than I am to trust all the statements which do duty for history. It is not only the traditions looming largely in popular interest, but some of the smallest local traditions which throw light on great historical events. They may tell us not merely of the great historical event, but of the peculiar relationship of parts of the kingdom to that event, which no purely historical evidence could by any possibility explain. One of the most striking examples is, perhaps, the Sussex tradition of "Duke" William as a conqueror.[45] The title Duke is here faithfully recorded of the great conqueror, who everywhere else in England, both in historical documents and in the popular language, is referred to as king. The explanation is, if the identification of this tradition with the great Norman king is correct, that Sussex being more or less separated from the rest of the country by its great weald, carried its own tradition of the bloody field at Hastings sufficiently long and uninterrupted for it to be stamped upon the minds of the people in its original form, and thus to remain. No better evidence could be found for the relationship of Sussex to this great event. All the chapters in Mr. Freeman's great history do not impress the imagination so strongly as this one fact, that William the Conqueror has always been Duke William to the Sussex folk. He was Duke William to the fen folk, too. They fought for their belief and were compelled to accept his kingship. The Sussex folk fought, too, and they handed down their conception of the great fight to their children.

A good example of a slightly different kind occurs in connection with Kett's rebellion in Norfolk. It was associated with a prophecy that said, "there shulde lande at Walborne hope the proudest prince of Christendome, and so shall come to Moshold heethe, and there shuld mete with other ij kinges, and shall fyght and shalbe put down: and the whyte lyon shuld optayne" the mastery. And yet this prophecy goes much further back, for the Danes are said to have landed at Weybourne Hope in their invasions, and the old rhyme is still remembered in the county:—

"He that would England win Must at Weybourn Hope begin."[46]

This is an example of the forcible revival of an ancient tradition to suit a later fact, and is evidence of the enormous impression which the event to which it refers had upon the locality. Kett's rebellion was one thing to the nation at large and quite another thing to this district of Norfolk, and the great events of the tenth century preserved in legend were equated with the minor events of the sixteenth century, thus enabling us to understand better the depth of the local feeling which produced these events.

Plan of the site of the "Heaven Walls" at Litlington, near Royston, Cambridgeshire (reprinted from "Archæologia"). **PLAN OF THE SITE OF THE "HEAVEN WALLS" AT LITLINGTON, ROYSTON, CAMBRIDGESHIRE**

Both local and personal traditions are of interest in the unravelling of the meaning of historical events, and the forces at the back of them, and I will add a note of one or two examples of those humbler traditions which confirm or enhance the value of the historical record. They are of the greatest importance if correctly understood. They include such examples, for instance, as Mr. Kemble notes when he says, "I have more than once walked, ridden, or rowed, as land and stream required, round the bounds of Anglo-Saxon estates, and have learned with astonishment that the names recorded in my charter were those still used by the woodcutter or the shepherd of the neighbourhood."[47] This is remarkable testimony to the persistence of tradition. It is the commencing point of a whole series of examples which go to show that embedded in the memories of the people, and supported by no other force but tradition, there are innumerable traces of historic fact.[48]

A stage forward, in the same class of tradition, are those examples of special names which indicate an important or impressive event, the real nature of which is only revealed by modern discovery. Thus perhaps the "White Horse Stone" at Aylesford, in Kent, the legend of which is that one who rode a beast of this description was killed on or about this spot,[49] may take us back to the great battle at Crayford, where Horsa was killed. Another kind of local tradition is perhaps more instructive. Immediately contiguous to the north side of the Roman road at Litlington, near Royston, were some strips of unenclosed, but cultivated, land, which in ancient deeds from time immemorial had been called "Heaven's Walls." Traditional awe attached to this spot, and the village children were afraid to traverse it after dark, when it was said to be frequented by supernatural beings. Here is subject for inquiry. Both words in the name are significant. Why the allusion to Heaven; why is a field called walls? The problem was solved in 1821, for in that year some labourers were digging for gravel on this spot, and they struck upon an old wall composed of flint and Roman brick. This accidental discovery was followed up by Dr. Webb, and the wall was found to enclose a rectangular space measuring about thirty-eight yards by twenty-seven, and containing numerous deposits of sepulchral urns containing ashes of the dead. It was clear from the results of the excavations that here was one of those large plots of ground environed by walls to which the name of *ustrinum* was given by the Romans,[50] a fact which was preserved in the name long after the site had lost every trace of its origin.

Sketch of Litlington Field, (reprinted from "Archæologia").
LITLINGTON FIELD

I will refer to one more local example. In Dorsetshire and Wiltshire fairs are held upon sites which are often marked by the remains of ancient works, or distinguished by some dim tradition of vanished importance.[51] One has only to refer to the history of the market as "a contribution to the early history of human intercourse" as Mr. Grierson puts it,[52] and to the extremely important and archaic constitution of the market, a glimpse of which has been afforded by Sir Henry Maine, alone among scholars who have investigated earliest English institutions, to know how valuable such a note as this must be if it can be confirmed by extended research. Local investigation of these places and their traditions would, no doubt, lead to many points in the tribal settlement of the district, an important fact of history nowhere found in history.

No one, I think, taking into consideration this view of the relationship of local and personal traditions to history will deny that history is likely to gain much by the proper interpretation of such traditions. Every yard of British territory has its historic interest, and there are innumerable peaks above the general level which should be worth much to national history. Every epoch of British history has its great personage, who in popular opinion stands out from among his fellows. When once it is understood that traditions attaching to places and persons yield facts of a kind worth searching for, there will arise the desire to obtain all that is now obtainable from this source, and to add thereto the deductions to be drawn from their geographical distribution.

II

If the accretion of myth around the lives of great historic personages, and the persistence of tradition in historic localities, may be accepted as one phase of the necessary relationship of tradition to history, we may proceed to inquire how far the unattached traditions, the folk-tales pure and simple, contain or are based upon historic details. These details will not tell us of any one historic personage, or relate to any one historic locality, but will relate to the peoples before personages and localities figured in their history, and will explain facts in culture-history rather than in political history. We shall be approaching the period before written history had begun, and for which, so far as written history is concerned, we are dependent upon foreign or outside authority. I think, perhaps, Dr. Karl Pearson has put the case for this view in the best form. "As we read fairy stories to our children," he says,

"we may study history for ourselves. No longer oppressed with the unreal and the *baroque*, we may see primitive human customs and the life of primitive man and woman cropping out at almost every sentence of the nursery tale. Written history tells us little of these things, they must be learnt, so to speak, from the mouths of babes. But there they are in the *Märchen*, as invaluable fossils for those who will stoop to pick them up and study them. Back in the far past we can build up the life of our ancestry—the little kingdom, the queen or her daughter as king maker, the simple life of the royal household, and the humble candidate for the kingship, the priestess with her control of the weather and her power over youth and maid. In the dimmest distance we can see traces of the earlier kindred group marriage, and in the near foreground the beginnings of that fight with patriarchal institutions which led the priestess to be branded by the new Christian civilization as the evil-working witch of the Middle Ages."[53]

I should not have ventured to quote this long passage if my own studies, before Dr. Pearson's book was published in 1897, had not led me to much the same conclusions.[54] But Dr. Pearson assists me in a special way. His methods are scientific. He is not a folklorist because he loves folklore, but because he sees in it the materials for elucidating the early life of man. He is not, so to speak, prejudiced in its favour. He brings to his aid the practical mind of the statistician and the psychologist, and his conclusions may not, therefore, be put on one side as easily as those of myself and other students of folklore.

It is due to the folklorist, however, to say that this aspect of the folk-tale had already been discovered by one of the greatest of the earlier collectors of traditional lore, the late Mr. J. F. Campbell. Thus, writing, in 1860, of his grand collection of "Highland Tales," Mr. Campbell very truly says: "The tales represent the actual everyday life of those who tell them, with great fidelity. They have done the same, in all likelihood, time out of mind, and that which is not true of the present is, in all probability, true of the past; and therefore something may be learned of forgotten ways of life."[55] Readers of Mr. Campbell's books well know how he has traced out from these traditions from the nursery, identical customs with Highland everyday life, and relics also of a long-forgotten past state of things; how he points to the records of the stone age and the iron age in these representatives of the scientific memoirs of the past; how very significantly he answers his own supposition, that if these tales "are dim recollections of savage times and savage people, then other magic gear, the property of giants, fairies, and bogles, should resemble things which are precious now amongst savage or half-civilized tribes, or which really have been prized amongst the old inhabitants of these islands or of other parts of the world."[56]

This is an extremely important conclusion on the relationship of history and tradition, and it will be well to illustrate it by turning to some obvious details of primitive life, which are to be seen with more or less clearness enshrined in the folk-tales which have been preserved in our own country.

In Kennedy's *Fireside Stories of Ireland*, it is related in one of the tales that there was no window to the mud-wall cabin, and the door was turned to the north;[57] and then, again, we have this picture given to us in another story: on a common that had in the middle of it a rock or great pile of stones overgrown with furze bushes, there was a dwelling-house, and a cow-house, and a goat's-house, and a pigsty all scooped out of the rock; and the cows were going into the byre, and the goats into their house, but the pigs were grunting and bawling before the door.[58] This takes us to the surroundings of the cave-dwelling people.

Then in other places we come across relics of ancient agricultural life preserved in these stories. In the Irish story of "Hairy Rouchy" the heroine is fastened by her wicked sisters in a pound,[59] an incident not mentioned in the parallel Highland tale related by Campbell.[60] Many Irish stories contain details of primitive life that the Scottish variants do not contain. The field that was partly cultivated with corn and partly pasture for the cow,[61] the grassy ridge upon which the princess sat, and the furrows wherein her two brothers were lying,[62] are instances.

A great question arises here. If the Scotch story does not mention the primitive incident mentioned in the Irish story, does it mean that the Irish story has retained for a longer time the details of its primitive original? Or does it mean that it has absorbed more of surrounding Irish life into it than the Scotch story has of surrounding Scottish life?

These details must have a place in the elucidation of Irish folk-tales, because they have a very distinct place indeed in primitive institutions; and it hence becomes a question to folklorists as to how they have entered into, or escaped from, the narrative of traditional story. It appears to me that the appearance or non-appearance of these phases of early life are typical of what has been going on with the plot and structure of folk-tales as long as they have remained the traditional treasures of the people. A story identical in all the main outlines of plot will be varied in matters of detail, according to the people who are using it in their daily routine of story-telling. But this variation is always from the primitive to the cultured, from the simple to the complex. The mud-cabin or cave-dwelling in Irish story would have developed into the palace in stories of a richer country like England; the old woman, young girl, master and servant, would become perhaps the queen, princess, king and vassal; just as in Spanish and Portuguese stories the giant of other European tales is represented by "the Moor." If this process of change is a factor in the life of the folk-tale, it follows that those folk-tales which contain the greatest number of primitive details are the most ancient, and come to us more directly from the prehistoric times which they represent.

We may gather warrant for such a conclusion if we pass from small details to a distinct institution. The institution which stands out most clearly in early history is the tribe, and I will therefore turn to an element of ancient tribal life, and an element which has to do with the practical organisation of that life, namely, the tribal assembly. We find that the folk-tale records under its fairy or non-historic guise many important recollections of the assembly of the tribe. One very natural feature of this assembly in early times was its custom of meeting in the open air—a custom which in later times still obtained, for reasons which were the outcome of the prejudices existing in favour of keeping up old customs. These reasons are recorded in the formula of Anglo-Saxon times, that meetings should not be held in any building, lest magic might have power over the members of the assembly.[63]

Before turning to the tales of our own country, I will first see whether savage and barbaric tales have recorded anything on the subject, for their picture of the tribal assembly, when revealed in the folk-tale, belongs to the period which might have witnessed the making of the story, and which certainly witnessed the tribal organisation of the people as a living institution. Dr. Callaway, in his *Nursery Tales and Traditions of the Zulus*, relates a story of "the Girl-King." "Where there are many young women," says the story, "they assemble on the river where they live, and appoint a chief over the young women, that no young woman may assume to act for herself. Well, then they assemble and ask each other, 'Which among the damsels is fit to be chief and reign well?' They make many inquiries; one after another is nominated and rejected, until at length they agree together to appoint one, saying, 'Yes, so and so shall reign.'"[64] However far this may be actually separated from the political assembly of the Zulus, there is no doubt we have here a folk-tale adaptation of events which were happening around the relators of the tale. This is all I am anxious to state, indeed. What in the folk-tale was related of the girl-king, was a reflex only of what happened when the political chieftain himself was concerned.

This, perhaps, is still better illustrated if we turn to India. In the story of "How the Three Clever Men outwitted the Demons," told by Miss Frere in her *Old Deccan Days*, it is related how "a demon was compelled to bring treasure to the pundit's house, and on being asked why he had been so long away, answered, 'All my fellow-demons detained me, and would hardly let me go, they were so angry at my bringing you so much treasury; and though I told them how great and powerful you are, they would not believe me, but will, as soon as I return, judge me in solemn council for serving you.' 'Where is your council held?' asked the pundit. 'Oh! very far, far away,' answered the demon, 'in the depths of the jungle, where our rajah daily holds his court.' The three men, the pundit, the wrestler, and the pearl-shooter, are taken by the demon to witness the trial.... They reached the great jungle where the durbar (council) was to be held, and there he (the demon) placed them on the top of a high tree just over the demon rajah's throne. In a few minutes they heard a rustling noise, and thousands and thousands of demons filled the place, covering the ground as far as the eye could reach, and thronging chiefly round the rajah's throne."[65]

A classical story told by Ælian gives us another interesting example of this feature of early political life. It is said of the Lady Rhodopis, who was alike fair and frail, that of all the beautiful women in Egypt, she was by far the most beautiful; and the story goes that one time when she was bathing, Fortune, which always was a lover of whatever may be the most unlikely and unexpected, bestowed upon her rank and dignity that were alone suitable for her transcendent charms; and this was the way what I am now going to tell came to pass. Rhodopis, before taking a bath, had given her robes in charge to her attendants; but at the same time there was an eagle flying over the bath, and it darted down and flew away with one of her slippers. The eagle flew away, and away, and away, until it got to the city of Memphis, where the Prince Psammetichus was sitting in the open air, and administering justice to those subject to his sway; and as the eagle flew over him it let the slipper fall from its beak, and it fell down into the lap of Psammetichus. The prince looked at the slipper, and the more he looked at it, the more he marvelled at the beauty of the material and the dainty minuteness of its size; and then he cogitated upon the wondrous way in which such a thing was conveyed to him through the air by a bird; and then it was he sent forth a proclamation to all parts of Egypt to try to discover the woman to whom the slipper belonged, and solemnly promised that whoever she might be he would make her his bride.[66]

A very beautiful legend, which has been preserved by the Rev. W. S. Lach-Szyrma,[67] carries into its fairy narrative more of the realities of tribal life. Mr. Lach-Szyrma obtained it from a peasant's chap-book, but it professes to be an ancient Slovac folk-tale:—

"An orphan girl is left with a cruel stepmother, who has a daughter who is bad-tempered and disagreeable, and extremely jealous of her. She becomes the Cinderella of the house, is ill-treated and beaten, but submits patiently. At last the harsh stepmother is urged by her daughter to get rid of her. It is winter, in the month of January; the snow has fallen, and the ground is frozen. The cruel stepmother in this dreadful weather bids the poor girl to go out in the forest, and not to come back till she brings some violets with her. After many entreaties for mercy the orphan is driven out, and goes out in the snow on the hopeless errand. As she enters the forest she sees a little way on in the deep glade, under the leafless trees, a large fire burning. As she draws near she perceives around the fire are twelve stones, and on the stones sit twelve men. The chief of them, sitting on the largest stone, is an old man with a long snowy beard, and a great staff in his hand. As she comes up to the fire the old man asks her what she wants. She respectfully replies by telling them, with many tears, her sad story. The old man comforts her. 'I am January; I cannot give you any violets, but brother March can.' So he turns to a fine young man near him and says, 'Brother March, sit in my place.' Presently the air around grows softer. The snows around the fire melt. The green grass appears, the flower-buds are to be seen. At the orphan girl's feet a bed of violets appear. She stoops and plucks a beautiful bouquet, which she brings home to her astounded stepmother."

Stone monuments erected as memorials in a Kasya village (reprinted from "Asiatic Researches"). **STONE MONUMENTS AS MEMORIALS (KASYA)**

Stone seats at a Kasya village (reprinted from "Asiatic Researches"). **STONE SEATS AT A KASYA VILLAGE (2 FEET TO 6 FEET IN DIAMETER)**

How clearly this is a representation of the tribal assembly worked into the folk-tale, where January and the months are the tribal chiefs, may be illustrated by a comparison with the actual events of Indian tribal life. Within the stockaded village of Supar-Punji, in Bengal, are two or three hundred monuments, large and small, all formed of circular, solid stone slabs, supported by upright stones, set on end, which enclose the space below. On these the villagers sit on occasions of state, each on his own stool, large or small, according to his rank in the commonwealth.[68]

Now evidence such as this, showing how the folk-tale among primitive people gets framed according to the social conditions within which it originates, will help us to realise the peculiar value of similar features which may be found in the folk-tales of our own country. English tales are nearly destitute of such illustrations of primitive tribal life as this. Some of the giant stories of Cornwall, such as that relating to the loose, uncut stones in the district of Lanyon Quoit, on whose tors "they do say the giants sit,"[69] may refer to the tribal assembly place, but it is shorn of all its necessary details, and we do not get many examples even in this shortened form.

Curiously enough, too, we find but little mention in the Scotch tales of the open-air gatherings of the tribe. The following quotation may refer to the custom perhaps, but it is not conclusive: "On the day when O'Donull came out to hold right and justice...." (there were twelve men with him).[70]

41

Another story is more exact. Mr. Campbell took it down from a fisherman in Barra (ii. 137). The hero-child Conall tends the sheep of a widow with whom he lodged. "To feed these sheep he broke down the dykes which guarded the neighbours' fields. The neighbours made complaint to the king, and asked for justice. The king gave foolish judgment, whereat his neck was turned awry, and the judgment-seat kicked. Conall gave a correct decision and released the king. He did this a second time, and the people said he must have king's blood in him." This allusion to the kicking of the judgment-seat is a very instructive illustration of tribal chieftainship and comes within that branch of the subject with which we are now dealing.

But when we pass from Britain to Ireland, there is at once a great storehouse of examples to be given. In Dr. Joyce's *Old Celtic Romances* there are some remarkable passages, which give us a good picture of the assemblies of primitive times. These passages, it should be noted, occur quite incidentally during the course of the story—they belong to the same era as the fairy-legend, the giant, and the witch, and taken as types of what was going on everywhere in prehistoric times, they tell us much that is very valuable.

View in the Kasya Hills, showing stone memorials (reprinted from "Asiatic Researches"). **VIEW IN THE KASYA HILLS SHOWING STONE MEMORIALS**

A great fair-meeting was held by the King of Ireland, Nuada of the Silver Hand, on the Hill of Usna. Not long had the people been assembled, when they beheld a stately band of warriors, all mounted on white steeds, coming towards them from the east, and at their head rode a young champion, tall and comely. "This young warrior was Luga of the Long Arms.... This troop came forward to where the King of Erin sat surrounded by the Dedannans, and both parties exchanged friendly greetings. A short time after this they saw another company approaching, quite unlike the first, for they were grim and surly-looking; namely, the tax-gatherers of the

42

Fomorians, to the number of nine nines, who were coming to demand their yearly tribute from the men of Erin. When they reached the place where the king sat, the entire assembly—the king himself among the rest—rose up before them." Here, without following the story further, the assembling in arms, the payment of the tributes at the council-hill, the sitting of the king and his assembly, are all significant elements of the primitive assembly. In a later part of the same story we have "the Great Plain of the Assembly" mentioned (p. 48). Another graphic picture is given a little later on, when the warrior Luga, above mentioned, demands justice upon the slayers of his father, at the great council on Tara hill. Luga asked the king that the chain of silence should be shaken; and when it was shaken, when all were listening in silence, he stood up and made his plea, which ended in the eric-fine being imposed upon the three children of Turenn, the accomplishment of which forms the basis of the fairy-tale which follows (p. 54). Then, in another place in the same tale, when the brothers are on their adventurous journey, fulfilling their eric-fine, they come to the house of the King of Sigar; and it "happened that the king was holding a fair-meeting on the broad, level green before the palace."

In another story the hero Maildun asks the island queen how she passes her life, and the reply is, "The good king who formerly ruled over this island was my husband. He died after a long reign, and as he left no son, I now reign, the sole ruler of the island. And every day I go to the Great Plain, to administer justice and to decide causes among my people."

The beginning of another story is—"Once upon a time, a noble, warlike king ruled over Lochlann, whose name was Colga of the Hard Weapons. On a certain occasion, this king held a meeting of his chief people, on the broad, green plain before his palace of Berva. And when they were all gathered together, he spoke to them in a loud, clear voice, from where he sat high on his throne; and he asked them whether they found any fault with the manner in which he ruled them, and whether they knew of anything deserving of blame in him as their sovereign lord and king. They replied, as if with the voice of one man, that they found no fault of any kind."

The last example is also a valuable one. A dispute has occurred respecting the enchanted horse, the Gilla Dacker, and "a meeting was called on the green to hear the award." Speeches are made and the awards are given.[71]

I think it will be admitted that the folk-tales of Britain refer back in such cases to the organisation of the tribe in early times, and the only possible conclusion to be drawn from this fact is that they too belong to early times and that they have brought with them to modern days these valuable fragments of history which are hardly to be discovered in any other historical document.

We have thus shown that the folk-tale contains many fragmentary details of ancient social conditions, and further that it contains more than mere details in the larger place it assigns to important features of tribal institutions. It now remains to see whether apart from incident the very structure and heart of the folk-tale is founded upon conceptions of life. I will take as an example the well-known story of Catskin. This story contains one remarkable feature running through many of the variants, and a second which is found in practically all of them. Both these features are perfectly impossible to modern creative fancy, and I venture to think we shall find their true origin in the actual facts of primitive life, not in the wondrous flight of primitive fancy.

The opening incidents of "Catskin" are thus related:—

"A certain king, having lost his wife, and mourned for her even more than other men do, suddenly determines, by way of relieving his sorrows, to marry his own daughter. The princess obtains a suspension of this odious purpose by requiring from him three beautiful dresses, which take a long time to prepare. These dresses are a robe of the colour of the sky, a robe of the colour of the moon, a third robe of the colour of the sun, the latter being embroidered with the rubies and diamonds of his crown. The three dresses being made and presented to her, the princess is checkmated, and accordingly asks for something even more valuable in its way. The king has an ass that produces gold coins in profusion every day of his life. This ass the princess asked might be sacrificed, in order that she might have his skin. This desire even was granted. The princess, thus defeated altogether, puts on the ass's skin, rubs her face over with soot, and runs away. She takes a situation with a farmer's wife to tend the sheep and turkeys of the farm."

The remainder of the story much resembles Cinderella's famous adventures, and I need not repeat it here. The pith of the story turns upon

44

the fact that a father purposes to marry his own daughter, or, in some versions, his daughter-in-law; and the daughter, naturally, as we say, objecting to this arrangement, runs away, and hence her many adventures. This famous story, told by English nurses to English children, long before literature stepped across the sacred precincts of the nursery, is also told in Ireland and Scotland. It is also current in France, Italy, Germany, Russia, Lithuania, and many other nations; and throughout all these versions, differing, of course, in some matters of detail, the selfsame incident is observable—the father wishing to marry his own daughter, and the daughter running away.[72] This incident, therefore, must be older than the several nations who have preserved it from their common home, where the tale was originally told with a special value that is now lost. It must then belong to primitive man, and not to civilised man, and must be judged by the standard of morals belonging to primitive man. It is not sufficient, or, indeed, in any way to the point, to say that the idea of marrying one's own daughter is horrible and detestable to modern ideas; we must place ourselves in a position to judge of such a state of affairs from an altogether different standpoint. And what do we find in primitive society? We find that women were the property, not the help-mates, of their husbands. And the question hence arises, in what relation did the children stand in respect to their parents? The answer comes from almost all parts of the primitive world that, in certain stages of society, the children were related to their mother only. It is worth while pausing one moment to give evidence upon the fact. Thus McLennan says of the Australians, "it is not in quarrels uncommon to find children of the same father arrayed against one another, or indeed, against their father himself; for by their peculiar law *the father can never be a relative of his children.*"[73] This is not the language, though it is the evidence, of the latest research, and another phase of it is represented by the custom, as among the Ahts of Vancouver Island, that in case of separation while the children are young, the children go always with the mother to their own tribe.[74]

Here we see that the relationship between father and daughter was in no way considered in ancient society of the type to which Australians and Ahts belonged, and it is now one of the accepted facts of anthropology that at certain stages of savage life fatherhood was not recognised. That this non-relationship of the father very often resulted in the further stage of the father marrying his daughter, is exemplified by many examples. The story of Lot and his daughters, for instance, will at once occur to the reader, and upon this Mr. Fenton has some observations, to which I may refer the student who wishes to pursue this curious subject further,[75] while Mr. Frazer, in his recent study of Adonis, has discussed the practice with his usual extent of knowledge.[76] Again, it should be remembered that in our own chronicle histories Vortigern is said to have married his own daughter, though the legend and the supposed consequences of the marriage have been twisted from their original primitive surroundings by the monkish chroniclers, through whom we obtain the story.[77] Turning next to the daughter-in-law, supposing that the difference between "daughter" and "daughter-in-law" (query stepdaughter) in the story variants is a vital difference, and not an accidental difference, there is curious and important evidence from India. The following custom prevails among certain classes of Sudras, particularly the Vella-lahs in Koimbator: "A father marries a grown-up girl eighteen or twenty years old to his son, a boy of seven or eight, after which he publicly lives with his daughter-in-law, until the youth attains his majority, when his wife is made over to him, generally with half a dozen children. These children are taught to address him as their father. In several cases this woman becomes the common wife of the father and son. She pays every respect due to her wedded husband, and takes great care of him from the time of her marriage. The son, in his turn, hastens to celebrate the marriage of his acquired son, with the usual pomps, ceremonies, and tumasha, and keeps the bride for himself as his father had done."[78] But even further than this, ancient Hindu law allowed the father, who had no prospect of having legitimate sons, to "appoint" or nominate a daughter who should bear a son to himself, and not to her own husband.[79] Sir Henry Maine gives the formula for this remarkable appointment, and then goes on to say that some customs akin to the Hindu usage of appointing a daughter appear to have been very widely diffused over the ancient world, and traces of them are found far down in history.[80]

What we have before us, therefore, to guide us in the view we take of the story incident of a father marrying his own daughter, may be summarised as follows:—

1. The father is not related to his daughter, and hence examples occur

46

of fathers marrying daughters.

2. The custom of marrying a daughter-in-law.

3. The custom of nominating a daughter to bear a son.

From any one of these facts of primitive life we arrive at the central incident in the story of Catskin: the father could marry his daughter without specially shocking the society of the primitive world, simply because, according to primitive ideas, father and daughter, as we call her, were not related.

We now arrive at the second incident—the running away of Catskin. This again is a very early form of marriage custom. Women of primitive times often objected to the forced marriages, and they expressed their objection very often by running away. In the instance of Catskin the running away was successful, as we all know; but in most instances the unwilling bride was captured and forced to surrender. Mr. Farrer, in his *Primitive Manners and Customs*, quite clears the ground for the refutation of an argument that might be applied if we did not know the customs of primitive society. It might be asked, why did Catskin run away if the custom was a usual one? For the same reason, we answer, that the women of savage society often do run away—objection to the marriage.[81]

Thus we have to note that the two principal features of our ordinary Catskin story are explainable by a reference to primitive manners and customs; and it seems to me much easier and much more reasonable to thus explain the origin of the Catskin story, than first of all to create a "lovely myth," as the mythologists would undoubtedly have a right to call it, of the Sun pursuing the Dawn, and then to say that the Catskin story is simply a relation of this myth.

The opening incident of the Catskin story, as thus interpreted, is not an isolated case of the survival of primitive marriage customs in popular stories. If it were so, there would be considerable difficulty in the way of supporting this interpretation. But it is only saying of Catskin what can be said of other stories. "There are traces," says Mr. Campbell, speaking of his Highland stories, "of foreign or forgotten laws and customs. A man buys a wife as he would a cow, and acquires a right to shoot her, which is acknowledged as good law."[82] Yes, this is good savage law and custom there is no doubt, and Lord Avebury and Mr. McLennan have illustrated it by examples. But in the Highland story of the "Battle of the Birds" the wife is sought to be purchased for a hundred pounds (Campbell, i. 36), and in the Irish story of the "Lazy Beauty and her Aunts" we find something like bride-capture and purchase as well.[83] So, again, if we turn to India the same kind of evidence is forthcoming of another part of the primitive ceremony. "Do not think," retorted the Malee in a story collected by Miss Frere, "that I'll make a fool of myself because I'm only a Malee, and believe what you've got to say because you're a great Rajah. If you mean what you say, if you care for my daughter and wish to be married to her, come and be married; but I'll have none of your new-fangled forms and court ceremonies hard to be understood; let the girl be married by her father's hearth, and under her father's roof."[84] And in another story of the "Chundun Rajah" we have "the scattering rice and flowers upon their heads;"[85] the significance of both of which customs are fully known.

These illustrations of the contact, the necessary contact, of tradition and history show that contact to be equally true of the folk-tale as it is of the local or personal legend. They all point to the substratum of fact underlying tradition, to the absorption by tradition of many features of the life by which it is surrounded, or to the absorption by some great historic person or event of the living tradition of his time or place. This contact is a fact equally important to history and to folklore. It cannot be neglected by either. It stands for something in the analysis which every student must give of the material with which he is working, and that something has a value, sometimes great and sometimes small, which must influence the estimate of the material which both history and folklore supply in the unravelling of man's past.

I will now finally give a more complicated example of the folk-tale as illustrative of the connection between history and tradition. Mr. J. F. Campbell printed a tale in the second volume of the *Transactions of the Ethnological Society* (p. 336), which had been sent to him in Gaelic by John Davan, in December, 1862—that is, after the publication of the fourth volume of his *Highland Tales*. The tale is only in outline, but in quite sufficient fulness for my present purpose, as follows:—

There was a man at some time or other who was well off, and had many children. When the family grew up the man gave a well-stocked farm to each of his children. When the man was old his wife died, and he divided all

48

that he had amongst his children, and lived with them, turn about, in their houses. The sons and daughters got tired of him and ungrateful, and tried to get rid of him when he came to stay with them. At last an old friend found him sitting tearful by the wayside, and learning the cause of his distress, took him home; there he gave him a bowl of gold and a lesson which the old man learned and acted. When all the ungrateful sons and daughters had gone to a preaching, the old man went to a green knoll where his grandchildren were at play, and pretending to hide, he turned up a flat hearthstone in an old stance,[86] and went out of sight. He spread out his gold on a big stone in the sunlight, and he muttered, "Ye are mouldy, ye are hoary, ye will be better for the sun." The grandchildren came sneaking over the knoll, and when they had seen and heard all that they were intended to see and hear, they came running up with, "Grandfather, what have you got there?" "That which concerns you not; touch it not," said the grandfather; and he swept his gold into a bag and took it home to his old friend. The grandchildren told what they had seen, and henceforth the children strove who should be kindest to the old grandfather. Still acting on the counsel of his sagacious old chum, he got a stout little black chest made, and carried it always with him. When any one questioned him as to its contents, his answer was, "That will be known when the chest is opened." When he died he was buried with great honour and ceremony, and then the chest was opened by the expectant heirs. In it were found broken potsherds and bits of slate, and a long-handled, white wooden mallet with this legend on its head:—

"So am favioche fiorum, Thabhavit gnoc annsa cheann, Do n'fhear nach gleidh maoin da' fein, Ach bheir a chuid go leir d'a chlann." "Here is the fair mall To give a knock on the skull To the man who keeps no gear for himself, But gives all to his bairns."

Wright, in his collection of Latin stories, published by the Percy Society in 1842 (pp. 28-29), gives a variant of this tale under the title of "De divite qui dedit omnia filio suo," and, so far as can be judged by the abstract, the parallel between the two narratives, separated by at least five centuries of time, is remarkably close. The latter part is apparently different, for the Latin version tells how the man pretended that the chest contained a sum of money, part of which was to be applied for the good of his soul, and the rest to dispose of as he pleased. But at the point of death his children opened the chest. "Antequam totaliter expiraret, ad cistam currentes nihil invenerunt nisi malleum, in quo Anglicè scriptum est:—

"'Wyht suylc a betel be he smyten, That al the werld hyt mote wyten, That gyfht his sone al his thing, And goht hym self a beggyn.'"

Here, then, is a case whereby to test the problem of the position of folk-tales as historical material. Did the people adopt this tale from literature into tradition and keep it alive for five centuries; or did some early and unconscious folklorist adapt it into literature? The literary version has the flavour of its priestly influence, which does not appear in the traditional version; and I make the preliminary observation that if literature could have so stamped itself upon the memory of the folk as to have preserved all the essentials of such a story as this, it must have been due to some academic influence (of which, however, there is no evidence), and this influence would have preserved a nearer likeness to literary forms than the peasant's tale presents to us. But the objection to this theory is best shown by an analysis of the tale, and by some research into the possible sources of its origin.

The story presents us with the following essential incidents:—

1. The gift of a well-stocked farm by a father to each of his children.
2. The surrender of all property during the owner's lifetime.
3. The living of the old father with each of his children.
4. The attempted killing of the old man.
5. The mallet bearing the inscription.
6. The rhyming formula of the inscription.

Mr. Campbell notes the first and third of these incidents in his original abstract of the story,[87] but of the remaining second, fourth, fifth, and sixth no note has hitherto been taken.

Of the first incident, the gift of a well-stocked farm by a father to each of his children, Mr. Campbell says: "This subdivision of land by tenants is the dress and declaration put on by a class who now tell this tale." But it also represents an ancient system of swarming off from the parent household when society was in a tribal stage. The incident of the tale is exactly reproduced in local custom. In the island of Skye the possessor of a few acres of land cut them up only a few years ago into shreds and patches to afford a separate dwelling for each son and daughter who married.[88] In Kinross, in 1797, the same practice prevailed. "Among the fecars the parents are in many instances disposed to relinquish and give up to their children their landed possessions or the principal part of them, retaining only for themselves some paltry pendicle or patch of ground."[89] In Ireland and in Cornwall much the same evidence is forthcoming, and elsewhere I have taken some pains to show that these local customs are the isolated survivals in late times of early tribal practices.[90]

We next turn to the second essential incident of the tale—the surrender of the estate during the owner's lifetime. This is a well-marked feature of early custom, and Du Chaillu has preserved something like the survival of the ritual observances connected with it in his account of the Scandinavian practice. On a visit to Husum he witnessed the ceremonial which attended the immemorial custom of the farm coming into possession of the eldest son, the father still being alive. The following is Mr. Du Chaillu's description, and the details are important: "The dinner being ready, all the members of the family came in and seated themselves around the board, the father taking, as is customary, the head of the table. All at once, Roar, who was not seated, came to his father and said, 'Father, you are getting old; let me take your place.' 'Oh, no, my son,' was the answer, 'I am not too old to work; it is not yet time: wait awhile.' Then, with an entreating look, Roar said, 'Oh, father, all your children and myself are often sorry to see you look so tired when the day's labour is over: the work of the farm is too much for you; it is time for you to rest and do nothing. Rest in your old age. Oh, let me take your place at the head of the table.' All the faces were now extremely sober,

51

and tears were seen in many eyes. 'Not yet, my son.' 'Oh, yes, father.' Then said the whole family, 'Now it is time for you to rest.' He rose, and Roar took his place, and was then the master. His father, henceforth, would have nothing to do, was to live in a comfortable house, and to receive yearly a stipulated amount of grain or flour, potatoes, milk, cheese, butter, meat, etc."[91] Without stopping to analyse this singular ceremony in detail, it is important to note that old age is the assigned cause of resignation by the father of his estate; that the ceremony is evidently based upon traditional forms, the meaning of which is not distinctly comprehended by the present performers; that the father is supported by his successor. As a proof that we have here a survival of very ancient practice, it may be noticed that in Spiti, a part of the Punjab, an exact parallel occurs. There the father retires from the headship of the family when his eldest son is of full age, and has taken unto himself a wife; on each estate there is a kind of dower-house with a plot of land attached, to which the father in these cases retires.[92] In Bavaria and in Würtemberg the same custom obtains,[93] and the sagas of the North also confirm it as an ancient custom.[94]

Of the third incident in the tale, the living of the father with his children, Mr. Campbell says this points to the old Highland cluster of houses and to the farm worked by several families in common,[95] and I think we have here the explanation why the father in Scotland did not have his "dower-house," as he did in Scandinavia and in Spiti.

We next come to the fourth incident, the attempted killing of the old father. Now, from some of the earliest accounts of travels in Britain, we know that the death of the aged by violence was a signal element of the native customs. "They die only when they have lived long enough; for when the aged men have made good cheere and anoynted their bodies with sweet ointments they leape off a certain rocke into the sea." That we have in this episode of the story, remains of customs which once existed in the North, Mr. Elton affords proof, both from saga-history and from the practice of later times, when "the Swedes and Pomeranians killed their old people in the way which was indicated by the passage quoted above."[96] It is the custom of many savage tribes, and the observances made use of are sometimes suggestive of the facts of the tale we are now analysing. Thus, among the Todas of the Nilgiri Hills, they place the old people in large earthen jars with some food, and leave them to perish;[97] while among the Hottentots, Kolben says, "when persons become unable to perform the least office for themselves they are then placed in a solitary hut at a considerable distance, with a small stock of provisions within their reach, where they are left to die of hunger, or be devoured by the wild beasts."[98]

The important bearing of these incidents of barbarous and savage life upon our subject will be seen when we pass on to our fifth incident, namely, the significant use of the mallet. Some curious explanations have been given of this. Mr. Thorns once thought it might be identified with Malleus, the name of the Devil.[99] Nork has attempted with more reason to identify it with the hammer of Thor.[100] But the real identification is closer than this. Thus, it is connected with the Valhalla practices, already noted, by the fact that if an old Norseman becomes too frail to travel to the cliff, in order to throw himself over, his kinsman would save him the disgrace of dying "like a cow in the straw," and would beat him to death with the family club.[101] Mr. Elton, who quotes this passage, adds in a note that one of the family clubs is still preserved at a farm in East Gothland.[102] Aubrey has preserved an old English "countrie story" of "the holy mawle, which (they fancy) hung behind the church dore, which, when the father was seaventie, the sonne might fetch to knock his father in the head, as effœte, & of no more use."[103] That Aubrey preserved a true tradition is proved by what we learn of similar practices elsewhere. Thus, in fifteenth-century MSS. of prose romances found in English and also in Welsh, Sir Perceval, in his adventures in quest of the Holy Grail, being at one time ill at ease, congratulates himself that he is not like those men of Wales, where sons pull their fathers out of bed and kill them to save the disgrace of their dying in bed.[104] Keysler cites several instances of this savage custom in Prussia, and a Count Schulenberg rescued an old man who was being beaten to death by his sons at a place called Jammerholz, or "Woful Wood;" while a Countess of Nansfield, in the fourteenth century, is said to have saved the life of an old man on the Lüneberg Heath under similar circumstances.

Our investigation of barbarous and savage customs, which connect themselves with the essential incidents of this Highland tale, has at this point taken us outside the framework of the story. The old father in the tale was not killed by the mallet, but he is said to have used it as a warning to others to stop the practice of giving up their property during lifetime. We have already seen that this practice was an actual custom in early times, appearing in local survivals both in England and Scotland. Therefore the story must have arisen at a time when this practice was undergoing a change. We must note, too, that the whole story leads up to the finding of a mallet with the rhyming inscription written thereon, connecting it with the instrument of death to the aged, but only on certain conditions. If, then, we can find that the rhyming inscription on the mallet has an existence quite apart from the story, and if we can find that mallets bearing such an inscription do actually exist, we may fairly conclude that the story, which, in Scotland, is the vehicle of transmission of the rhyme, is of later origin than the rhyme itself.

First of all, it is to be noted under this head that Wright, in a note to the Latin story we have already quoted, gives from John of Bromyard's *Summa Predicantium* another English version of the verse—

"Wit this betel the smieth And alle the worle thit wite That thevt the ungunde alle thing, And goht him selve a beggyng,"

which shows, I think, the popularity of the verse in the vernacular. Clearly, then, the Latin version is a translation of this, and not *vice versâ*. It must have been a rhyming formula in the vernacular, which had a life of its own quite outside its adoption into literature.

This inferential proof of the actual life of the English rhyming formula is confirmed by actual facts in the case of the corresponding German formula. Nork, in the volume I have already quoted, collects evidence from Grimm, Haupt, and others, which proves that sometimes in front of a house, as at Osnabrück, and sometimes at the city gate, as in several of the cities of Silesia and Saxony, there hangs a mallet with this inscription:—

"Wer den kindern gibt das Brod Und selber dabei leidet Noth Den schlagt mit dieser keule todt"—

which Mr. Thoms has Englished thus:—

"Who to his children gives his bread And thereby himself suffers need, With this mallet strike him dead."[105]

These rhymes are the same as those in the Scottish tale and its Latin analogue, and that they are preserved on the selfsame instrument which is mentioned in the story as bearing the inscription is proof enough, I think, that the mallets and their rhyming formulæ are far older than the story. They are not mythical, the story is; their history is contained in the facts we have above detailed; the life of the folk-tale commences when the use or formula of the mallet ceases to be part of the social institutions.

To the rhyming formulæ, then, I would trace the rise of the mythic tale told by the Highland peasant in 1862 to Mr. J. F. Campbell. The old customs which we have detailed as the true origin of the mallet, and its hideous use in killing the aged and infirm, had died out, but the symbol of them remained. To explain the symbol a myth was created, which kept sufficiently near to the original idea as to retain evidence of its close connection with the descent of property; and thus was launched the dateless, impersonal, unlocalised story which Mr. Campbell has given as a specimen of vagrant traditions, which "must have been invented after agriculture and fixed habitations, after laws of property and inheritance; but it may be as old as the lake-dwellings of Switzerland, or Egyptian civilisation, or Adam, whose sons tilled the earth."[106] I would venture to rewrite the last clause of this dictum of the great master of folk-tales, and I would suggest that the story, whatever its age as a story, tells us of facts in the life of its earliest narrators which do not belong to Teutonic or Celtic history. The Teuton and the Celt, with their traditional reverence for parental authority, at once patriarchal and priestly, would retain, with singular clearness, the memory of traditions, or it may be observations, of an altogether different set of ideas which belonged to the race with which they first came into contact. But whether the story is a mythic interpretation by Celts of pre-Celtic practices, or a pre-Celtic tradition, varied as soon as it became the property of the Celt to suit Celtic ideas, it clearly takes us back to practices very remote, to use Mr. Elton's forcible words, from the reverence for the parents' authority which might have perhaps been expected from descendants of "the Aryan household."[107] These practices lead us back to a period of savagery, of which we have to speak in terms of race distinction if we would get at its root.[108] The importance of such a conclusion cannot be overrated, for it leads directly to the issue which must be raised whenever an investigation of tradition leaves us with materials, which are promptly rejected as fragments of Celtic history because they are too savage, but which need not therefore be rejected as history, because they may be referred further back than Celtic history.

If we proceed by more drastic methods, by the methods of statistics, we shall arrive at much the same conclusion.[109] Taking the first twelve stories in Grimm's great collection, we find that seven of them yield elements which we are entitled to call savage, because they are so far removed from the European culture amidst which the folk-tales have lived, and because these elements belong not to the accidentals of the stories but to the essentials. Thus, if we divide the folk-tale into its components, we shall find that it consists of three features:—

    1. The story radicals, or essential plot;

    2. The story accidentals, or illustrative points;

    3. Modern gloss upon the events in the story—

and if we go on to allocate the various incidents of the stories to these three heads, we get the following common results with regard to seven out of the twelve first stories of Grimm's great collection:—

I.—Frog Prince

Story radicals Story accidentals Added features Modern gloss 1. Savage elements Youngest daughter

Fountain or well the locality of leading incident

Frog prince—totem

Frog prince stays at the house of his future wife

Exogamous marriage, the prince coming from a foreign country — — — 2. Fantastic element — — Faithful servant whose heart is bound by iron bands — 3. Rank and splendour — — — Kingly state and its trappings—the princess wears a crown on ordinary occasions, and yet opens the door to a visitor while at dinner

III.—Our Lady's Child

Story radicals Story accidentals Added features Modern gloss 1. Savage elements — Naked forest woman captured for wife

Suspicion that she is a cannibal — — 3. Rank and splendour — — —
Virgin Mary and heaven the central features of the heroine's
adventures 4. Moral characteristics Punishment for curiosity — — —
IV.—The Youth who Wants to Learn to Shudder

Story radicals Story accidentals Added features Modern gloss 1.
Savage elements Winning of wife by service

Succession to kingship through wife—female kinship

Treasure guarded by spirits — — — 2. Fantastic element — The
adventures in the haunted castle — — 3. Rank and splendour — — —
*Kingly state 4. Moral characteristics Bravery — — — V.—***The Wolf**
and Seven Little Kids

Story radicals Story accidentals Added features Modern gloss 1. Savage
elements Talking animals

Cutting open of the animal to free the swallowed kids, and refilling the
stomach with stones Criticism upon men as compared with animals, 'truly
men are like that' — —
VI.—Faithful John

Story radicals Story accidentals Added features Modern gloss 1.
Savage elements Capture of bride

Talking of animals

Three taboos—
  Horse
  Garment

Sucking of breasts

Sacrifice of children and sprinkling of their blood on a stone

*Human origin of stone pillar — — — 3. Rank and splendour — — — Kingly state and great wealth in gold and riches 4. Moral characteristics — Punishment for curiosity — — IX.—*The Twelve Brothers

Story radicals Story accidentals Added features Modern gloss 1. Savage elements Going [causing to go] away of sons, so that the inheritance should fall to the daughter

Change of brothers into ravens

Life dependent on an outside object Forest life — — 3. Rank and splendour — — — Kingly state 4. Moral characteristics — — — — XI.—Brother and Sister

Story radicals Story accidentals Added features Modern gloss 1. Savage elements Transformation of hero into roebuck after drinking at stream — —
—

There are thus savage elements in seven out of twelve stories, and the question becomes an important one as to how this is. They are the stories of the nursery, told by mothers to children, stories kept alive by tradition, and the only possible answer to our question is that they contain fragments of the early culture-history of the ancestors, or at all events the predecessors, of those who have preserved them for our use. An occasional savage incident might have been considered a freak of the original narrator, or a borrowing by one of the countless late narrators of these stories brought home from savage countries; but statistics disprove both of these suppositions. It is not accidental but persistent savagery we meet with in the folk-tale. It is also the savagery to be found amongst modern peoples still in the savage stage of culture.

This is proved in a very complete manner by Mr. MacCulloch, whose study provides the material for a statistical survey of story incidents founded on primitive custom and belief.[110] They are the most ancient history to which we have access. That this history is contained in the folk-tales of modern peasantry shows it to have come from that far-off period which saw the earliest condition of these people. It is still history, if it tells us of a life which preceded the written record. It is history of the most valuable description, for it is to be found nowhere else as relating to the remotest period of European civilisation. The modern savage is better off in this respect. He has an outside historian in the traveller and the anthropologist of modern days. The savage who was ancestor to our own people had no such means of becoming known to history, or had but very limited means, and it is only in the deathless tradition that we can trace him out.

These conclusions have been drawn from that great class of tradition preserved by historic peoples in historic times, and yet unmistakably pointing to prehistoric culture. We have been able to show the methods to be adopted for, and the results of, disengaging the myth which has gravitated to the historic person or place from the historic facts which have become part of the legend, and to trace out in the folk-tale facts which belong to a culture far removed from civilised life. There are thus revealed two distinct centres of influence, the traditional centre and the historic centre, and it is obvious that the question must be asked—which is the more important? It seems to me equally obvious that the answer must be given in favour of the historic. History is indebted to tradition for preserving some of the most remote facts of racial or national life, which but for tradition would have been lost, and if we are content to use this tradition as a storehouse from which we may provide ourselves with ancient historical documents, we can trace out therefrom points in the history of any given country wherever the traditions have been preserved.

The folk-tale, in point of fact, equally with the personal and local legend, comes into close contact with history. The periods of history in the folk-tales are different from those in the legends, but together these periods reach from prehistoric culture to historic event. We cannot, however, call this extent of time a continuous period, and we cannot point to definite stages within the detached periods. Much more research must be accomplished before it will be possible to claim such results as these. I have indicated some points of difficulty, some methods of treatment which appear to me to be wrong, and to which I shall have again to refer later on; but in the meantime, from the necessarily incomplete evidence which I have been able to produce, it is, I think, abundantly clear that folklore has to be studied from its historical surroundings if we would draw from it all that it is capable of telling.

III

In the meantime it is well to bear in mind that there is one important department of history which has always been frankly and unhesitatingly accepted as history and yet which has no stronger foundation than tradition, and tradition of the most formal kind. I allude to the early laws of most of the peoples who have become possessed of an historic civilisation. These laws have all been preserved by tradition, are in rhyme or rhythm in order to assist the memory, have become the sacred repository of a school or class of priests, and have finally been reduced to writing by a great lawgiver, who by the act of giving the people written laws has had attributed to him supernatural origin and powers. That history should have accepted from tradition such an important section of its material is worth consideration by itself, apart from its bearing on the present study, and I shall proceed, therefore, to set out some of the chief facts in this connection.

There can be no doubt that in the tribal society of Indo-European peoples the laws and rules which governed the various members of the tribe were deemed to be sacred and were preserved by tradition. The opening clauses of the celebrated Laws of Manu illustrate this position. "The great sages approached Manu, who was seated with a collected mind, and having worshipped him spoke as follows: Deign, divine one, to declare to us precisely and in due order the sacred laws of each of the four chief castes and of the intermediate ones. For thou, O Lord, alone knowest the purport, the rites, and the knowledge of the soul taught in this whole ordinance of the self-existent which is unknowable and unfathomable."[111] They were not only sacred in origin but they dealt with sacred things, and Sir Henry Maine has drawn the broad conclusion that "there is no system of recorded law, literally from China to Peru, which, when it first emerges into notice, is not seen to be entangled with religious ritual and observance."[112] In Greece the lawgivers were supposed to be divinely inspired, Minôs from Jupiter, Lykurgos from the Delphic god, Zaleukos from Pallas.[113] The earliest notions of law are connected with Themis the Goddess of Justice.[114] In Rome it is to Romulus himself that is attributed the first positive law, and it is by a college of priests that the laws were preserved.[115] In Scandinavia the laws were in the custody and charge of the temple priests, and the accumulated evidence for the sacred origin and connection of the laws is to be found in the sagas.[116] Among the Celtic peoples it is well known that the laws were preserved and administered by the Brehons, who are compared with the Hindu Brahmins by Sir Henry Maine, "with many of their characteristics altered, and indeed, their whole sacerdotal authority abstracted by the influence of Christianity."[117] In the Isle of Man the laws were deemed sacred and known only to the Deemsters.[118]

In all cases laws were preserved by tradition and not by writing and evidence, and the superior value attached to the traditional record appears everywhere. The oldest record of Hindu law agrees with the best authority that it was not founded on writing but "upon immemorial customs which existed prior to and independent of Brahminism."[119] In Greece the very nature of the *themistes* shows that they were judgments dependent upon traditional custom. In Rome it is the subject of definite research that the "greater part of Roman law was founded on the *mores majorum*."[120] In Scandinavia the law speaker was obliged to recite the whole law within the period to which the tenure of his office was limited.[121] The Celtic laws are based upon customs handed down from remote antiquity,[122] and late down in English law it was admitted as a principle that if oral declarations came into conflict with written instruments the former had the more binding authority.[123]

One of the means by which this sacred tradition was preserved was through the medium of rhythm and verse. Thus, as Sir Henry Maine explains,

"The law book of Manu is in verse, and verse is one of the expedients for lessening the burden which the memory has to bear when writing is

61

unknown or very little used. But there is another expedient which serves the same object. This is Aphorism or Proverb. Even now in our own country much of popular wisdom is preserved either in old rhymes or in old proverbs, and it is well ascertained that during the middle ages much of law, and not a little of medicine, was preserved among professions, not necessarily clerkly, by these two agencies."[124]

In Greece the same word, νόμος, was used for custom and law as for song. The ῥήτρα (declared law) of Sparta and Taras was in verse; the laws of Charondas were sung as σκόλια at Athens,[125] and Strabo refers to the Mazacenes of Cappadocia as using the laws of Charondas and appointing some person to be their law-singer (νομωδός), who is among them the declarer of the laws.[126]

Sir Francis Palgrave, noticing the same characteristic of Teutonic law, says:—

"It cannot be ascertained that any of the Teutonic nations reduced their customs into writing, until the influence of increasing civilisation rendered it expedient to depart from their primeval usages; but an aid to the recollection was often afforded as amongst the Britons, by poetry or by the condensation of the maxim or principle in proverbial or antithetical sentences like the Cymric triads. The marked alliteration of the Anglo-Saxon laws is to be referred to the same cause, and in the Frisic laws several passages are evidently written in verse. From hence, also, may originate those quaint and pithy rhymes in which the doctrines of the law of the old time are not unfrequently recorded."[127]

Again, the editors of the Brehon Law Tracts point out that early laws are handed down "in a rhythmical form; always in language condensed and antiquated they assume the character of abrupt and sententious proverbs. Collections of such sayings are found scattered throughout the Brehon Law Tracts."[128] The sagas contain many verses which partake of the character of legal formulæ, and in Beowulf there seems to be a definite example. It occurs in the passage describing Beowulf engaged in his fatal combat with the fiery dragon, when his "companions," stricken with terror, deserted him, on which Wiglaf pronounced the following malediction:—

"Now shall the service of treasure, and the gifts of swords, all joy of paternal inheritance, all support of all your kin depart; every one of your family must go about deprived of his rights of citizenship; when far and wide the nobles shall learn your flight, your dishonourable deed. Death is better to every warrior than disgraced life."

Mr. Kemble remarks on this passage, that it is not improbable that the whole denunciation is a judicial formula, such as we know early existed, and in regular rhythmical measure.[129]

These early examples may be followed up by others preserved to modern times. The most significant of these occurs in the Church ceremony of marriage, which preserves in the vernacular the ancient rhythmical formula of the marriage laws, and the antiquity of the Church ritual is proved from the fact that it is accompanied and enforced by the old rhythmical verse, which is indicative of early legal or ceremonious usage.

"With this rynge I the wed And this gold and silver I the geve, and with my body I the worshipe, and with all my worldely cathel I the endowe."[130]

Sir Francis Palgrave has noticed the subject, and points out that the wife is taken

"to have and to hold[131] from this day forward for better, for worse, for richer, for poorer,[132] in sickness and in health, to love and to cherish, till death us do part and thereto I plight thee my troth."

These words are inserted in our service according to the ancient canon of England, and even when the Latin mass was sung by the tonsured priest, the promises which accompany the delivery of the symbolical pledge of union were repeated by the blushing bride in a more intelligible tongue.[133] This is a curious and significant fact, and as we trace out these rhythmical lines farther back in their original vernacular, the more clearly distinct is their archaic nature. According to the usage of Salisbury the bride answered:—

"I take thee, John, to be my wedded husband, to have and to hold fro' this day forward for better, for worse, for richer, for poorer, in sycknesse, in hele, to be bonere and buxom [obedient] in bedde and at borde till death do us part and thereto I plight thee my trothe."[134]

The Welsh manual in the library of the Dean and Chapter of Hereford has a slight variation in the form, and an older spelling:—

"Ich N. take thee N. to my weddid wyf, for fayroure for foulore, for ricchere for porer, for betere for wers, in sicknesse and in helthe, forte deth us departe, and only to the holde and tharto ich plygtte my treuthe."[135]

To this may be added the many local examples of the preservation of laws or legal formulæ by means of their form in verse. The most interesting of these, perhaps, is that by which the Kentishman redeemed his land from the lord by repeating, as it was said, in the language of his ancestors:—

"Nighon sithe yeld And nighon sithe geld, And vif pund for the were, Ere he become healdere."

The first verse,

"Dog draw Stable stand Back berend And bloody hand"

justified the verderer in his punishment of the offender. In King Athelstane's grant to the good men of Beverley, and inscribed beneath his effigy in the Minster,

"Als fre Mak I the As heart may think Or eigh may see,"

we have perhaps the ancient form of manumission or enfranchisement,[136] just as we have the surrender by a freeman who gave up his liberty by putting himself under the protection of a master, and becoming his man, still preserved among children, when one of them takes hold of the foretop of another and says:—

"Tappie, tappie, tousie, will ye be my man?"[137]

All over the country we meet with these rhyming or rhythmical formulæ which have legal significance. In the north the chief of the Macdonalds gave grants in the following form:—

"I, Donald, chief of the Macdonalds, give here, in my castle, a right to Mackay, to Kilmahumag, from this day till to-morrow and so on for ever."

"Mise Donull nau Donull, Am shuidh air Dun Donuill, Toirt còir do Mhac-aigh air Kilmahumaig, O'n diugh gus a màireach 'S gu la bhràth mar sin."[138]

At Scarborough there is an old proverbial saying as to "Scarborough Warning," which has had various accounts given of its origin,[139] but the true explanation of which is that it is the fragment of an ancient legal formula of the kind we are investigating. Abraham De la Pryme describes it in his seventeenth-century diary as follows:—

"Scarburg Warning is a proverb in many places of the north, signifying any sudden warning given upon any account. Some think it arose from the sudden comeing of an enemy against the castle there, and haveing dischargd a broad side, then commands them to surrender. Others think that the proverb had it's original from other things, but all varys. However, this is the true origin thereof.

"The town is a corporation town, and tho' it is very poor now to what it was formerly, yet it has a ... who is commonly some poor man, they haveing no rich ones amongst them. About two days before Michilmass day the sayd ... being arrayed in his gown of state he mounts upon horseback, and has his attendants with him, and the macebear[er] carrying the mace before him, with two fidlers and a base viol. Thus marching in state (as bigg as the lord mare of London) all along the shore side, they make many halts, and the cryer crys thus with a strange sort of a singing voyce, high and low:—

"'Whay! Whay! Whay! Pay your gavelage, ha! Between this and Michaelmas Day, Or you'll be fined I, say!'

"Then the fiddlers begins to dance, and caper and plays, fit to make one burst with laughter that sees and hears them. Then they go on again and crys as before, with the greatest majesty and gravity immaginable, none of this comical crew being seen so much as to smile all the time, when as spectators are almost bursten with laughing. This is the true origin of the proverb, for this custome of gavelage is a certain tribute that every house pays to the ... when he is pleased to call for it, and he gives not above one day warning, and may call for it when he pleases."[140]

Rhyming tenures have been frequently noted but never understood. They occur in many parts of the country. The tithingman of Combe Keynes, in Dorsetshire, is obliged to do suit at Winforth Court, and after repeating the following incoherent lines, pays threepence and goes away without saying another word:—

"With my white rod And I am a fourth post That three pence makes three God bless the King, and the lord of the franchise Our weights and our measures are lawful and true Good morrow Mr. Steward I have no more to say to you."[141]

It is hardly necessary to quote more examples. They are not unknown to the historian, but because they are in rhyme they have been hastily assumed to be spurious or even burlesque.[142] But the evidence of a rhyming formula is the opposite to this. It is evidence of their genuineness,

65

and if some of the words appear to be nonsensical it is due to the fact that the sense of the old formula has been misunderstood, and has then become gradually altered.

All these rhyming tenures, indeed, find their place among the traditional examples of legal formulæ. They are the local offshoots preserved because of their legal significance, preserved by those interested from their legal side. Because they are not preserved in the formal codes they need not be neglected, and they must not be misunderstood. They are not to be put on one side by the historian as freaks of local landowners. They are real descendants by traditional lines from the times when laws were not written, but kept alive in the memory by means of such assistance as rhyme could supply, and from the tribesmen who thus treasured the law they obeyed.[143]

That this branch of recorded law is not only early but tribal is undoubted, but perhaps it will be well to refer to tribal rhyming formulæ of an independent kind in order to show by parallel evidence the tribal characteristics. In 1884 Mr. Posnett drew attention to this important subject, and noted that

"Dr. Brown, in an attempt to sketch the origin of poetry—an attempt which attracted the attention of Bishop Percy in his remarks introductory to the *Reliques*—proposed more than one hundred years ago to discover the source of the combined dance, song, melody, and mimetic action of primitive compositions in the common festivals of clan life. The student of comparative literature will probably regard Dr. Brown's theory as a curious anticipation of the historical method in a study which, in spite of M. Taine's efforts, has made so little progress as yet. The clan ethic of inherited guilt and vicarious punishment has attracted considerable attention. But the clan poetry of the ancient Arabs and of the bard-clans, surviving in the Hebrew sons of Asaph or the Greek Homeridæ, has not received that light from comparative inquiry which the closely connected problems of primitive music and metre would alone amply deserve."[144]

Not much has been done since this was penned. Max Müller had previously, in 1847, declared that the Rig Veda consisted of the clan songs of the Hindu people,[145] but the importance of such a conclusion has been entirely neglected. In the meantime evidence is accumulating that in Britain there are still preserved many examples of clan songs. Thus Lord Archibald

Campbell has published, in the first volume of his *Waifs and Strays of Celtic Tradition*, some sixteen or seventeen sagas. Some of these are clan-traditions; and the editor notes as evidence of their antiquity the fact that none of them makes any mention of firearms. These clan-traditions all relate to feuds and vendettas; and in one case it is expressly recorded that the descendants of one of the foes of the clan, in their account of the incident narrated, "altered this tradition and reversed the main facts." This has been followed by a volume definitely devoted to "clan-traditions,"[146] while in the *Carmina Gadelica* and many of the Highland incantations there are preserved specimens of ancient clan songs.

The most interesting of the tribal songs is that preserved at the Hawick Common riding. The burgh officers form the van of a pageant which insensibly carries us back to ancient times, and in some verses sung on the occasion there is a refrain which has been known for ages as the slogan of Hawick. It is "Teribus ye teri Odin," which is probably a corruption of the Anglo-Saxon, "Tyr habbe us, ye Tyr ye Odin"—May Tyr uphold us, both Tyr and Odin.

Fortunately Dr. Murray has investigated this formula, and I will quote what he says:—

"A relic of North Anglian heathendom seems to be preserved in a phrase which forms the local slogan of the town of Hawick, and which, as the name of a peculiar local air, and the refrain, or 'owerword' of associated ballads, has been connected with the history of the town back to 'fable-shaded eras.' Different words have been sung to the tune from time to time, and none of those now extant can lay claim to any antiquity; but associated with all, and yet identified with none, the refrain '*Tyr-ibus ye Tyr ye Odin*,' Tyr hæb us, ye Tyr ye Odin! Tyr keep us, both Tyr and Odin! (by which name the tune also is known) appears to have come down, scarcely mutilated, from the time when it was the burthen of the song of the gleó-mann or scald, or the invocation of a heathen Angle warrior, before the northern Hercules and the blood-red lord of battles had yielded to the 'pale god' of the Christians."

The Auld Ca-knowe: calling the Burgess Roll at Hawick (reprinted from Craig and Laing's "Hawick Tradition"). **THE AULD CA-KNOWE: CALLING THE BURGESS ROLL**

The Hawick Moat at sunrise (reprinted from Craig and Laing) **HAWICK MOAT AT SUNRISE**

And in a note Dr. Murray adds:—

"The ballad now connected with the air of 'Tyribus' commemorates the laurels gained by the Hawick youth at and after the disastrous battle, when, in the words of the writer,

"'Our sires roused by "Tyr ye Odin," Marched and joined their king at Flodden.'

Annually since that event the 'Common-Riding' has been held, on which occasion a flag or 'colour' captured from a party of the English has been with great ceremony borne by mounted riders round the bounds of the common land, granted after Flodden to the burgh; part of the ceremony consisting in a mock capture of the 'colour' and hot pursuit by a large party of horsemen accoutred for the occasion. At the conclusion 'Tyribus' is sung, with all the honours, by the actors in the ceremony, from the roof of the oldest house in the burgh, the general population filling the street below, and joining in the song with immense enthusiasm. The influence of modern ideas is gradually doing away with much of the parade and renown of the Common-Riding. But 'Tyr-ibus ye Tyr ye Odin' retains all its local power to fire the lieges, and the accredited method of arousing the burghers to any political or civil struggle is still to send round the drums and fifes, 'to play Tyribus' through the town, a summons analogous to that of the Fiery Cross in olden times. Apart from the words of the slogan, the air itself bears in its wild fire all the tokens of a remote origin."[147]

We could not get better evidence than this of the survival of tribal custom, custom that is distinctly connected with tribes rather than with places or individuals, with groups of people who, now bound together by local considerations and influences, have only recently passed away from the far more ancient influences of the tribe. Alike in the forms of historical codes and in traditional local remains, we have found evidence of the use of rhyme for the preservation of unwritten rules and forms; and this use restores to tradition an important branch of its material.

We have thus ascertained that there is direct and acknowledged indebtedness of history to tradition. Its extent covers a wide area of culture progress, and of unbroken continuity from tribal to historic times. The legal codes of the barbaric tribes of Western Europe are the direct successors of the traditional originals; and because these legal codes, equally with their unwritten predecessors, cannot be dispensed with by the historian, they find their place unquestioned among genuine historical material. They are no more, and no less, historical than other traditional material. They are part of the life of the people rescued from prehistoric days, and they tell us of these days by the same sanction and the same methods as the rest of the traditional material which has been so strangely and so persistently neglected by the historian. The whole of tradition, and not selected parts of it, must be brought into use if we would follow scientific method, and I claim this for the study of folklore on the strength of the results which have now been brought together.

One of five stone circles in the fields opposite the Glebe of Nymphsfield (reprinted from Sir William Wilde's "Lough Corrib") **ONE OF FIVE STONE CIRCLES IN THE FIELDS OPPOSITE THE GLEBE OF NYMPHSFIELD**

Carn-an-Chluithe to commemorate the defeat and death of the youths of the Dananns (reprinted from Wilde) **CARN-AN-CHLUITHE TO COMMEMORATE THE DEFEAT AND DEATH OF THE YOUTHS OF THE DANANNS**

The cairn of Ballymagibbon, near the road passing from Cong to Cross (reprinted from Wilde) **THE CAIRN OF BALLYMAGIBBON NEAR THE ROAD PASSING FROM CONG TO CROSS**

IV

Here, however, we are close up to an important point of controversy. The mythologists claim tradition as theirs. It does not, they assert, give us the history but the mythology of our race. It tells us not of the men but of the gods. In explaining how this comes about, however, they have fallen into errors which it is not only necessary to correct but which are fundamental in their effects. We shall be better able later on to discuss the extremely important question of the position of the prehistoric tradition amidst historic life and surroundings, if we try to understand what the mythologists have done and not done in their attempts to claim exclusive property in the folk-tale. They have entirely denied or ignored all history contained in the folk-tale, and they have proceeded upon the assumption, the bald assumption not accompanied by any kind of proof, that the folk-tale contains nothing but the remnants of a once prevalent system of mythology. They ignore all the proofs brought forward by folklorists to the contrary, such proofs, for instance, as Mr. Knowles, Sir Richard Temple and others have produced concerning the Hindu folk-tale. What is not true of the Hindu folk-tale cannot be true of its Celtic or Teutonic or Scandinavian parallel, and yet in the most recent study of Celtic tradition, Mr. Squire takes its mythic origin for granted, and works through his ingenious statement without let or hindrance from other points of view. But even his thorough-going methods compel him to stop short at certain points, and to admit that he has come across historic fact. Thus he agrees that the Fir-Bolgs "were not really gods but the pre-Aryan race which the Gaels, when they landed in Ireland, found already in occupation,"[148] and yet when he treats of the fight of the Fir-Bolgs with the Tuatha dé Danann, and is confronted with Sir William

70

Wilde's proofs that the monuments on the plain of Moytura are in agreement with the traditions concerning them, and point to the account of the battle being historical,[149] all that Mr. Squire can admit is that "certainly the coincidences are curious." He disposes of them on the ground that the "people of the goddess Danu are too obviously mythical to make it worth while to seek any standing ground for them in the world of reality." That standing ground might be found connected with the Tuatha dé Danann in many places, but Mr. Squire will have it that it is impossible, because "it was about this period that the mythology of Ireland was being rewoven into spurious history."[150] It is not, however, upon the mistakes of other inquirers[151] that the mythologists may rest a good claim for their own view. The *Historia Britonum* of Geoffrey of Monmouth disposes of neither the myths nor the history of the Celts. It shows myth in its secondary position, in the handling of those who would make it all history, just as now there are scholars who would make it all myth. In front of the legends attaching to persons and places is the history of these persons and places. Behind these legends lies the domain of the unattached and primitive folk-tale, Mr. Campbell's *Highland Tales*, Kennedy's *Fireside Stories of Ireland*, and those English tales which have been rescued by Mr. Clodd and others. This makes it impossible to see in the hero-legends naught else than the intangible realm of Celtic gods and goddesses.

Equally impossible is it to create for them a home in a system of "state religion," and yet a state religion is a necessary part of the evidence for mythological origins.[152] There was no Celtic state. Emphatically this was so. Everything we know about the Celts of Britain, both before and after the Roman conquest, both in Britain, where the Roman power was upheld for four centuries, and in Ireland, where the Roman power never penetrated, the Celts were possessed of a tribal, not a state polity; lived in tribal strongholds, not in Celtic cities; occupied tribal territories, not countries formed into states; elected tribal chiefs in primitive fashion, and not kings with state ceremonial; and when they come under the dominion of an incipient state policy after the conquest of the English and the Northmen, their laws are promulgated and codified, and show that both Welsh and Irish codes are tribal, not state law.

Not only do I fail to discover a state religion of the Celts, but I do not find it among the Teutons. There is greater evidence of discrepancies than of agreement in all the European religions, but these have not been dwelt upon by scholars. Professor York Powell, in one of his illuminating studies on Teutonic heathendom, is the only authority I know of who argues against the idea of a systematised religion. "It is important that we should at once throw aside the idea that there was any *system*, any organized pantheon in the religion of these peoples. Their tribes were small and isolated, and each had its own peculiar gods and observances, although the mould of each faith was somewhat similar. Hence there were varieties of religious customs among the Goths, Swedes, Saxons, and Angles."[153]

Altar dedicated to the field deities of Britain, found at Castle Hill on the wall of Antoninus Pius **ALTAR DEDICATED TO THE FIELD DEITIES OF BRITAIN**
FOUND AT CASTLE HILL ON THE WALL OF ANTONINUS PIUS

Now if there was no state there could be no state religion. What existed of worship and religion was tribal. These are the historical facts, which have been neglected by students of myth and saga. I shall have to point out in greater detail presently what these tribal conditions mean to studies in folklore, but the word of warning and protest must come here, for it is unconsciously the conception of a Celtic state religion which gives even the semblance of possibility for Celtic mythology to be found in every hero-legend. It is, in short, the neglect of this among other historical facts which has led the folklorist into error of a somewhat magnificent kind. He attempts to create out of the myths of a people a mythology which provides gods to be worshipped, faiths to be organised, and beliefs to be the standards of life and conduct. Thus, as I have pointed out elsewhere,[154] Sir John Rhys has, in his acute identification of the worship of the water-god Lud on the Thames and of Nod on the Severn,[155] introduced the idea of a great Celtic worship established on these two great rivers as parts of a definite system of Celtic religion, whereas examination proves that the parallel faiths of two perfectly distinct Celtic tribes, the Silures on the Severn and the Trinovantes on the Thames, were welded into a common worship of the god of the waters by the masters of Celtic Britain, the Romans. There was no Celtic organisation which commanded both Severn and Thames until the Romans occupied the country, and occupying the country they adopted into their own religion the native gods and, fortunately for us, recorded their adoption in the pavements of their houses or their temples.[156]

Mr. A. B. Cook goes much further than Sir John Rhys. He attempts to dig out the European sky-god from all sorts of queer places, all sorts of forgotten records, thereby producing a wealth of folklore parallels for which every student must be profoundly thankful. But he does not make it anywhere clear that this universal god was gloriously apparent to his worshippers. There is no established connection between the sky-god and those who worshipped the sky-god, and we seek in vain amidst all the brilliant researches, which have been held to produce evidence of the sky-god, for evidence that he was worshipped by the Aryan-speaking Celt and Teuton. In point of fact, we never get at the worshippers at all. There is the assumption of a state mythology without any evidence for the existence of the state.

In place of this obvious necessity we get an immense abstraction, worked out with all the subtle ingenuity and learning of the Cambridge professor. Mr. Cook has, in fact, used the materials he has collected with such amazing care to project therefrom just those mythological conceptions which Celt and Teuton would have worked out for themselves if they, like the Hindu and the Greek, had developed the state while they were still free to develop their own native beliefs. This they never did, and so their fire worship did not advance beyond its early stages. It was separated from nature worship to become the servant of the European tribes. It helped them to develop tribal and family institutions. It produced for them a tribal and family worship. It did not get beyond this, because Roman institutions and Christianity stood in the way and prevented tribal fire worship from becoming anthropomorphised into a mythology. This need not cause us to doubt that the analogies claimed by these scholars are true analogies. There were among the Celtic peoples, as among other branches of the race to which

Celt, Greek, Teuton, Scandinavian, and Hindu belonged, the incipient elements which would go to make up a national or state mythology, when the nation or the state emerged, as it did emerge in the case of Greece and of Rome, from its tribal originals. But the Celtic state did not emerge from tribalism in Britain; the Celtic heroes were always tribal heroes. They were, as Hereward and Arthur were, real human flesh and blood, fighting and raiding and loving and feasting in their tribal fashion as the later heroes did in their national fashion; because of their success as tribal heroes they had attached to them the tribal myths; because they died as nobly as Cuchulain died they left imperishable records among those for whom they died. They were more than gods to the Celtic tribesman—they were kinsmen.

The false conception of a state religion before there was a state, appears in other studies not primarily based upon folklore research, and not having in view anthropological results. It is the basis of the remarkable researches of Sir Norman Lockyer as to the astrological and solar origin of Stonehenge and other circles, and in his chapter which deals with the question, "Where did the British worship originate?" he finds himself bound to the theory of a borrowed civilisation which established the solar system.[157] This borrowed civilisation is Egyptian, but it is too much to ask mythology to supply not only a complete system of belief but a civilisation which belongs to it. What is needed is independent evidence of the civilisation. Without such independent evidence it is impossible to accept the deduction drawn only from one sphere of information.

The error of transferring to the domain of mythology events and occurrences which belong to history, is followed by an error of another sort, namely, the transferring to some general department of human belief the particular beliefs of a people, or of tribes of people. It is wrong to continue to label particular cults as nature myths, when they have already been transferred from that position to a more definite position among the beliefs of a people. Thus even so good a scholar as Mr. A. B. Cook, rightly interpreting Greek evidence of the hill-top fires and of the house fire, yet denies to the exactly corresponding Irish evidence the same interpretation, and argues that "the ritual of Samain, at which all the hearths in Ireland were supplied with fresh fire from a common centre at Tlachtga [is] almost certainly solar," and that "we shall not be far wrong if we suppose that the solar fires of Beltaine were the ritual of the sky god connected with the Ash of Uisnech."[158] Mr. Frazer, too, has interpreted these bonfires as mainly sun charms, and he sees in the Balder myth, and in the peasant customs all over Europe, which he asserts illustrate this myth, an ancient ritual which originally marked the beginning of the new year, when the tree spirit, or spirit of vegetation, was burned, the special reasons why the deity of vegetation should die by fire being that as "light and heat are necessary to vegetable growth, on the principle of sympathetic magic, by subjecting the personal representative of vegetation to their influence you secure a supply of these necessaries for trees and crops."[159] Mr. Frazer goes far afield for evidence. He does not see that the fire ceremonies which he collects from all Europe have a specialised significance, even in their last stages of existence as survivals, which is not found among the Incas, the African tribes, the hill tribes of India, and the Chinese, whom he cites as providing the required parallels. Parallel practices are not necessarily evidence of parallels in culture, and it is the failure to locate properly the several examples in relationship to each other which produces a loose and inadequate conception of the relics of fire worship in European countries, and the refusal to recognise its special place as the cult of a tribal people.[160] Another example of this fundamental error takes us in the very opposite direction to that of Dr. Frazer. Thus Dr. Gummere, in a recent study dealing with Germanic origins,[161] sees nothing in the fire cult of the Indo-European people but a branch, and apparently an undeveloped branch, of general nature worship, not specially Germanic or Indo-European, not specialised by the tribes and clans of these people into a cult far more closely connected with their doings and their life than mere participation in the general primitive nature worship could have afforded.

The danger of searching for a general system of belief and worship from the beliefs and rites of peoples not ethnically, geographically, or politically connected is very great, and I venture to think that even Mr. Frazer's remarkable researches into the agricultural rites of European peoples do not take count of one important consideration. I think his constructive hypothesis is too complex in process and too systematic in form to have been the actual living faith of the varied paganism of the European peoples. It would have meant as organised an institution as the Christian Church itself, and of this there is no evidence whatever. It would have meant an exclusive agricultural ceremony, and of this there is strong evidence to the contrary. It would have meant a deep system of philosophy, penetrating from the highest to the lowest of the people, and of this there is no evidence. The plain fact is that the historical conditions have been altogether left out of consideration in these matters, and we consequently do not get a complete study. We get the advocate's position. The case for the mythological interpretation of folklore has been put with full strength, but it is not the entire case.

V

This short survey of the relationship of tradition to history would not answer its purpose if we did not consider the complementary position which history bears to tradition. This may best be done by reference to the period before that occupied by contemporary native record. The history here alluded to is, properly speaking, only derived from one source, namely, the works of foreign or outside authorities. It is written by observers from a civilised country, travelling among the more primitive peoples of another land, and the Greek and Latin authors who relate particulars of early Britain were of this class. Their narratives have to be compared with the traditions written down as history by professed historians, who lived long after the events happened to which the traditions are said to relate, but who recorded the traditions of the people preserved in the monasteries by devotees who were of the people, or by the songs and rhymes which, as Henry of Huntingdon states explicitly, were used for the purpose.

Both the observations of the foreign historians and travellers and the recorded traditions from native sources have been treated with scant courtesy whenever they cannot be explained according to the views of each particular inquirer into the period to which they refer. They have been alternatively the subject of dispute or neglect by students for a long series of years. They consist of items which do not fit in with Celtic or Teutonic institutions as we know them from other and more detailed sources. They offend against the national pride because they tell of a condition of savagery. They do not appeal to the historian, because the historian knows little and cares nothing at all about the condition of savagery. If, therefore, they are not rejected as true history, they are purposely neglected. They are in any event never taken into consideration by the right method, and they stand over for examination by any one who will take the trouble to deal with them by the light and test of modern research.

It is not my purpose to deal with these matters now, but it is advisable that we should try to understand two things—first, how they have been dealt with by the historian; secondly, their true place in history.

The Greek and Latin authors who have stated of peoples living in Britain many characteristics which do not belong to civilisation or even to the borders of civilisation, range from Pytheas the Greek in the middle of the fourth century before our era down to the Latin poets of the early fifth century anno Domini. They all refer to the British savage. He is cannibalistic, incestuous, naked, possesses his wives in common, lives on wild fruits and not cultivated cereals, indulges in head-hunting, has no settled living-place which can be called a house, and generally betrays the characteristics of pure savagery.[162] Altogether there is a fairly substantial range of material for the formation of a reasonable conception of the condition of savagery in Britain.

Roman sculptured stone found at Arniebog, Cumbernauld, Dumbartonshire, showing a naked Briton as a captive **ROMAN SCULPTURED STONE FOUND AT ARNIEBOG, CUMBERNAULD, DUMBARTONSHIRE, SHOWING A NAKED BRITON AS A CAPTIVE**

We need not dwell long upon the earlier of our historians who have neglected or contested the statements of the authorities they use. They hardly possessed the material for scientific treatment, and personal predilections were the governing factors of any opinion which is expressed. John Milton, in his brave attempt to tell the story of early England, does not so much as allude to these disagreeable points. Hume disdainfully passes by the whole subject and practically begins with the Norman conquest. Lappenberg says of the group marriage of the Britons that it "is probably a mere Roman fable."[163] Innes accepts the views of the classical authorities and argues from them in his own peculiar way,[164] but Sullivan will have it that the materials afforded from classical sources are worthless: "they consist of mere hearsay reports without any sure foundation, and in many cases not in harmony with the results of modern linguistic and archæological investigations."[165] Neither Turner nor Palgrave has any doubt as to the authority of these early accounts,[166] and Dr. Giles accepts the accounts which he so usefully collected from the original authorities.[167]

The modern historian cannot, however, be so incidentally treated. He lives in the age of the comparative sciences and of anthropological research. He sometimes uses, though in a half-hearted and incomplete fashion, the results of inquirers in these fields of research, but he nowhere deals with the problem fully. His sins are not general, but special. He agrees with one statement of his original authority and disagrees with another, and we are left with a chaos of opinion founded upon no accepted principle. If the earlier historians accepted or rejected historical records without much reason for either course, the later historians have no right to follow them. The terms "savage" and "barbarian," indulged in by the Greek and Roman writers, cannot be rejected by modern authorities simply because they are too harsh. They cannot be considered merely in the nature of accusations against the standing and position of our ancestors, made by advocates anxious to blacken the national character. Even scholars like Mr. Skene, Mr. Elton, and Sir John Rhys, though inclined to weigh these passages by the light of ethnographic research, throw something like doubt upon the exact extent to which they may be taken as evidence. Mr. Elton, though admitting that the early "romances of travel" afford some evidence as to the habits of our barbarian ancestors, cannot quite get as far in his belief as to think that the account of "the Irish tribes who thought it right to devour their parents" is much more than a traveller's tale.[168] Sir John Rhys is not quite sure that the account by Cæsar of the communal marriages of the British is "not a passage from some Greek book of imaginary travels among imaginary barbarians which Cæsar had in his mind,"[169] though he notes elsewhere that "the vocabulary of the Celts will be searched in vain for a word for son or daughter as distinguished from boy or girl" as a fact of no little negative importance in relation to Cæsar's "ugly account;"[170] and he has similar doubts to express, noteworthy among them being the passage from Pliny which illustrates the Godiva story.[171] Mr. Skene lays stress upon the fact that Tacitus "neither alludes to the practice of their staining their bodies with woad nor to the supposed community of women among them;" and he offers some kind of excuse for the Roman evidence as to the tattooing with representations of animals,[172] evidence which Sir John Rhys, too, is chary of accepting in its full sense. Mr. Pearson reluctantly accepts Cæsar's account of the group marriage and the human sacrifice of the Druids, but he ignores all else, including the attested cannibalism of the Atticotti, though he mentions that tribe in another connection.[173] Sir James Ramsay agrees that the Britons tattooed their bodies with woad, recognises the fact that their matrimonial customs were polyandric, and that brother-and-sister marriage obtained, and generally accepts the prevalent ideas as to Celtic Druidism with its sacrificial rites and the system of "state worship." He rests his views for much of this upon the anthropological evidence in support of it.[174] Mr. Lang on behalf of Scotland, and Dr. Joyce on behalf of Ireland, have their say on the evidence. Mr. Lang seems to accept Cæsar's evidence "if correctly reported," throws doubts upon the ethnological value of such customs, and declares roundly that to found theories upon such evidence as archæology provides "is the province of another science, not of history."[175] Dr. Joyce says that in early Greek and Roman writers there is not much reliable information about Ireland, though he believes them when they talk of students from Britain residing in Ireland and of books existing in Ireland in the fourth century.[176]

This meagre result from the historians seems to me to be most unfortunate. Even when the testimony of early writers is accepted, it is accepted without the necessary filling in which such an acceptance warrants. Bare acceptance does not tell us much. Each recorded fact has a relationship to surrounding facts, should lead us to associated facts which, escaping observation by early writers, can nevertheless be restored. In history they are isolated and unconnected, because of the faults of the historian who records them. Anthropologically they belong to a wider grouping, reveal a connection with each other which is otherwise unsuspected, and prepare themselves for treatment on a larger platform. The historian has used them for the unprofitable controversy ranging round the question of early Celtic civilisation, whereas they clearly belong to the history of early man, and even the folklorist does not disdain to cast them on one side when they do not suit his purpose.[177]

It is still more unfortunate that Sir Henry Maine should have sought to enhance the value of his Indian evidence by contrasting it with what he calls "the slippery testimony concerning savages which is gathered from travellers' tales,"[178] and that Mr. Herbert Spencer should have replied to this in an angry note, declaring that he was aware "that in the eyes of most, antiquity gives sacredness to testimony, and that so what were travellers' tales when they were written in Roman days have come in our days to be regarded as of higher authority than like tales written by recent or living travellers."[179] The scorn passed upon "travellers' tales," the application of the term "romance" to the early descriptions of voyages, have done the same amount of mischief to these early chapters of history as the constant disbelief in the value of tradition has done to the testimony of folklore.

Now I do not recall these controversies, or lay stress upon what appear to me to be the shortcomings of the historian and folklorist in their relationship to each other, for the purpose of reawakening old antagonisms. I have merely selected a few illustrations of the present position of the subject in order that it may be seen how essential it is to proceed on other lines. All the items which have formed the subject of dispute, together with others which have escaped attention—items which have found their way into history by accident, which are by nature fragmentary and isolated, which do not connect up with anything that is distinctively Celtic or Teutonic, and which do not apparently fit in with any standard common to themselves—must command attention if only because they alone cannot be cut out of history when items standing side by side with them are allowed to remain, and in the end it can, I think, be shown that they command attention because of their inherent value.

The method of investigation as to the importance and significance of these earliest historical records must be anthropological. They are in point of fact so much anthropological data relating to Britain. It is no use calling them history, and then defining that history as bad history simply because as history the recorded facts do not appear to be credible. As a matter of fact they belong to the prehistory period of Britain, and to test their value scientific methods are required.

In the first place, anthropology shows that there is no *primâ facie* necessity for calling them Celtic, thus identifying them with that portion of our ancestry which is Celtic in race; for there is evidence of a non-Celtic race existing in prehistoric times, and existing down to within historic times, if not to modern times. Mr. Willis Bund has recently summarised the evidence from archæology, philology, and tradition as it appears in a particularly valuable local study of ancient Cardiganshire, stating it "to be agreed that there was more than one race of early inhabitants, and two of the sources say that there was an original race and at least two distinct races of invaders," and further, "that whoever the original inhabitants were they were not Celts."[180] These original inhabitants, who were not Celts, have left their remains in the barrows and megalithic monuments which still exist in various parts of the country, and anthropologists show that they have not entirely disappeared from among the race distinctions observable among the people of these islands. If it is possible to proceed from this to another stage, and to show from the British evidence what Mr. Risley has so well illustrated from the Indian evidence, namely, that gradations of race types as shown by anthropometrical indices correspond with gradations of social precedence and social organisation,[181] it may yet be possible to prove that the people who were not Celts were the people with whom originated those recorded customs and beliefs which are rejected as too savage for the Celt. Unfortunately, we know nothing about them, except the isolated scraps which are to be picked up from the early historians. This compels us to turn to other sources of information, and when we do this we find that British folklore preserves in traditional custom, rite, belief, and folk-tale, parallels to each and every item of savagery mentioned by the early historians of Britain; and further, that anthropology shows clearly enough that among the customs and beliefs of primitive races there are to be found parallels to every item of custom and belief recorded of early Britain. This gets rid of one of our greatest difficulties, and disposes of Dr. Sullivan's unwarranted assertion to the contrary (*ante*, p. 113). The recorded customs and beliefs of early Britain are proved by this means not to be impossible or improbable factors in the elements of the British prehistoric race. It will not be possible to term them inventions of romance or of false testimony, simply on the ground that they are not found elsewhere. On the contrary it will, I think, be difficult to resist the conclusion that inventions such as these, covering a wide and ascertained area of sociological and early religious development, could hardly have been made by historians having the limited range of knowledge possessed by the native and classical writers who are responsible for the facts. It is an easy, but not a satisfactory method of criticism to declare what is not to one's liking to be invention and romance, and it has until late years been difficult to combat such an argument. The battle has raged round wordy disputes, the merits of which are governed by the abilities of the respective disputants; that this is no longer possible is due to the fact that there have entered into the fray the methods and results of folklore which prevent the terms invention and romance from being applied, except where there is good independent reason for their use.

I have now dealt with all the points which appear to be necessary in order to show the inherent relationship of folklore to history, and I have shown causes for resisting the claims of mythology to appropriate what it chooses of folklore, and then to reject all the rest from consideration. I have dealt (1) with examples of local traditions and hero-traditions, in their relation to history and historical conditions; (2) with the folk-tale in its retention of details of early historic conditions, and of the picture of early tribal organisation, and in that its structure is based upon the events of savage social conceptions; (3) with the early laws and rules of tribal society preserved by tradition and accepted in historical times; (4) with the claims of mythology to interpret the meaning of folk-tales, and the reasons for rejecting this claim; and (5) with the treatment by historians of statements by classical writers as to the condition of the peoples inhabiting Britain before the dawn of civilisation. I think it will be admitted that, without pretending in any way to have exhausted the evidence, or even to have thoroughly comprehended and satisfactorily stated it under each of these heads, a very considerable claim has been made out for the historical value of folklore. If so much has been gained it will rest with folklorists to pursue investigations on these lines, and it will remain with the historian to consider the results wherever his research leads him into domains where the evidence of folklore is obtainable.

It will be seen that the problems which the two sciences, history and folklore, have to solve in conjunction are not a few and that they are extremely complex. They cannot be solved if history and folklore are separated; they may be solved if the professors in each work together, both recognising what there is of value in the other. History in its earliest stages is either entirely dependent upon foreign authorities, or it has to follow the practice of the earlier and unscientific historian and to deny that there is any history, or at all events any history worth recording, before the advent, perhaps the accidental advent, of an historian on native ground. History in its later stages is dependent upon the personal tastes or ability of each historian for the record of events and facts. Folklore in its earliest stages has brought down from the most ancient times memories of ancient polity, faith, custom, rite, and thought. In its later stages it has preserved custom, rite, and belief amid the attacks of the progressive civilisation which has been developed, and it has clothed heroes of later times with the well-worn trappings of those of old. Combined history and folklore can restore much of the picture of early times, and can work through the fulness of later times with some degree of success. There is needed for this work, however, a clear conception of the position properly held by both sciences, together with established rules of research. This is more particularly needed in the department of folklore. I do not pretend to be able to formulate these rules. In the subjects dealt with in this chapter I have indicated a few of the points which must be raised, and my object will be in the remaining chapters to set forth some of the conditions which it appears to me necessary to consider in connection with the problems with which folklore is concerned as one of the historical sciences.

FOOTNOTES:

[1] Mr. Kemble gives an important illustration of this proposition in his *Saxons in England*, i. 331.

[2] I would refer the reader to Prof. York Powell's brilliant lecture on "A Survey of Modern History," printed in his biography by Mr. Oliver Elton, ii. 1-13, for an admirable summary of this view.

[3] *View of the State of Ireland*, 1595, p. 478.

[4] Asser's *Life of Alfred*, by W. H. Stevenson, 262.

[5] It is not worth while unduly emphasising this point, but the peculiar habit of classing fictional literature as folklore and thereupon

condemning the value of tradition is very prevalent. Mr. Nutt, in dealing with the Troy stories in British history, adopts this method, and denies the existence of historic tradition on the strength of it, *Folklore*, xii. 336-9.

[6] This expression was recently allowed in our old friend *Notes and Queries* in a singularly unsuitable case, 10th ser. vii. 344.

[7] I am not sure this is always the fault of those who are not folklorists. I recently came across a dictum of one of the most distinguished folklorists, Mr. Andrew Lang, which is certainly much in the same direction. "As a rule tradition is the noxious ivy that creeps about historical truth, and needs to be stripped off with a ruthless hand. Tradition is a collection of venerable and romantic blunders. But a tradition which clings to a permanent object in the landscape, a tall stone, a grassy, artificial tumulus, or even an old tree, may be unexpectedly correct."—*Morning Post*, 2 November, 1906.

[8] It is worth while referring to Mr. MacRitchie's article in *Trans. International Folklore Congress* on the historical aspect of Folklore; but Professor York Powell has said the strongest word in its favour in his all too short address as President of the Folklore Society, see *Folklore*, xv. 12-23.

[9] Chapter xi. of Tylor's *Early History of Mankind*.

[10] Spenser, *View of the State of Ireland*, 1595 (Morley reprint), 77.

[11] Perhaps the most remarkable testimony to the foundation of the folk-tale and ballad in the events of history is to be found in a statement made to the *Tribune*, 14 September, 1906, by Mr. Mitra, once proprietor and editor of the *Deccan Post*, with regard to the agitation against the partition of Bengal into two provinces. Mr. Mitra deliberately states that "the best test of finding out Hindu feeling towards the British Government is to see whether there are any ballads or nursery rhymes in the Bengali language against the British. You can have it from me, and I challenge contradiction, that there is no single ballad or nursery rhyme in the Bengali language which is against the British." This is where the soul of the people speaks out.

[12] It is printed, and I have used this print, in Blomefield's *History of Norfolk* (1769), iii. 506, from which source I quote the facts concerning it. Sir William Dugdale's account goes on to connect it with a monument in the church, but this part of the local version is to be considered presently.

[13] See the *Diary* printed by the Surtees Society, p. 220.

[14] The legend was also printed in that popular folk-book, *New Help*

to Discourse, so often printed between 1619 and 1656, and Mr. Axon transcribed this version for the *Antiquary*, xi. 167-168; and see my notes in *Gent. Mag. Lib. English Traditions*, 332-336.

[15] I happen to possess the original cutting of this version preserved among my great-grandfather's papers.

[16] These words are, "I am not a Bigot in Dreams, yet I cannot help acknowledging the Relation of the above made a strong Impression on me."

[17] *Leeds Mercury*, January 3rd, 1885, communicated by Mr. Wm. Grainge of Harrogate.

[18] Mr. Axon says it is current in Lancashire and in Cornwall, *Antiquary*, xi. 168; Sir John Rhys gives two Welsh versions in his *Celtic Folklore*, ii. 458-462, 464-466; a Yorkshire version in ballad form is to be found in Castillo's *Poems in the North Yorkshire Dialect* (1878), under the title of "T' Lealholm Chap's lucky dreeam," *Antiquary*, xii. 121; an Ayrshire variant relates to the building of Dundonald Castle, and is given in Chambers's *Pop. Rhymes of Scotland*, 236.

[19] Blomefield, *Hist. of Norfolk*, iii. 507, suggests that the animal carving represents a bear. There is nothing to confirm this and readers may judge for themselves by reference to the illustrations, which are from photographs taken in Swaffham Church.

[20] I discussed the details in the *Antiquary*, vol. x. pp. 202-205.

[21] This story was communicated by "W.F." to the *St. James's Gazette*, March 15th, 1888. Its continuation, in order to point a moral, does not belong to the real story, which is contained in the part I have quoted.

[22] *Saga Library, Heimskringla*, iii. 126.

[23] These have been collected and commented upon with his usual learning and research, by Mr. Hartland in the *Antiquary*, xv. 45-48. Blomefield, in his *History of Norfolk*, iii. 507, points out that the same story is found in Johannes Fungerus' *Etymologicon Latino-Græcum*, pp. 1110-1111, though it is here narrated of a man at Dort in Holland, and in *Histoires admirables de nostre temps*, par Simon Goulart, Geneva, 1614, iii. p. 366. Professor Cowell, in the third volume of the *Cambridge Antiquarian Society Transactions*, p. 320, has printed a remarkable parallel of the story which is to be found in the great Persian metaphysical and religious poem called the Masnavi, written by Jaláluddin, who died about 1260. J. Grimm discussed

these treasure-on-the-bridge stories in *Kleinere Schriften*, iii. 414-428, and did not attach much value to them.

[24] It is not unimportant in this connection to find that London itself assumes an exceptional place in tradition. Mr. Frazer notes a German legend about London, *Golden Bough* (2nd ed.), iii. 235; Pausanias, v. 292. Mr. Dale has drawn attention to the Anglo-Saxon attitude towards Roman buildings in his *National Life in Early English Literature*, 35.

[25] See *Archæologia*, xxv. 600; xxix. 147; xl. 54; *Arch. Journ.*, i. 112.

[26] I have worked this point out in my *Governance of London*.

[27] Bishop Kennett, quoted in *Notes and Queries*, fourth series, ix. 258.

[28] Mommsen's account of the Pontifex Maximus should be consulted, *Hist. Rome*, i. 178; and *cf.* Fowler, *Roman Festivals*, 114, 147, 214.

[29] Mrs. Gomme, *Traditional Games*, i. 347.

[30] Bingley, *North Wales*, 1814, p. 252.

[31] See my *Folklore Relics of Early Village Life*, 29; Tylor, *Primitive Culture*, i. 97. This case was reported in the newspapers at the time of its occurrence. It came to England from the *London and China Telegraph*, from which the *Newcastle Chronicle*, 9 February, 1889, copied the following statement:—

"The boatmen on the Ganges, near Rajmenal, somehow came to believe that the Government required a hundred thousand human heads as the foundation for a great bridge, and that the Government officers were going about the river in search of heads. A hunting party, consisting of four Europeans, happening to pass in a boat, were set upon by the one hundred and twenty boatmen, with the cry 'Gulla Katta,' or cut-throats, and only escaped with their lives after the greatest difficulty."

[32] I have worked out this fact in my *Governance of London*, 46-68, 202-229.

[33] See Turner, *Hist. of Anglo-Saxons*, ii. 207-222; *Y Cymmrodor*, xi. 61-101.

[34] A passage in William of Malmesbury points to the fact of the Bretons in the time of Athelstan looking upon themselves as exiles from the land of their fathers. Radhod, a prefect of the church at Avranches, writes to King Athelstan as "Rex gloriose exultator ecclesiæ ... deprecamur atque humiliter invocamus qui in exulatu et captivitate nostris meritis et peccatis, in

Francia commoramur" etc., *De Gestis Regum Anglorum* (Rolls Ed.), i. 154.

[35] Rhys, *Celtic Folklore*, ii. 466. Sir John Rhys acknowledges his indebtedness to me for lending him my Swaffham notes, but at that time I had not formed the views stated above and Sir John Rhys confessed his difficulty in classifying and characterising these stories (p. 456).

[36] In the *Anglo-Saxon Chronicle*, anno 418, and in *Ethelward's Chronicle*, A.D. 418, it is recorded that "those of the Roman race who were left in Britain bury their treasures in pits, thinking that hereafter they might have better fortune, which never was the case."

[37] Buried treasure legends are worth examining carefully, especially with reference to their geographical distribution, with a view of ascertaining how far they follow the direction of the Roman, English, Danish and Norman Conquests. See Henderson, *Folklore of Northern Counties*, 320, for Yorkshire examples, and *Folklore Record*, i. 16, for an interesting Sussex example.

The Danish part of Lincoln, near Sleaford, has numerous treasure legends, see Rev. G. Oliver, *Existing Remains of Ancient Britons between Lincoln and Sleaford*, pp. 29 *et seq.*

Mr. W. J. Andrew has proved in the *British Numismatic Journal* (1st ser. i. 9-59) that traditions of buried treasure may be verified a thousand years after the laying down of the hoard. This has reference to the famous Cuerdale find of coins. The people of Walton-le-Dale, on the Ribble, had a legend that if you stood on a certain headland and looked up the valley to Ribchester "you would gaze over the greatest treasure that England had ever seen." The farmers tried excavations, and the divining rod is said to have been used.

The tradition was true. In May, 1840, the hoard was accidentally found, near Cuerdale Hall, within forty yards of the stream, by men who were repairing the southern bank. A willow tree, still in its prime, was planted to mark the spot. We do not know how much bullion was scattered by the finders, but there was recovered a mass of ingots, armlets, chains, rings, and so on, amounting to 1000 oz., with over 7000 silver coins. They lay in a crumbling leaden case, within a decomposed chest of wood. There were about 1060 English silver coins, whereof 919 were of the reign of King Alfred. There were 2020 from Northumbrian ecclesiastical mints, and 2534 of King Canute, with 1047 foreign coins, mainly French. The treasure had belonged to the Scandinavian invaders in the host of the Danish Kings of Northumbria, and very many bore the mark of York, the Danish capital. The chest was the treasure-chest of the Danes. The money had been seized in England, 890-897; on French coasts, 897-910; and collected among the Danes of Northumbria about 911. In that year, we know, the Danes raided Mercia, and were followed by the English King and thoroughly defeated. Their treasurer, Osberth, was killed, and it is argued that the Danes fell back by the Roman road, and were trying to cross into Northumbria by the ford at Cuerdale, but that, the ford being dangerous, they were obliged to bury their treasure-chest forty yards on the southern bank of the river. They were unable to cross, were cooped up in a bend of the stream, and were all put to the sword. Mr. Lang discussed this from the folklore point of view in the *Morning Post*, 2nd November, 1906, and concludes that "granting that none who knew the site of the deposit escaped, the theory marches well, and quite accounts for the presence of the hoard where it was found. The Danish rearguard defending the line of the Darwen would know that their treasure was hurried forward and probably concealed, but would not know the exact spot."

Another good example is recorded in the *Antiquary*, xiv. 228. Further Henderson notes that the Borderers of England and Scotland entrusted their buried treasure to the brownie (*Folklore of Northern Counties*, 248). This is exactly the same idea which exists throughout India. "Hidden treasures are under the special guardianship of supernatural beings. The Singhalese, however, divide the charge between demons and cobra capellas. Various charms are resorted to by those who wish to gain the treasures. A pujâ is sufficient with the cobras, but the demons require a sacrifice. Blood of a human being is the most important, but the Kappowas have hitherto confined themselves to a sacrifice of a white cock, combining its blood with their own, drawn by a slight puncture in the hand or foot. A Tamil, however, has resorted to human sacrifice as instanced by a case reported in the *Ceylon Times*."—*Indian Antiquary*, 1873. ii. p. 125.

[38] Morris, *Heimskringla*, ii. 13.

[39] Laing's *Heimskringla*, ii. 260.

[40] Rhys, *The Arthurian Legend*, 7. Squire, in his recent *Mythology of the British Islands*, states the case for "the mythological coming of Arthur" in cap.

xxi. of his book.

[41] As, for instance, in the case of Taliesin and Ossian, see Squire, *Mythology of the British Islands*, 318; Rhys, *Celtic Mythology*, 551; Nutt's Notes to *Mabinogion*.

I suppose the most ancient example of the duplication process is that of Dion Cassius (iii. 5), who suggests an earlier Romulus and Remus in order to account for the early occupation of the Palatine Hill at Rome. Middleton's *Anc. Rome*, 45.

[42] It is interesting to find that, with independent investigation, Mr. Bury explains on the lines I adopt the traditional part of the life of St. Patrick. See his *Life of St. Patrick*, p. 111.

[43] Freeman, *Hist. Norm. Conq.*, iv. 467.

[44] Wright, *Essays*, i. 244, notes this point; see also Freeman, *Hist. Norm. Conq.*, iv. 828, and the preface to my edition of Macfarlane's *Camp of Refuge* (Historical Novels Series), where I have discussed this subject at length.

[45] *Journ. Anthrop. Inst.*, iii. 52.

[46] Russell, *Kett's Rebellion*, p. 6.

[47] Kemble's *Horæ Ferales*, 108.

[48] Perhaps the most interesting example in a minor way comes from Shrewsbury. In the Abbey Church, forming part of a font, is the upper stone of a cross (supposed to have been the Weeping Cross) which was discovered at St. Giles's churchyard. It had been immemorially fixed in the ditch bank, and all traces of its origin were quite lost, except that an old lady, who was born in 1724, remembered having seen in her youth, persons kneeling before this stone and praying. The transmission of the tradition through very nearly three centuries proved correct, for on its being loosened by the frosts of a severe winter, it fell, and its religious distinction became immediately apparent from the sculpture with which it was adorned.—*Eddowes' Shrewsbury Journal*, 5th October, 1889.

[49] *Gent. Mag. Lib. Popular Superstitions*, 121. The importance of this tradition may be tested by reference to my book on the *Governance of London*, 96-98.

[50] *Archæologia*, xxvi. 369-370. One could give many additional examples from all parts of the country, and undoubtedly they are worth collecting. I cannot refrain from quoting the following, as it is from an

out-of-the-way source. At Seagry, in Wilts, is an ancient farm, one field of which was known as "Peter's Orchard." The author of a local history records the following: "It has been handed down from generation to generation that in a field on this farm a church was built on the site of an ancient heathen burial ground. In order to test the accuracy of this tradition, in the autumn of 1882 I had excavations made on the spot, which I will now describe. The field contains about ten acres, and presents a very singular appearance. In removing the sods, about two feet from the surface we discovered extensive stone foundations, extending for a considerable distance over the field. From the charred appearance of the stones they had evidently suffered from fire, thus supporting the tradition of some of the oldest inhabitants that the ancient church had been destroyed by fire. On continuing the search we found, about two feet below these foundations, a quantity of early British pottery, the remains of broken urns, some charred bones, and heads of small spears. The following is an extract from a letter which I have received from a gentleman, whose family have been connected with this parish for over two hundred years, and who has given me great assistance. He says: My father was born at Startley in 1784, and remained there until about 1840. Both he and my grandfather were deeply imbued with old folklore. I well remember them constantly speaking of the firm belief handed down to them of the heathen burial places at Seagry, and of the supposed ruins of a church and some religious house at Seagry. I think the discoveries made (on the very spot mentioned by tradition) in August, 1882, are abundant proof that after the lapse of more than nine centuries actual verification of the carefully transmitted tradition has at last been found."—*Bath Herald*, 1st September, 1883. If references to other examples were needed I should like to note Sir William Wilde's illustration as to "how far the legend, the fairy tale, the local tradition, or the popular superstition may have been derived from absolute historic fact."—*Lough Corrib*, 121, 123.

[51] *Echoes from the Counties* (1880), p. 30.

[52] Grierson, *The Silent Trade* (1903).

[53] Pearson's *Chances of Death*, ii. 90. The reader should consult Dr. Pearson's entire study on this subject, chapters ix. and x., which may be compared with Mr. MacCulloch's *Childhood of Fiction*, 5-15, and more particularly with Mr. Hartland's *Science of Fairy Tales*.

[54] In 1881 I read a paper before the Folklore Society on "Some Incidents in the story of the Three Noodles by means of reference to facts," *Folklore Record*, iv. 211, and in 1883 I published in the *Antiquary*, two papers on "Notes on Incidents in Folk-tales," based upon the same idea.

[55] Introduction, p. lxix.

[56] Introduction, p. lxxvii.

[57] Page 12.

[58] *Ibid.*, p. 26.

[59] *Ibid.*, p. 5.

[60] *Tales of the Highlands*, i. p. 251.

[61] Kennedy, *loc. cit.*, p. 77.

[62] *Ibid.*, p. 90.

[63] See Beda, *Hist. Ecclesia*, lib. i. cap. 25.

[64] See vol. i. p. 253.

[65] Miss Frere's *Old Deccan Days*, p. 279.

[66] Ælian, *Var. Hist.*, lib. xiii. cap. xxxiii.

[67] *Folklore Record*, vol. iv. p. 57.

[68] *Asiatic Researches*, xvii. p. 502.

[69] *Folklore Record*, vol. iii. p. 284.

[70] Campbell's *Popular Tales of the West Highlands*, i. 308.

[71] Joyce, *Old Celtic Romances*, 38, 75, 153, 177, 270. In the *Silva Gadelica*, by Mr. Standish O'Grady, the assembly is described sitting in a circle, vol. ii. p. 159, and Tara is also described, vol. ii. 264, 358, 360, 384.

[72] Miss Cox's admirable study and analysis of the Cinderella group of stories includes the Catskin variants, which number seventy-seven.—*Cinderella*, pp. 53-79.

[73] *Studies in Ancient History*, p. 62.

[74] Sproat's *Scenes and Studies of Savage Life*, p. 96.

[75] See his *Early Hebrew Life*, p. 85.

[76] Frazer, *Adonis, Attis, and Osiris*, 27-28.

[77] Todd and Herbert, *Irish Version of Nennius*, p. 89.

[78] *Indian Antiq.*, iii. 32.

[79] *Laws of Manu* (Bühler), ix. 127; *Apastamba Gautama* (Bühler), xxviii. 18.

[80] Sir Henry Maine in his *Early Law and Custom*, p. 91.

[81] A most remarkable instance of an actual case of running away from a marriage, resulting in adventures which might easily become folk-tale adventures if the story were once started on its traditional life, is to be found in Shooter's *Kafirs of Natal and the Zulu Country*, pp. 60-71.

[82] *West Highland Tales*, vol. i. p. lxix.

[83] Kennedy's *Fireside Stories of Ireland*, p. 64.

[84] *Old Deccan Days*, p. 52.

[85] *Ibid.*, p. 233.

[86] "Standing-place."

[87] *Journ. Ethnol. Soc., loc. cit.*

[88] *New Statistical Account of Scotland*, xiv. 273.

[89] Ure's *Agriculture of Kinross*, 57.

[90] *Archæologia*, l. 195-214.

[91] Du Chaillu's *Land of the Midnight Sun*, i. 393.

[92] Tupper, *Punjab Customary Law*, ii. 188.

[93] *Cobden Club Essays—Primogeniture.*

[94] Morris, *Saga Library*, ii. 194.

[95] *Journ. Ethnol. Soc.*, ii. 336.

[96] Elton, *Origins of English History*, 91; *cf.* Du Chaillu, *Land of the Midnight Sun*, i. 393; Morris's *Sagas*, ii. 194.

[97] Breeks, *Hill Tribes of India*, 108.

[98] Mavor's *Collection of Voyages*, iv. 41.

[99] *Anecdotes and Traditions* (Camden Soc.), 85.

[100] *Mythologie der Volkssagen und Volksmärchen.*

[101] Geiger, *Hist. Sweden*, 31, 32.

[102] Elton, *Origins of English History*, 92.

[103] Aubrey, *Remaines of Gentilisme and Judaisme*, 14.

[104] Nutt, *Legend of the Holy Grail*, 44.

[105] *Gentleman's Magazine*, 1850, i. 250-252.

[106] *Journ. Ethnol. Soc.*, ii. 337.

[107] Elton's *Origins*, 92.

[108] Mr. Jacobs (*Folklore*, i. 405) objected to my interpretation of this story because—first, the Latin rhyme appearing in the Gaelic tale, the twelfth-century Latin story and the German inscription "tell for the origination of the story in one single place in historic times;" and, secondly,

because a Kashmir story (Knowles' *Folk-tales of Kashmir*, 241), based on the same main incident, omits the minor incident of the mallet altogether. The answer to the first objection is that the Latin rhyme has been attached, in historic times, to the ancient folk-tale; and to the second objection, that the Kashmir story preserves the main incident of surrender of property upon reaching old age, and omits the more savage incident of killing, because the Kashmir people are in a stage of culture which still allowed of the surrender of property, but, like the Scandinavians, did not allow of the killing of the aged. Similarly, an English parallel to this form of the variant is preserved by De la Pryme in his *Diary* (Surtees Society), 162. It must be remembered that the Kashmiris occupy a land which is referred to by Herodotos (iii. 99-105) as in the possession of people who killed their aged (*cf.* Latham, *Ethnology of India*, 199); and if my reading of the evidence is correct, this is also the case of the Highland peasant.

[109] Dr. Pearson advocates statistical methods in his *Chances of Death*, ii. 58, 75-77, and shows by examples the value of them.

[110] MacCulloch, *Childhood of Fiction*: "Some of the things which in these old-world stories form their fascination, have had their origin in sordid fact and reality" (p. vii).

[111] Bühler, *Laws of Manu*, i.: "In Vedic mythology Manu is the heros eponymos of the human race and by his nature belongs both to gods and to men" (p. 57). *Cf.* Burnell and Hopkins, *Ordinances of Manu*, p. 25.

[112] *Early Law and Custom*, 5.

[113] Pausanias, iii. 2(4).

[114] Maine, *Ancient Law*, 4; Grote, *Hist. of Greece*, iii. 101.

[115] Ortolan, *Hist. Roman Law*, 50; Maine, *Early Law and Custom*, 6.

[116] Morris, *Saga Library*, i. p. xxx; Dasent, *Burnt Njal*, i. xlvi.

[117] *Early Law and Custom*, 162.

[118] Manx Society Publications, xviii. 21-22.

[119] Strabo, lib. xv. cap. 1, pp. 709, 717; J. D. Mayne, *Hindu Law and Usage*, 4, 13.

[120] Mackenzie, *Roman Law*, 11; *cf.* Pais, *Anc. Legends of Roman Hist.*, 139.

[121] Dasent, *Burnt Njal*, i. p. lvii, and Vigfusson and Powell, *Origines Islandicæ*, i. 348.

[122] *Anc. Laws of Ireland*, iv. p. vii.

[123] This appears very strongly in the famous twelfth-century law case which Longchamp pleaded so successfully. *Rotuli curia Regis*, i. p. lxii.

[124] *Early Law and Custom*, 9; *cf.* Burnell and Hopkins, *Ordinances of Manu*, pp. xx, xxxi. It is worth while quoting here the following interesting note from a letter from the Marquis di Spineto printed in Clarke's *Travels*, viii. 417:—

"From the most remote antiquity men joined together, and wishing either to amuse themselves or to celebrate the praises of their gods sang short poems to a fixed tune. Indeed, generally speaking, *the laws by which they were governed*, the events which had made the greatest impression on their minds, the praises which they bestowed upon their gods or on their heroes were all sung long before they were written, and I need not mention that according to Aristotle this is the reason why the Greeks gave the same appellation to laws and to songs."

[125] The references are all given in Smith's *Dict. of Greek and Roman Antiquities* sub νόμος. Aristotle in the *Problems*, 19, 28, definitely says, "Before the use of letters men sang their laws that they might not forget them, as the custom continues yet among the Agathyrsoi."

[126] Lib. xii. cap. ii. 9.

[127] *Hist. English Commonwealth*, 43.

[128] *Anc. Laws of Ireland*, iv. pp. viii, x.

[129] Hampson's *Origines Patriciæ*, 106-107; Kemble, line 5763 *et seq.*

[130] Proctor's *History of the Book of Common Prayer*, p. 410.

[131] *Hist. Eng. Commonwealth*, ii. p. cxxxvi. Littleton points out the legal antiquity and importance of these words: "no conveyance can be made without them." See Wheatley's *Book of Common Prayer* (quoting Littleton), p. 406.

[132] The York manual had the additional clause, "for fairer for fouler." See Wheatley, *loc. cit.*, p. 406.

[133] Palgrave, *loc. cit.*

[134] *Ibid.*

[135] *Manuale et processionale ad usum insiquis ecclesiæ Evoracensis*, Surtees Society, 1875. See also *Gentleman's Magazine*, 1752, p. 171; Proctor's *History of the Book of Common Prayer*, p. 409, for other examples.

[136] Palgrave, *English Commonwealth*, i. 43.

[137] Chambers, *Popular Rhymes of Scotland*, 115.

[138] Sinclair's *Stat. Acc. of Scotland*, x. 534.

[139] Chambers, *Book of Days*, January 19; Nichols, *Fuller's Worthies*, 494.

[140] *Diary of De la Pryme* (Surtees Society), 126. It may be noted here that Kelly, *Curiosities of Indo-European Traditions*, 179, notes the preservation of an ancient law for the preservation of the oak and the hazel in a traditional proverbial rhyme.

[141] Hazlitt, *Tenures of Land*, 80; other examples refer to the Hundred of Cholmer and Dancing, in Essex, 75; to Kilmersdon, in Somersetshire, 182; to Hopton, in Salop, 165. John of Gaunt is responsible for many of these curious and interesting remains of tribal antiquity. Bisley's *Handbook of North Devon*, 28, refers to one relating to the manor of Umberleigh, near Barnstaple, and I have a note from Mr. Edmund Wrigglesworth, of Hull, of a parallel to this being preserved by tradition only. There is a tradition respecting the estate of Sutton Park, near Biggleswade, Bedfordshire, which states that it formerly belonged to John of Gaunt, who gave it to an ancestor of the present proprietor, one Roger Burgoyne, by the following grant:—
"I, John of Gaunt, Do give and do grant, To Roger Burgoyne And the heirs of his loin Both Sutton and Potton Until the world's rotten."
Potton was a neighbouring village to Sutton. There is a moated site in the park called "John o' Gaunt's Castle," see *Notes and Queries*, tenth series, vi. 466. *Cf.* Aubrey, *Collections for Wilts*, 185, for an example at Midgehall; Cowell's *Law Interpreter*, 1607, and the *Dictionarum Rusticum*, 1704, for the custom of East and West Enborn, in Berks, which was made famous by Addison's *Spectator* in 1714.

[142] Sometimes these are called "burlesque conveyances." See an example quoted in *Hist. MSS. Commission*, v. 459.

[143] It is well to bear in mind the great force of ancient tribal law, which was personal, upon localities. Nottingham is divided into two parts, one having primogeniture and the other junior right as the rule of descent. Southampton and Exeter have also local divisions. But perhaps the most striking example is at Breslau, where there co-existed, until 1st January, 1840, five different particular laws and observances in regard to succession, the

property of spouses, etc., the application of which was limited to certain territorial jurisdictions; not unfrequently the law varied from house to house, and it even happened that one house was situated on the borders of different laws, to each of which, therefore, it belonged in part; Savigny, *Private Int. Law*, cap. i. sect. iv.

[144] *Academy*, February, 1884; *Percy Reliques*, edit. Wheatley, i. 384.

[145] *Trans. British. Association*, 1847, p. 321.

[146] Series No. V., published in 1895.

[147] *Philological Society Papers*, 1870-2, pp. 18, 248; Dr. Murray gives the air in an appendix. See also a note by Mr. Danby Fry in the *Antiquary*, viii. 164-6, 269-70; and *The Hawick Tradition*, by R. S. Craig and Adam Laing, published at Hawick in 1898.

[148] Squire, *Mythology of the British Islands*, 69.

[149] Wilde, *Lough Corrib*, 210-248. Sir William Wilde has studied the details of this great fight with great care, and it is impossible to ignore his evidence as to the monuments of it being extant to this day among the recorded antiquities of Ireland. The battle lasted four days. The first day the Fir-Bolg had the best of the fighting, and pillar-stones erected to the heroes who fell are still in situ. Clogh-Fadha-Cunga, or long stone of Cong, which stood on the old road to the east of that village and a portion of which, six feet long, is still in an adjoining wall, being erected to Adleo of the Dananians, and Clogh-Fadha-Neal, or long stone of the Neale, at the junction of the roads passing northwards from Cross and Cong, commemorating the place where the king stood during the battle. After the battle each Fir-Bolg carried with him a stone and the head of a Danann to their king who erected a great cairn to commemorate the event, and this must be the cairn of Ballymagibbon which stands on the road passing from Cong to Cross. The well of Mean Uisge is identified as that mentioned in the MS. accounts of the battle, connected with a striking incident. After a careful examination of the locality, says Sir William Wilde, with a transcript of the ancient MS. in his hand, he was convinced of the identity of a stone heap standing within a circle as the place where the body of the loyal Fir-Bolg youth was burned. The second day's battle surged northwards, and at the western shores of Lough Mask, Slainge Finn, the king's son, pursuing the two sons of Cailchu and their followers, slew them there, and "seventeen flag

stones were stuck in the ground in commemoration of their death," and by the margin of the lake in the island of Inish-Eogan there stands this remarkable monument to this hour. The line of the Fir-Bolg camp can still be traced with wonderful accuracy. Caher-Speenan, the thorny fort, was a part of this camp, and still exists. More to the south-east, on the hill of Tongegee, are the remains of Caher-na-gree, the pleasant fort, and still further to the east are Lisheen, or little earthen fort, and Caher-Phætre, pewter fort. Other forts also exist to give evidence both of the Fir-Bolg and the Danann lines. The Danann monuments are situate in the fields opposite the glebes of Nymphsfield. Five remarkable stone circles still remain within the compass of a square mile, and there are traces of others. The Fir-Bolgs were defeated on the fourth day and their king Eochy fell fighting to the last. "A lofty cairn was raised over his body, and called Carn Eathach, from his name." On the grassy hill of Killower, or Carn, overlooking Lough Mask, stands to this hour the most remarkable cairn in the west of Ireland, and there is little doubt this is the one referred to in the ancient tradition as commemorating the death of the last Fir-Bolg king in Erin.

[150] Squire, *op. cit.*, 76, 138.

[151] Squire, *op. cit.*, 230.

[152] Squire, *Mythology*, 399.

[153] See *Life and Writings* by Oliver Elton, ii. 224.

[154] *Governance of London*, 110-113.

[155] *Celtic Heathendom*, 125-133.

[156] See Bathurst, *Roman Antiquities of Lydney Park*, plates viii., xiii., for the famous example dealt with by Sir John Rhys; and Stuart, *Caledonia Romana*, 309, plate ix. fig. 2, for a dedication to the "Deities of Britain."

[157] See his *Stonehenge and Other British Stone Monuments*, chap. xxii.

[158] See *Folklore*, xv. 306-311, for the Greek evidence; and xvii. 30, 164, for the Irish evidence.

[159] Frazer, *Golden Bough* (2nd ed.), iii. 236-316. Mr. Frazer, however, is inclined to review his explanation of bonfires as sun-charms; see his *Adonis, Attis and Osiris*, 151, note 4.

[160] The specialisation of the fire cult is illustrated by the Hindu myth of the Angiras, see Wilson, *Rig Veda Sanhita*, i. p. xxix.

[161] Gummere, *Germanic Origins*, 400-2.

[162] It will be convenient to give the references for the various details of savage life in Britain. The original extracts are all given in *Monumenta Historica Britannica* and in Giles' *History of Ancient Britons*, vol. ii. Ireland—cannibalism: Strabo, iv. cap. 5, 4, p. 201, Diodoros, v. 32; promiscuous intercourse: Strabo; birth ceremony: Solinus, xxii. Scotland—human sacrifice: Solinus, xxii.; promiscuous intercourse, Solinus, cap. xxii., Xiphilinus from Dio in *Mon. Brit. Hist.*, p. lx., and St. Jerome adv. Jovin., v. ii. 201; nakedness, Herodian in *Mon. Brit. Hist.*, p. lxiv, and Xiphilinus, *ibid.*, p. lx. Britain—head-hunting, Strabo, iv. 1-4, pp. 199-201, Diodoros, v. 29; tattooing, Cæsar, *De bello Gallico*, v. 12, Pliny, *Nat. Hist.*, xxii. i. (2); promiscuous intercourse, Cæsar, *ibid.*, v. 14, Xiphilinus in *Mon. Brit. Hist.*, p. lvii.

[163] *History of England under the Anglo-Saxon Kings*, i. 14.

[164] Innes' *Critical Essay*, 45, 51, 56, 240.

[165] O'Curry's *Manners and Customs of Ancient Irish*, i. p. vi. Dr. Whitley Stokes has criticised O'Curry's translations as bad, "not from ignorance, but to a desire to conceal a fact militating against theories of early Irish civilisation."—*Revue Celtique*, iii. 90-101.

[166] Turner, *Hist. of Anglo-Saxons*, i. 64-74; Palgrave, *Eng. Com.*, i. 467-8.

[167] Giles' *History of Anc. Britons*, i. 231, referring to parallel customs among the Chinese.

[168] Elton, *Origins of English History*, 82.

[169] Rhys, *Celtic Britain*, 55.

[170] *Celtic Heathendom*, 320, note.

[171] I have dealt with this in my *Ethnology in Folklore*, 36-40.

[172] Skene, *Celtic Scotland*, i. 59, 84.

[173] Pearson, *Hist. of England during the Early and Middle Ages*, i. 15, 21, 35.

[174] Ramsay, *Foundations of England*, i. 9, 11, 30.

[175] Lang, *Hist. of Scotland*, i. 3-5.

[176] Joyce, *Social Hist. of Ireland*, i. 19.

[177] In addition to Mr. Lang and Dr. Joyce, who are folklorists as well as historians, and who as we have seen do deal with these records scientifically, the folklorist goes out of his way to reject these records. Thus

Mr. Squire says that "the imputation" which Cæsar makes as to polyandrous customs "cannot be said to have been proved," *Mythology of the British Islands*, 30.

[178] *Village Communities*, 17.

[179] *Principles of Sociology*, i. 714.

[180] *Arch. Cambrensis*, 6th ser. v. 3.

[181] *Journ. Anthrop. Inst.*, xx. 259.

Chapter II

MATERIALS AND METHODS

The materials of folklore consist of traditional tales (so called) and traditional customs and superstitions (so called), the feature of both groups being that at the time of first being recorded and reduced to writing they existed only by the force of tradition. There is no fixed time for the record. It is sometimes quite early, as, for instance, the examples which come to us from historians; it is generally quite late, namely, the great mass of examples which, during the past century or so, have been collected directly from the lips or observances of the people, sometimes by the curious traveller or antiquary, lately by the professed folklorist.

The consideration of the relationship of history and folklore has cleared the ground for definitions and method. Before the material of which folklore consists can be considered by the light of method, we must get rid of definitions which are often applied to folklore in its attributed sense. Folk-tales are not fiction or art, were not invented for amusement, are not myth in the sense of being imaginative only.[182] Customs and superstitions are not the result of ignorance and stupidity. These attributes are true only if folk-tales, customs, and superstitions are compared with the literary productions and with the science and the culture of advanced civilisation; and this comparison is exactly that which should never be undertaken, though unfortunately it is that which is most generally adopted. The folk-tale may be lent on occasion to the artist—to Mr. Lang, to Mr. Jacobs, and their many copyists; and these artists may rejoice at the wonderful results of the unconscious art that resides in these products of tradition, but the folk-tale must not be wholly surrendered. It does not belong to them. It does not belong to art at all, but to science. That it is artistic in form is an addition to its characteristics, but has nothing whatever to do with its fundamental features. Similarly with legend. It may be lent to Malory, to Tennyson, to Longfellow, to the literary bards of the romance period, for the purpose of weaving together their story of the wonderful; but it must not be surrendered to the romancist, and, above all things, the romances must never be allowed to enter the domain of folklore. Romances may be stripped of their legends so that the source of legendary material may be fully utilised, but the romances themselves belong to literature, and must remain within their own portals. And so with customs. They may be pleasing and reveal some of the beauties of the older joyousness of life which has passed away, it is to be regretted, from modern civilisation; they may be revived in May-day celebrations, in pageants, in providing our schools with games which tell of the romance of living. But they do not belong to the lover of the beautiful or to the revivalists. Equally with the folk-tale they belong to science. And so also with superstitions. The Psychical Research Society, the spiritualists, the professional successors of the mediæval witch and wizard, may turn their attention to traditional superstitions; but the folklorist refuses to hand them over, and claims them for science.

This use of traditional material for modern purposes is not the only danger to proper definitions. There is also its appearance in the earlier stages of literature. The traditional narrative, the myth, the folk-tale or the legend, is not dependent upon the text in which it appears for the first time. That text, as we have it, was not written down by contemporary or nearly contemporary authority. Before it had become a written document it had lived long as oral tradition.[183] In some cases the written document is itself centuries old, the record of some early chronicler or some early writer who did not make the record for tradition's sake. In other cases the written document is quite modern, the record of a professed lover of tradition. This unequal method of recording tradition is the main source of the difficulty in the way of those who cannot accept tradition as a record of fact. In all cases the test of its value and the interpretation of its testimony are matters which need special study and examination before the exact value of each tradition is capable of being determined. The date when and the circumstances in which a tradition is first reduced to literary form are important factors in the evidence as to the credibility of the particular form in which the tradition is preserved; but they are not all the factors, nor do they of themselves afford better evidence when they are comparatively ancient than forms of much later date and of circumstances far different. It cannot be too often impressed upon the student of tradition that the tradition itself affords the chief if not the only sure evidence of its age, its origin, and its meaning; for the preservation of tradition is due to such varied influences that the mere fact of preservation, or the particular method or date of preservation, cannot be relied upon to give the necessary authority for the authenticity of the tradition. Tradition can never assume the position of written history, because it does not owe its origin, but only its preservation, to writing.

Documentary material is examined as to its palæographical features, as to the testimony afforded by its author or assumed author, as to its credibility in dealing with contemporary events or persons, as to its date, and in other ways according to the nature of the document. Traditional material has nothing to do with all this. It has no palæography; it has no author, and if a personal author is assigned to any given fragment or element it is generally safe to ignore the tradition as the product of a later age; it does not deal with persons nor, as a rule, with specific events; it has no date. It has therefore to undergo a process of its own before it can be accepted as historical evidence, and this process, if somewhat tedious, is all the more necessary because of the tender material of which tradition is composed. This will be made clearer if we understand exactly what the different classes of tradition are and how they stand to each other.

Considering the materials of folklore in their true sense and not their attributed sense then, we may proceed to say something as to methods. Definitions and rules are needed. No student can attack so immense a subject without the aid of such necessary machinery, and it is because the attempt has been so often made ill-equipped in this respect, that the science of folklore has suffered so much and has remained so long unrecognised. Already, in dealing with the relationship of history and folklore, one or two necessary distinctions in terms have been anticipated. We have discovered that the impersonal folk-tale is distinguished in a fundamental manner from the personal or local legend, and that the growth of mythology is a later process than the growth of myth. These distinctions need, however, to be systematised and brought into relationship with other necessary distinctions. The myth and the folk-tale are near relations, but they are not identical, and it is clear that we need to know something more about myth. Because mythic tradition has been found to include many traditions, which of late years have been claimed to belong to a definitely historical race of people, it must not be identified with history. This claim is based upon two facts, the presence of myth in the shape of the folk-tale and the preservation of much mythic tradition beyond the stage of thought to which it properly belongs by becoming attached to an historical event, or series of events, or to an historical personage, and in this way carrying on its life into historic periods and among historic peoples. The first position has resulted in a wholesale appropriation of the folk-tale to the cause of the mythologists; the second position has hitherto resulted either in a disastrous appropriation of the entire tradition to mythology, or in a still more disastrous rejection both of the tradition and the historical event round which it clusters. Historians doubting the myth doubt too the history; mythologists doubting the history reject the myth from all consideration, and in this way much is lost to history which properly belongs to it, and something is lost to myth.

If, therefore, I have hitherto laid undue stress upon the foundation of tradition in the actual facts of life, and upon the close association of tradition with historic fact, it is because this side of the question has been so generally neglected. Everything has been turned on to the mythic side. Folk-tales have been claimed as the exclusive property of the mythologists, and those who have urged their foundation on the facts of real life have scarcely been listened to. There is, however, no ground for the converse process to be advocated. If tradition is not entirely mythology it is certainly not all founded on sociology, and the mythic tradition in the possession of a people advanced in culture has to be considered and accounted for. It is myth in contact with history, and the contact compels consideration of the result.

I

The first necessity is for definitions. Careful attention to what has already been said will reveal the fact that tradition contains three separate classes, and I would suggest definition of these classes by a precise application of terms already in use: The *myth* belongs to the most primitive stages of human thought, and is the recognisable explanation of some natural phenomenon, some forgotten or unknown object of human origin, or some event of lasting influence; the *folk-tale* is a survival preserved amidst culture-surroundings of a more advanced stage, and deals with events and ideas of primitive times in terms of the experience or of episodes in the lives of unnamed human beings; the *legend* belongs to an historical personage, locality, or event. These are new definitions, and are suggested in order to give some sort of exactness to the terms in use. All these terms—myth, folk-tale, and legend—are now used indiscriminately with no particular definiteness. The possession of three such distinct terms forms an asset which should be put to its full use, and this cannot be done until we agree upon a definite meaning for each.

The first place must be given to mythic tradition. This is not special to our own, or to any one branch of the human race. It belongs to all—to the Hindu, the Greek, the Slav, the Teuton, the Celt, the Semite, and the savage. It goes back to a period of human history which has only tradition for its authority, in respect of which no contemporary records exist, and which relates to a time when the ancestors of now scattered peoples lived together, and when they were struggling from the position of obedient slaves to all the fears which unknown nature inflicted on them, to that of observers of the forces of nature.

Traditions which are properly classed as myth are those which are too ancient to be identified with historical personages, and too little realistic to be a relation of historical episodes. They are rather the explanations given by primitive philosophers of events which were beyond their ken, and yet needed and claimed explanation. In this class of tradition we are in touch with the struggles of the earliest ancestors of man to learn about the unknown. Our own research in the realms of the unknown we dignify by the name and glories of science. The research of our remote ancestors was of like kind, though the domain of the unknown was so different from our own. It was primitive science.

The best type of this class of myth is, I think, the creation myth.[184] Everywhere, almost, man has for a moment stood apart and asked himself the question, Whence am I?—stood apart from the struggle for existence when that struggle was in its most severe stages. The answer he has given himself was the answer of the Darwin of his period. From the narrow observation of the natural man and his surroundings, governed by the enormous impressions of his own life, the answer has obviously not been scientific in our sense of the term. But it was scientific. It was the science of

104

primitive man, and if we have to reject it as science not so good as our science, nay, as not science at all judged by our standard, we must not deny to primitive man the claim of having preceded modern man in his observation and interpretation of the world of nature.

The range of the creation myth is almost world-wide. It includes examples from all quarters, and examples of great beauty as well as of singular, almost grotesque hideousness; the New Zealand myth is surely the best type of the former, and perhaps the Fijian of the latter. As Mr. Lang says: "all the cosmogonic myths waver between the theory of construction, or rather of reconstruction and the theory of evolution very rudely conceived."[185]

It is not necessary to quote a large number of examples, because I am not concerned with their variety nor with their essentials. I am only anxious to point out their existence as evidence of the scientific character of primitive myth.[186] It is not to the point to say that the science was all wrong. What is to the point is to say that the attempt was made to get at the origin of man and his destiny. Mr. Lang thinks that "the origin of the world and of man is naturally a problem which has excited the curiosity of the least developed minds," but in the use of the term "naturally," I think the stupendous nature of the effort made by the least developed minds is entirely neglected, and we miss the opportunity of measuring what this effort might mean.

When savages ask themselves, as they certainly *do* ask themselves, whence the sky, whence the winds, the sun, moon, stars, sea, rivers, mountains and other natural objects, they reply in terms of good logic applied to deficient knowledge. All the knowledge they possess is that based upon their own material senses. And therefore, when they apply that knowledge to subjects outside their own personality, they deal with them in terms of their own personality. How did the sky get up there, above their heads—the sky evidently so lovingly fond of the earth, so intimately connected with the earth?

The New Zealand answer to these questions is a great one, by whatever standard it is measured. Heaven and earth, they say, were husband and wife, so locked in close embrace that darkness everywhere prevailed. Their children were ever thinking amongst themselves what might be the difference between darkness and light. At last, worn out by the continued darkness, they consulted amongst themselves whether they should slay their parents, Rangi and Papa, *i.e.* heaven and earth, or whether they should rend them apart. The fiercest of their children exclaimed, "Let us slay them!" but the forest, another of the sons, said, "Nay, not so. It is better to rend them apart, and to let heaven stand far above us and the earth to lie under our feet. Let the sky become as a stranger to us, but the earth remain close to us as our nursing-mother." The brothers consented to this proposal with the exception of Tawhiri-ma-tea, the father of winds and storms; thus five of the brothers consented and one would not agree. Then each of the brothers tries to rend his parents, heaven and earth, asunder. First the father of cultivated food tries and fails; then the father of fish and reptiles; then the father of uncultivated food; then the father of fierce human beings. Then at last slowly uprises Tane-mahuta, the father of forests, birds, and insects, and he struggles with his parents; in vain he strives to rend them apart with his hands and arms. Lo, he pauses; his head is now firmly planted on his mother, the earth; his feet he raises up and rests against his father, the skies; he strains his back and limbs with mighty effort, and at last are rent apart Rangi and Papa, who shriek aloud with cries and groans. But Tane-mahuta pauses not, he regards not their shrieks and cries; far, far beneath him he presses down the earth; far, far above him he thrusts up the sky. Then were discovered a multitude of human beings whom heaven and earth had begotten, and who had hitherto lain concealed. But Tawhiri-ma-tea, the wind and storm, the brother who had not consented, is angry at this rending apart of his parents, and he rises and follows his father, the sky, and fights fiercely with the earth and his brothers.[187]

The explanation of this myth is simple. Unaided by the facts of science, the New Zealand savages could only think of the facts of their own experience. Only two personalities could produce the various products of the world; therefore the earth was the mother and the sky the father. But they are now separated and apart. Only a personality could have separated, and the forest, root-sown in the earth, branch-up in the sky, is evidently the means of this separation. And so, satisfactorily to their own minds, these rude savages settled the question of the origin of heaven and earth.

The close similarity of this to the story of Kronos has frequently been pointed out; but a Greek story is always worth repeating. Near the beginning of things Earth gave birth to Heaven. Later, Heaven became the husband of Earth, and they had many children. Some of these became the gods of the various elements, among whom were Okeanos, and Hyperion, the sun. The youngest child was Kronos of crooked counsel, who ever hated his mighty sire. Now the children of Heaven and Earth were concealed in the hollows of Earth, and both the Earth and her children resented this. At last they conspired against their father, Heaven, and, taking their mother into the counsels, she produced Iron and bade her children avenge her wrongs. Fear fell upon all of them except Kronos, and he determined to separate his parents, and with his iron weapon he effected his object. All the brothers rejoiced except one, Okeanos, and he remained faithful to his father.[188]

It would be well for the sake of the story itself to give a creation myth from India, but I shall have other use for it than its particular charm.

"'In the beginning, when Twashtri came to the creation of woman, he found that he had exhausted his materials in the making of man, and that no solid elements were left. In this dilemma, after profound meditation, he did as follows. He took the rotundity of the moon, and the curves of creepers, and the clinging of tendrils, and the trembling of grass, and the slenderness of the reed, and the bloom of flowers, and the lightness of leaves, and the tapering of the elephant's trunk, and the glances of deer, and the clustering of rows of bees, and the joyous gaiety of sunbeams, and the weeping of clouds, and the fickleness of the winds, and the timidity of the hare, and the vanity of the peacock, and the softness of the parrot's bosom, and the hardness of adamant, and the sweetness of honey, and the cruelty of the tiger, and the warm glow of fire, and the coldness of snow, and the chattering of jays, and the cooing of the *kókila*, and the hypocrisy of the crane, and the fidelity of the *chakrawáka*, and compounding all these together, he made woman and gave her to man. But after one week, man came to him and said: Lord, this creature that you have given me makes my life miserable. She chatters incessantly and teases me beyond endurance, never leaving me alone; and she requires incessant attention, and takes all my time up, and cries about nothing, and is always idle; and so I have come to give her back again, as I cannot live with her. So Twashtri said: Very well; and he took her back. Then after another week, man came again to him and said: "Lord, I find that my life is very lonely, since I gave you back that creature. I remember how she used to dance and sing to me, and look at me out of the corner of her eye, and play with me, and cling to me; and her laughter was music, and she was beautiful to look at, and soft to touch; so give her back to me again. So Twashtri said: Very well; and gave her back again. Then after only three days, man came back to him again and said: Lord, I know not how it is; but after all I have come to the conclusion that she is more of a trouble than a pleasure to me; so please take her back again. But Twashtri said: Out on you! Be off! I will have no more of this. You must manage how you can. Then man said: But I cannot live with her. And Twashtri replied: Neither could you live without her. And he turned his back on man, and went on with his work. Then man said: What is to be done? for I cannot live either with her or without her.'"[189]

Now this myth has, so far as its central fact is concerned, its

108

counterpart in Celtic folklore. In the Welsh Mabinogi of Math, son of Mathonwy, it is related how Arianrod laid a destiny upon her son, whom she would not recognise, that he should never have a wife of the race that now inhabits the earth, and how Gwydion declared that he should have a wife notwithstanding. "They went thereupon unto Math, the son of Mathonwy, and complained unto him most bitterly of Arianrod. Well, said Math, we will seek, I and thou, by charms and magic, to form a wife for him out of flowers. So they took the blossoms of the oak, and the blossoms of the broom, and the blossoms of the meadow-sweet, and produced from them a maiden, the fairest and most graceful that man ever saw." No one can doubt that this interesting fragment of Welsh tradition takes us back to a creation legend of the same order as the Indian legend, and that the two widely separated parallels belong to the period when men were carving out for themselves theories as to the origin of women in relation to men.

It is impossible to deny a place among these myths of creation to the Hebrew tradition of Adam and Eve in the Garden of Eden. The first chapter of Genesis is the answer which the early Hebrews gave to the scientific question as to the origin of man. How much it cost them to arrive at this conclusion one cannot guess, one only knows that it has become a glory to the ages of Hebrew history, as well as to the civilisation of Christianity. Unfortunately it has become much more. The science of the primitive Hebrew has been adopted as the God-given revelation to all mankind. It is the function of folklore to correct this error, to restore the Hebrew tradition to its proper place among the myths of the world which have answered the cry of early man for the knowledge of his origin. There is no degradation here. Science is no longer in doubt as to the origin of man within the evolutionary process of the natural world, and it rightly rejects the first chapter of Genesis as of value to modern research. But science should accept it as a chapter in the history of anthropology, a chapter which has only proved not to be true, because of the limited range of early man in the facts about man, but a chapter, nevertheless, which has the inherent value of a faithful record of man's search after truth. This is a great position. This is the revelation which is made to us from the first chapter of Genesis, and when the theologian is bold and able enough to step outside the formularies of his ancient faith, and reach the magnificent world of thought which lies in front of him by the revelations of scientific discovery, he will consider the anthropological interpretation of the Hebrew Bible as one of the necessary elements of his equipment. There is on present lines a whole world of thought between science and religion, although they both have the same object. They both seek the great unknown. Science, however, gives up all efforts in the past which have proved futile and erroneous, cheerfully surrenders all errors of research and interpretation, starts investigation afresh, begins new discoveries, and rewrites the story they have to tell. Religion, on the other hand, comes to a full stop when once she has made or accepted a discovery, when once she has pronounced that the great unknown has become known to her votaries and supporters. She is skilful to use the results of science up to the point where they serve her purpose, and to use the terms of science in order to build up her shattering position. But she does not advance. She does not accept the first chapter of Genesis as a wonderful revelation of the early stages of human investigation into the realms of the unknown, but still keeps to her old formula of a revelation of the deity as to the origin of man, and she does not see that by this attitude she is lessening every day her capacity for teaching truth.

I think the attitude of science to the Hebrew tradition is only a little less unfortunate than that of religion. Professor Huxley employed all the resources of his great knowledge to disprove the scientific accuracy of the tradition, and when one rereads his chapters on this subject[190] one wonders at the absence of the sense of proportion. Perhaps it was necessary, considering the place which the Hebrew tradition occupies in civilised thought, to show its utter inconsistency with the facts of nature, but it was equally necessary to show that it has its place in the history of human thought. The folklorist replaces it among the myths of creation, and then proceeds to analyse and value it. The Hebrew is shown by the myth he adopted to have frankly acknowledged that the origin of man and of the world was undiscoverable by him. Whatever older myths he once possessed, he discarded them in favour of a mythic God-creator, and this is only another way of stating that the mystery of man's origin could not, to the Hebrew mind, be met by such a myth as the New Zealander believed in, or as the Kumis believed in, but could only be met by the larger conception of a special creation. The Hebrew could not find his answer in nature, so he appealed to super-nature. His God was the unknown God, and the realm of the unknown God was the unknowable. Though in terms this may not be the interpretation of the Hebrew creation myth, its ultimate resolve is this; and because modern science has penetrated beyond this confession of the unknown origin of man to the evolution of man, it should not therefore treat contemptuously the effort of early Hebrew science. Because it is not possible to admit this effort as part of modern science, it must not be rejected from the entire region of science. It must be respected as one of the many efforts which have made possible the last effort of all which proclaims that man has kinship with all the animal world.

These points illustrate the unsatisfactory attitude of science and religion to myth. There is still to notice the unsatisfactory attitude of the folklorist. Wrong interpretation of special classes of myth is, of course, to be anticipated in the commencement of a great study such as folklore; but there are also wrong interpretations of the fundamental basis of myth. Thus even Mr. Frazer, with all his vast research into savage thought and action, doubts the possession of good logical faculty by mankind. If mankind, he says, had always been logical and wise, history would not be a long chronicle of folly and crime.[191] But surely we cannot doubt man's logical powers. They have been too strong for his facts. He has applied mercilessly all the powers of his logical faculties upon isolated observations of phenomena, and it is this limited application which has produced the folly and crime. I venture to think that civilised man shares with the savage of to-day, and with the primitive ancestors of all mankind, the charge of applying perfectly good logic to an insufficiency of facts, and producing therefrom fresh chapters of folly and crime.

If myth is correctly defined as primitive science, as I have ventured to suggest, it is important to know how it assumes a place among the traditions of a people. Primitive science was also primitive belief. If it accounted for the origin of mankind, of the sun, moon, and stars, of the earth and the trees, it accounted for them as creations of a higher power than man, or, at all events, of a great and specially endowed man, and higher powers than man were of the unknown realm. The unknown was the awful. Primitive science and primitive belief were therefore on one and the same plane.[192] They were subjects to be treated with reverence and with awe. The story into which the myth was so frequently woven is not a story to those who believe in the truth of the myth. It assumes the personal shape, because the personal is the only machinery by which primitive man is capable of expressing himself. It was held only by tradition, because tradition was the only means of transmitting it, and it was of a sacred character, because sacred things and beliefs were the only forces which influenced primitive thought. When it was repeated to new generations of learners, it was not a case of story-telling—it was a matter of the profoundest importance. Everywhere among the lowest savagery we find the secrets of the group kept from all but the initiated, and these secrets are the traditions which have become sacred, traditions expressed sometimes in ceremonial, sometimes in rites, sometimes in narratives. Thus the mythological and religious knowledge of the Bushmen is imparted in dances, and when a man is ignorant of some myth, he will say, "I do not dance that dance," meaning that he does not belong to the group which preserves that particular sacred chapter.[193] The Ashantees have an interesting creation myth which is stated to be the foundation of all their religious opinions.[194] Mr. Howitt, in his important chapter on "Beliefs and Burial Practices,"[195] seems to me to exactly interpret the savage mind. The first thing he notes is the belief—a belief that "the earth is flat, surmounted by the solid vault of the sky," that "there is water all round the flat earth," that the sun is a woman, and that the moon was once a man who lived on earth, and so on. Then, secondly, he notes the manner in which these beliefs are translated to and held by the people, the myth in point of fact—unfortunately, Mr. Howitt calls it a legend—wherein it is perfectly obvious that the Australian is interpreting the facts of nature in the only language known to him to be applicable, namely, that of his own personality. Messrs. Spencer and Gillen produce much the same kind of evidence,[196] and describe a ceremony among the northern tribes connected with the myth of the sun, which ends in a newly initiated youth being brought up, "shown the decorations, and had everything explained to him."[197] Among the central tribes the same authorities describe minutely the initiation ceremonies, during which the initiate boy "is instructed for the first time in any of the sacred matters referring to totems, and it is by means of the performances which are concerned with certain animals, or rather, apparently with the animals, but in reality with Alcheringa individuals who were the direct transformations of

112

such animals, that the traditions dealing with this subject, which is of the greatest importance in the eyes of the natives, are firmly impressed upon the mind of the novice, to whom everything which he sees and hears is new and surrounded with an air of mystery."[198] Sir George Grey, speaking of the traditions of the Maori which he collected, says his reader will be in "the position of one who listens to a heathen and savage high priest, explaining to him in his own words and in his own energetic manner, the traditions in which he earnestly believes, and unfolding the religious opinions upon which the faith and hopes of his race rest."[199] This "school of mythology and history," as it is significantly termed in John White's *Ancient History of the Maori*, was "Whare-Kura, the sacred school in which the sons of high priests were taught our mythology and history," and it "stood facing the east in the precincts of the sacred place of Mua." The school was opened by the priests in the autumn, and continued from sunset to midnight every night for four or five months in succession. The chief priest sat next to the door. It was his duty to commence the proceedings by repeating a portion of history; the other priests followed in succession, according to rank. On the south side sat the old and most accomplished priests, "whose duty it was to insist on a critical and verbatim rehearsal of all the ancient lore."[200] The American-Indian account, by the Iroquois, of how myths were told to an ancient chief and an assembly of the people on a circular open space in a deep forest, wherein was a large wheel-shaped stone, from beneath which came a voice which told the tale of the former world, and how the first people became what they are at present,[201] is in exact accord with this evidence. The priestly novice among the Indians of British Guiana is taught the traditions of the tribe, while the medicine man of the Bororó in Brazil has to learn certain ritual songs and the languages of birds, beasts, and trees.[202]

I do not want to press the point too far, because evidence is not easy to get on account of the incomplete fashion in which it has been collected and presented to the student. The records of native life are divided off into chapters arranged, not on the basis of native ideas, but on the basis of civilised ideas, and from this cause we get myth and belief in different chapters as if they had no connection with each other; we get myths treated as if they were but the fancy-begotten amusements of the individual, instead of the serious ideas of the collective people about the elements of nature to

113

which they have directed their attention. Mr. J. A. Farrer comes practically to this correct conclusion,[203] while Mr. Jevons seems to me to have arrived at the same result in spite of some false intermediate steps, due to his failure to discriminate between myth and mythology.[204] Failures of this kind are of almost infinite loss to scientific research. They stop the results which might flow from the stages correctly reached, and hide the full significance which arises from the fact that man's aspirations are always so much in excess of his accomplished acts. Poetry, philosophy, prayer, worship, are all short of the ideal; and the question may surely arise whether the actual accomplishments of man in civilisation, as compared with those of man in savagery, afford any sort of indication of the distance between man's accomplishment and his aspiration at any age. If man has never travelled at one moment of time, or at one definite period of life, all this distance in thought, it may still be possible to use this distance between savage and cultured accomplishment as a standard of measurement between accomplishment and ideal, wherever the material for such a purpose is available. If folklorists will keep such a possibility in mind, whenever they are called upon to investigate myth, it will at all events save them from proceeding upon lines which cannot lead to progress in the investigation of human history.

The primitive myth does not include all that properly comes within the definition of myth. There must be included the myth formed to explain a rite or ceremony, which originating in most ancient times has been kept up at the instance of a particular religion or cult, but the meaning and intent of which has been forgotten amidst the progress of a later civilisation. Pausanias is the great storehouse of such myths as this, and Mr. Lang has, more than any other scholar, examined and explained the process which has gone on.

There is also included in this secondary class of myth, the myths upon which are founded the great systems of mythology. The Hindu mythology, in spite of all that has been done to place it on the pedestal of primitive original thought, is definitely relegated to the secondary position by its best exponents. The Vedic religion is tribal in form, and in the pre-mythological stage.[205] In the Rámáyaná and Mahábhárata, on the contrary, "we trace unequivocal indications of a departure from the elemental worship of the Vedas, and the origin or elaboration of legends which form the great body of the mythological religion of the Hindus."[206] The

114

pre-mythological and the mythological stages of Hindu religion, therefore, are both discoverable from the traditional literature which has descended from both ages, and this fact is important in the classification of the various phases of tradition. When once it is admitted that the beginnings of mythology are to be traced in one section of the people who are supposed to derive a common system of mythology from a common home, future research will hesitate to interpret, as Kuhn and Max Müller and their school have done, the traditions of Celts, Teutons, and Scandinavians as the detritus of ancient mythologies instead of the beginnings of what, under favourable conditions, might have grown into mythologies. Mythological tradition is essentially a secondary not a primary stage. This fact is overlooked by many authorities, and I have noted some of the unfortunate results. It is not overlooked by those who study the principles of their subject as well as the details. Thus, as Robertson-Smith has so well explained, "mythology was no essential part of ancient religion, for it had no sacred sanction and no binding force on the worshippers.... Belief in a certain series of myths was neither obligatory as a part of true religion, nor was it supposed that by believing a man acquired religious merit and conciliated the favour of the gods. What was obligatory or meritorious was the exact performance of certain sacred acts prescribed by religious tradition. This being so, it follows that mythology ought not to take the prominent place that is too often assigned to it in the scientific study of ancient faiths."[207] This is exactly the position, and all that I have advanced for the purpose of aiming at a classification of the various kinds of tradition is in accord with this view.

All that I am anxious to prove, all that it is possible to prove, from these considerations of the position occupied by myth, is that myths constitute a part of the serious life of the people. They belong to the men and women, perhaps some of them to the men only and others to the women only, but essentially to the life of the people.

I do not think that even Mr. Hartland in his special study of the subject has quite understood this. He begins at a later period in the history of tradition, the period of story-telling proper, when myths have become folk-tales,[208] and he treats this period as the earliest instead of the secondary stage of myth. In this stage something has happened to push myth back from the centre of the people's life to a lesser position—a new religious influence, a new civilisation, a new home, any one of the many influences, or any combination of influences, which have affected peoples and sent them along the paths of evolution and progress.

It is in this way that we come upon the folk-tale. The folk-tale is secondary to the myth. It is the primitive myth dislodged from its primitive place. It has become a part of the life of the people, independently of its primary form and object and in a different sense. The mythic or historic fact has been obscured, or has been displaced from the life of the people. But the myth lives on through the affections of the people for the traditions of their older life. They love to tell the story which their ancestors revered as myth even though it has lost its oldest and most impressive significance. The artistic setting of it, born of the years through which it has lived, fashioned by the minds which have handed it down and embellished it through the generations, has helped its life. It has become the fairy tale or the nursery tale. It is told to grown-up people, not as belief but as what was once believed; it is told to children, not to men; to lovers of romance, not to worshippers of the unknown; it is told by mothers and nurses, not by philosophers or priestesses; in the gathering ground of home life, or in the nursery, not in the hushed sanctity of a great wonder.[209]

The influence of changing conditions upon the position of mythic tradition is well illustrated by Dr. Rivers in his account of the Todas. This people, he says, "are rapidly forgetting their folk-tales and the legends of their gods [that is, their myths], while their ceremonial remains to a large extent intact and seems likely to continue so for some time." Dr. Rivers attributes this to the effect of intercourse with other people. This intercourse has had no missionary results and has not therefore affected their religious rites and ceremonies, but has shown itself largely in the form of loss of interest in the stories of the past.[210] In other words, and in accordance with the definitions I am suggesting, the primitive myths of the Todas have definitely assumed a secondary position as folk-tale, and not a strong position at that, while religion has clung to rite and formula.

Primitive myth dislodged in this fashion is sometimes preserved in a special manner and for religious purposes in its ancient setting as a belief, or as a tradition belonging to sacred places and appertaining to sacred things. This is what has happened to the Genesis myth of the Hebrews; it has also

116

happened to some of the sacred myths of the Hindus, and perhaps to some of the sacred myths of the Greeks. In this position the myth may even be reduced to writing, and where this happens all the sacredness appertaining to tradition is transferred to the written instrument.

Thus in Arkadia, Pausanias tells us, was a temple of Demeter, and every second year, when they were celebrating what they called the greater mysteries, they took out certain writings which bore on the mysteries, and having read them in the hearing of the initiated, put them back in their place that same night.[211] In India examples occur of land being held for telling stories at the Uchàos or festivals of the goddess Dévi.[212] The colleges of Rome, composed of men specially skilled in religious lore, and charged with the preservation of traditional rules regarding the more general religious observances, the proper fulfilment of which implied a certain amount of information, and rendered it necessary for the state in its own interest to provide the faithful transmission of that information, have been described by Mommsen.[213]

I pass to the third class of tradition, namely, the legend, and this need not detain us long. We have already illustrated it by the notes on history and folklore, and by its very nature it belongs essentially to the historic age. In dealing with legend, there is first to determine whether its characters are historical, or are unknown to history. If the former, there is next to disengage those parts of the tradition which, by their parallels to other traditions, or by their nature, may be safely certified as not belonging to the historical hero or to the period of the historical hero. If the latter, the details must be analysed to see what elements of culture are contained therein. In both cases tradition will have served a purpose, and that purpose must be sought. Tradition does not attach itself to an historical personage without cause. There is necessity for it, and in the case of Hereward the necessity was proved to have been the great gap in the history of a national hero. Tradition does not preserve details of primitive culture-history without cause, and in the examples already quoted it has been shown that this cause rests upon the indissoluble links which the uncultured peasant of to-day has with the pre-cultured past of his race. He will have forgotten all about his tribal life and its consequences, but will retain legends which are founded upon tribal life. He will have lost touch with ideas which proclaim that man or woman not of his tribe is an enemy to be feared or attacked, but will gladly relate legends which deal with events growing out of a state of perpetual strife among the ancestors of people now in friendship. He will not understand the personal tie of ancient times, but will listen to the legends attached to places in such strange fashion as to make places seem to possess a personal life full of events and happenings. He will know nothing of giants and ogres, but will love the legends which tell of heroes meeting and conquering such beings. The history of the school books is nothing to him, but the history unknowingly contained in the legends is very real, and is applied over and over again to such later events as by force of circumstances become stamped upon the popular mind and thus succeed in displacing the original. It would be an important contribution to history to have these legends collected and examined by a competent authority. They would be beacon lights of national history preserved in legend.

It will be readily conceded, I think, that in attempting these definitions of the various classes of tradition, and in illustrating them from the records of man's life in various parts of the world, it has been impossible for me to deal with certain points in the problem before us. In particular I have not considered the favourite subject of the diffusion of folk-tales. I do not believe in a general system of diffusion, such a system, I mean, as would suffice to account for the parallels to be found in almost all countries.[214] I think diffusion occupies a very small part indeed of the problem, and that it only takes place in late historical times. It is a large subject, and I have virtually stated my answer to the theory of diffusion in the definitions and classifications which I have ventured to put forward. It may be considered by some that other facts in the conditions of myth, folk-tale, and legend would not confirm the general outline I have given of the three classes of tradition to which I have applied these terms; and of course there are many side issues in so great a problem. I would not urge the correctness of the views I have put forward as applicable to every part of the world, or to every phase in the history of tradition; but I would urge that in the great centres of traditional life they are practically the only means of arriving at the position occupied by tradition, and that in all cases they form a working hypothesis upon which future inquirers may well base their researches.

II

Of late years there have been placed alongside of the traditional myth, folk-tale, and legend many other products of tradition—customs, ceremonies, practices, and beliefs, and it has been argued, and argued strongly and convincingly, that the tradition which has brought down the saga and song as far-off echoes of an otherwise unrecorded past has also brought down these other elements which must also belong to the same distant past. This argument is now no longer seriously disputed. But there still remains open for discussion the exact kind of evidence which these elements of tradition supply, the particular period or people from which they have descended, the particular department of history to which they relate. All this is highly disputed.

Folklore has in this department been greatly aided by Dr. Tylor's impressive terminology, whereby the custom, ceremony, practice, and belief which have come down by tradition are classed as "survivals." This term implies an ancient origin, and the necessary work of the student is to get back to the original. Until very lately the fact of survival has carried with it the presumption of ancient origin, but Mr. Crawley has raised an objection which I think it is well to meet. He urges that "the history of religious phenomena exemplifies in the most striking manner the continuity of modern and primitive culture; but there is a tendency on the part of students to underestimate this continuity, and, by explaining it away on a theory of survivals, to lose the only opportunity we have of deducing the permanent elements of human nature."

This sentence at once prepares us for much that follows; but Mr. Crawley leaves the point itself untouched, except by implication, until he is in the middle of his book, and then we have his dictum that "it may be finally asserted that nothing which has to do with human needs ever survives as a mere survival."[215] It will at once be seen that we have here a new estimate of the force which survivals play in the evidence of human progress. They prove the continuity of modern and primitive culture. They are part and parcel of modern life, filling a vacuum which has not been filled by modern thought, carrying on, therefore, the standard of religious belief and religious ideal from point to point until they can be replaced by newer ideas and concepts. This definition of survivals is very bold. It answers Mr. Crawley's purpose and argument in a way which no other fact in human history, so far as we can judge, could answer it. It is the basis upon which his whole argument is founded. Occupying such an important place, it should have received explicit investigation, instead of being treated as a sort of side issue of incidental importance.

When explicit investigation is undertaken, Mr. Crawley's case must, I think, break down. Survivals are carried along the stream of time by people whose culture-status is on a level with the culture in which the survivals originated. It matters not that these people are placed in the midst of a higher civilisation or alongside of a higher civilisation. When once the higher civilisation penetrates to them, the survival is lost. There is not continuity between modern and primitive thought here, but, on the contrary, there is strong antagonism, ending with the defeat and death of the primitive survival. This is the evidence wherever survivals can be studied, whether in the midst of our own civilisation, or even of primitive civilisations, which constantly exhibit traces of older beliefs and ideas being pushed out of existence by newer. It is, indeed, a mistake to suppose, as some authorities apparently do, that survivals can only be studied when they are embedded in a high civilisation. It is almost a more fruitful method to study them when they appear in the lower strata; and even in such a case as the Australian aborigines I think that it is the neglect of observing survivals that has led to some of the erroneous theories which have recently been advanced against Messrs. Spencer and Gillen's conclusions.

For the purpose of examining survivals in custom, rite, and belief, we have nothing more than a series of notes of customs and beliefs obtaining among the lower and lowest classes of the people, and not being the direct teaching of any religious or academic body. These notes are very unequal in value, owing to the manner in which they have been made. They are often accidental, they are seldom if ever the result of trained observation, and they are often mixed up with theories as to their origin and relationship to modern society and modern religious beliefs. To a great extent the two first of these apparent defects are real safeguards, for they certify to the genuineness of the record, a certificate which is more needed in this branch of inquiry than perhaps in any other. But with regard to the third defect there is considerable danger. An inquirer with an object is so apt to find what he wishes to find, either by the exercise of his own credulity or the ingenuous extension of inquiry into answer; whereas the inquirer who is content to note with the simplicity of those who occupy themselves by collecting what others have not collected, may be deficient in the details he gives, but is seldom wrong or violently wrong in what he has recorded. In every direction, however, great caution is needed, and especially where any section of custom and belief has already been the subject of inquiry. It is indeed almost safe to say that all research into custom and belief, even that of such masters as Tylor, Lang, Hartland, Frazer, and others, needs re-examination before we can finally and unreservedly accept the conclusions which have been arrived at.

Such an examination must be directed towards obtaining some necessary points in the life-history of each custom, rite, and belief. We have to approach this part of our work guided by the fact that folklore cannot by any possibility develop. The doctrine of evolution is so strong upon us that we are apt to apply its leading idea insensibly to almost every branch of human history. But folklore being what it is, namely the survival of traditional ideas or practices among a people whose principal members have passed beyond the stage of civilisation which those ideas and practices once represented, it is impossible for it to have any development. When the original ideas and practices which it represents were current as the standard form of culture, their future history was then to be looked for along the lines of development. But so soon as they dropped back behind the standard of culture, whatever the cause and whenever the event happened, then their future history could only be traced along the lines of decay and disintegration. We are acquainted with some of the laws which mark the development of primitive culture, but we have paid no attention to the influences which mark the existence of survivals in culture. For this purpose we must first ascertain what are the component parts of each custom or superstition; secondly, we must classify the various elements in each example; and thirdly, we must group the various examples into classes which associate with each other in motif and character.

By this treble process we shall have before us examples of the changes in folklore, and demonstrably they are changes of decay, not of development. By grouping and arranging these changes it may be possible to

121

ascertain and set down the laws of change—for that there are laws I am nearly certain. It is these laws which must be discovered before we can go very far forward in our studies. Every item of custom and superstition must be tested by analysis to find out under which power it lives on in survival, and according to the result in each case, so may we hope to find out something about the original from which the survival has descended.

Each folklore item, in point of fact, has a life history of its own, and a place in relationship to other items. Just as the biography of each separate word in our language has been investigated in order to get at Aryan speech as the interpretation of Aryan thought, so must the biography of each custom, superstition, or story be investigated in order to get at Aryan belief or something older than Aryan belief. We must try to ascertain whether each item represents primitive belief by direct descent, by symbolisation, or by changes which may be discovered by some law equivalent to Grimm's law in the study of language.

Analysis of each custom, rite, or belief will show it to consist of three distinct parts, which I would distinguish by the following names:—

1. The formula.
2. The purpose.
3. The penalty or result.

It will be found that these three component parts are not equally tenacious of their original form in all examples. In one example we may find the formula either actually or symbolically perfect, while the purpose and penalty may not be easily distinguishable. Or it may happen that the formula remains fairly perfect; the purpose may be set down to the desire of doing what has always been done, and the penalty may be given as luck or ill-luck. Of course, further variations are possible, but these are usually the more general forms.

I will give an example or two of these phases of change or degradation in folklore. First, then, where the formula is complete, or nearly so, and the purpose and penalty have both disappeared. At Carrickfergus it was formerly the custom for mothers, when giving their child the breast for the last time, to put an egg in its hand and sit on the threshold of the outer door with a leg on each side, and this ceremony was usually done on a Sunday. Undoubtedly I think we have here a very nearly perfect formula; but what is its purpose, and what is the penalty for non-observance? Upon both these latter points the example is silent, and before they can be restored we must search among the other fragments of threshold customs and see whether they exist either separately from the formula or with a less perfect example. Secondly, where the formula has disappeared and the purpose and penalty remain, nearly the whole range of those floating beliefs and superstitions which occupy so largely the collections of folklore would supply examples. But I will select one example which will be to the point. When the Manx cottager looks for the traces of a foot in the ashes of his firegrate for the purpose of seeing in what direction the toes point, the penalty being that, if they point to the door, a death will occur, if to the fireplace, a birth,[216] there is no trace of the ancient formula. It is true we may find the missing formula in other lands; for instance, among some of the Indian tribes of Bombay. There the formula is elaborate and complete, while the purpose and the penalty are exactly the same as in the Isle of Man. But this hasty travelling to other lands is not, I contend, legitimate in the first place. We must begin by seeing whether there is not some other item of folklore, perhaps now not even connected with the house-fire group of customs and superstitions, whose true place is that of the lost formula of this interesting Manx custom. And when once we have taught ourselves the way to restore these lost formulæ to their rightful places, the explanation of the mere waifs and strays of folklore will be attended with some approach to scientific accuracy, and we shall then be in a position to get rid of that shibboleth so dear to the non-folklore critic, that all these things we deal with are "mere superstitions."

Thirdly, when the formula is complete, or nearly so, and the purpose and penalty become generalised. At St. Edmundsbury a white bull, which enjoyed full ease and plenty in the fields, and was never yoked to the plough or employed in any service, was led in procession in the chief streets of the town to the principal gate of the monastery, attended by all the monks singing and a shouting crowd. Knowing what Grimm has collected concerning the worship of the white bull, knowing what is performed in India to this day, there is no doubt that this formula of the white bull at St. Edmundsbury has been preserved in very good condition. The purpose of it was, however, not so satisfactory. It is said to have taken place whenever a married woman wished to have a child; and the penalty is lost in the obvious

123

generalisation that not to perform the ceremony is not to obtain the desired end.[217]

The second process, that of classification of the various elements in each example, will reveal some characteristics of folklore, which, so far as I know, have never yet been taken count of. One very important characteristic is the prevalence of a particular belief attached to different objects in different places. Thus Sir John Rhys in his examination of Manx folklore stopped short in his explanation of the superstition of the first-foot, because he had heard that, while in the Isle of Man it was attached to a dark man, elsewhere it was attached to a fair man. Of the examples where, on New Year's morning, it is held to be unlucky to meet a dark person, I may mention Lincolnshire, Durham, Yorkshire, and Northumberland. It is, on the contrary, *lucky* to meet, as first-foot, a dark-haired man in Lancashire, the Isle of Man, and Aberdeenshire.[218] In these cases we get the element of "dark" or "fair" as the varying factor of the superstition; but instances occur in Sutherlandshire, the West of Scotland, and in Durham, where the varying factor rests upon sex—a man being lucky and a woman being unlucky.

Similarly of the well-known superstition about telling the bees of the death of their owner, in Berkshire, Bucks, Cheshire, Cornwall, Cumberland, Lincolnshire, Lancashire, Monmouthshire, Notts, Northumberland, Shropshire, Somersetshire, Suffolk, Surrey, Sussex, Wilts, Worcestershire, it appears that a relative may perform the ceremony, or sometimes a servant merely, while in Derbyshire, Hants, Northants, Rutland, and Yorkshire it must be the heir or successor of the deceased owner. Again, while in the above places the death of the owner is told to the bees, in other places it is told to the cattle, and in Cornwall to the trees;[219] and, in other places, marriages as well as death are told to the bees.[220]

In some cases the transfer from one object to another of a particular superstition is a matter of absolute observation. Thus, the labourers in Norfolk considered it a presage of death to miss a "bout" in corn or seed sowing. The superstition is now transferred to the drill, which has only been invented for a century. Again, in Ireland, it is now considered unlucky to give any one a light for his pipe on May-day—a very modern superstition, apparently. But the pipe in this case has been the means of preserving the old superstition found in many places of not giving a light from the homestead

124

fire.

I will just refer to one other example, the well-known custom of offering rags at sacred wells. Sir John Rhys thought that the object of these scraps of clothing being placed at the well was for transferring the disease from the sick person to some one else. But I ventured to oppose this idea, and considered that they were offerings, pure and simple, to the spirit of the well, and referred to examples in confirmation. Among other items, I have come across an account of an Irish "station," as it is called, at a sacred well, the details of which fully bear out my view as to the nature of the rags deposited at the shrine being offerings to the local deity. One of the devotees, in true Irish fashion, made his offering accompanied by the following words: "To St. Columbkill—I offer up this button, a bit o' the waistband o' my own breeches, an' a taste o' my wife's petticoat, in remimbrance of us havin' made this holy station; an' may they rise up in glory to prove it for us in the last day."[221] I shall not attempt to account for the presence of the usual Irish humour in this, to the devotee, most solemn offering; but I point out the undoubted nature of the offerings and their service in the identification of their owners—a service which implies their power to bear witness in spirit-land to the pilgrimage of those who deposited them during lifetime at the sacred well.[222]

Now, in all these cases there is an original and a secondary, or derivative, form of the superstition, and it is our object to trace out which is which. Do the rags deposited at wells symbolise offerings to the local deity? If so, they bring us within measurable distance of a cult which rests upon faith in the power of natural objects to harm or render aid to human beings. Does the question of first-foot rest upon the colour of the hair or upon the sex of the person? I think, looking at all the examples I have been able to examine, that colour is really the older basis of the superstition, and, if so, ethnological considerations are doubtless the root of it. Again, if the eldest son of the deceased owner of bees appears in the earliest form of the death-telling ceremony, we have an interesting fragment of the primitive house-ritual of our ancestors.

When, however, we come upon the worship of local deities, when we can suggest ethnological elements in folklore, and when we can speak of the house-father, and can see that duties are imposed upon him by traditional custom, unknown to any rules of civilised society, we are in the presence of facts older than those of historic times. It is thus that folklore so frequently points back to the past before the age of history. Over and over again we pause before the facts of folklore, which, however explained, always lead us back to some unexplored epoch of history, some undated period, which has not revealed its heroes, but which has left us a heritage of its mental strivings.

The method of using these notes of custom, rite, and belief for scientific purposes is therefore a very important matter. It is essential that each single item should be treated definitely and separately from all other items, and, further, that the exact wording of the original note upon each separate item should be kept intact. There must be no juggling with the record, no emendations such as students of early literary work are so fond of attempting. Whatever the record, it must be accepted. The original account of every custom and belief is a corpus, not to be tampered with except for the purpose of scientific analysis, and then after that purpose has been effected all the parts must be put together again, and the original restored to its form.

The handling of each custom or belief and of its separate parts in this way enables us, in the first place, to disentangle it from the particular personal or social stratum in which it happens to have been preserved. It may have become attached to a place, an object, a season, a class of persons, a rule of life, and may have been preserved by means of this attachment. But because every item of folklore of the same nature is not attached to the same agent wherever that particular item has been preserved, it is important not to stereotype an accidental association as a permanent one. Moreover, the modern association is not necessarily the ancient association, and there is the further difficulty created by writers on folklore classifying into chapters of their own creation the items they collect or discuss.[223] In the second place, we are enabled to prepare each item of folklore for the place to which it may ultimately be found to belong. The first step in this preparation is to get together all the examples of any one custom, rite, or belief which have been preserved, and to compare these examples with each other, first as to common features of likeness, secondly as to features of unlikeness. By this process we are able to restore what may be deficient from the insufficiency of any particular record—and such a restoration is above all things essential—and to present for examination not an isolated specimen but a

126

series of specimens, each of which helps to bring back to observation some portion of the original. The reconstruction of the original is thus brought within sight.

Generally, it may be stated that the points of likeness determine and classify all the examples of one custom or belief; the points of unlikeness indicate the line of decay inherent in survivals.

This partial equation and partial divergence between different examples of the same custom or belief allows a very important point to be made in the study of survivals. We can estimate the value of the elements which equate in any number of examples, and the value of the elements which diverge; and by noting how these values differ in the various examples we shall discover the extent of the overlapping of example with example, which is of the utmost importance. A given custom consists, say, of six elements, which by their constancy among all the examples and by their special characteristics may be considered as primary elements, in the form in which the custom has survived. Let us call these primary elements by algebraical signs, a, b, c, d, e, f. A second example of the same custom has four of these elements, a, b, c, d, and two divergences, which may be considered as secondary elements, and which we will call by the signs g, h. A third example has elements a, b, and divergences g, h, i, k. A further example has none of the primary elements, but only divergences g, h, i, l, m. Then the statement of the case is reduced to the following:—

$1 = a, b, c, d, e, f.$ $2 =$ $a, b, c, d + g, h.$ $3 =$ $a, b + g, h,$ $i, k.$ $4 =$ $+ g, h, i, l, m.$ The first conclusion to be drawn from this is that the overlapping of the several examples (No. 1 overlapping No. 2 at a, b, c, d, No. 2 overlapping No. 3 at $a, b + g, h$, No. 3 overlapping No. 4 at $+ g, h, i$) shows all these several examples to be but variations of one original custom, example No. 4, though possessing none of the elements of example No. 1, being the same custom as example No. 1. Secondly, the divergences g to m mark the line of decay which this particular custom has undergone since it ceased to belong to the dominant culture of the people, and dropped back into the position of a survival from a former culture preserved only by a fragment of the people.[224]

The first of these conclusions is not affected by the order in which the examples are arranged; whether we begin with No. 4 or with No. 1, the relationship of each example to the others, thus proved to be in intimate association, is the same. The second conclusion is necessarily dependent upon what we take to be "primary elements" and "secondary elements;" and the question is how can these be determined? As a rule it will be found that the primary elements are the most constant parts of the whole group of examples, appearing more frequently, possessing greater adherence to a common form, changing (when they do change) with slighter variations; while the secondary elements, on the other hand, assume many different varieties of form, are by no means of constant occurrence, and do not even amongst themselves tend to a common form. The primary elements, therefore, constitute the form of the custom which represents the oldest part of the survival. They alone will help us to determine the origin of the custom, whether by features represented in the elements thus brought together or by comparison with ancient custom elsewhere or with survivals elsewhere similarly reconstituted. Altogether these elements, thus linked together by the tie of common attributes, are parts of one organic whole, and it is on this reconstructed organism we have to rely for the evidence from tradition.

When any given custom or belief has undergone this double process of analysis of its component parts and classification of its several elements, another process has to be undertaken, namely, to ascertain its association with other customs or beliefs, in the same country or among the same people, each of which customs or beliefs, being treated in exactly the same manner, is found to exhibit some degree of relationship in origin, condition, or purpose to the whole group under examination. In this way classification, analysis, and association go hand in hand as the necessary methods of studying survivals. Without analysis we cannot properly arrive at a classification; without classification we cannot work out the association of survivals.

The process is perhaps highly technical and complicated. It may not be of interest to all to discuss the process by which results are attained when what is most desired are the results themselves. But in truth the two parts of this study cannot well be separated. To judge of the validity of the results one must know what the process has been, and too often results are jumped at without warrant; items of custom and usage or of belief and myth are docketed as belonging to a given phase of culture, a given group of people, when they have no right to such a place in the history of man. It is not only distasteful to the inquirer, but almost impossible to dislodge any item of folklore once so placed, and thus much of the value of the material supplied by folklore is lost or discounted.

Custom, rite, and belief treated in this fashion become veritable monuments of history—a history too ancient to have been recorded in script, too much an essential part of the folk-life to have been lost to tradition. We may hope to restore therefrom the surviving mosaic of ancient institutions, ancient law, and ancient religion, and we may further hope, with this mosaic to work upon, to restore much of the entire fabric which has been lying so many centuries beneath the accumulated and accumulating mass of new developments representing the civilisation of the Western world.

III

It is only here that we can discover the point where we may properly commence the work of comparative folklore. An item of folklore which stands isolated is practically of no use for scientific investigation. It may be, as we have seen, that the myth is in its primary stage as a sacred belief among primitive people, in its secondary or folk-tale stage as a sacred memory of what was once believed, in its final or legendary stage when it does duty in preserving the memory of a hero or a place of abiding interest. It may be, as we have seen, that the custom, rite, or belief is a mere formula without purpose or result, a mere traditional expression of a purpose without formula or result, a mere statement of result without formula or purpose. We must know the exact position of each item before we begin to compare, or we may be comparing absolutely unlike things. The exact position of each item of folklore is not to be found from one isolated example. It has first to be restored to its association with all the known examples of its kind, so that the earliest and most complete form may be recorded. That is the true position to which it has been reduced as a survival. This restored and complete example is then in a position to be compared either with similar survivals in other countries on the same level of culture, or within the same ethnological or political sphere of influence, or with living customs, rites, or beliefs of peoples of a more backward state of culture or in a savage state of culture.

Comparison of this kind is of value. Comparison of a less technical or comprehensive kind may be of value in the hands of a great master; but it is often not only valueless but mischievous in the hands of less experienced writers, who think that comparison is justified wherever similarity is discovered.

Similarity in form, however, does not necessarily mean similarity in origin. It does not mean similarity in motive. Customs and rites which are alike in practice can be shown to have originated from quite different causes, to express quite different motifs, and cannot therefore be held to belong to a common class, the elements of which are comparable. Thus to take a very considerable custom, to be found both in folk-tales and in usage, the succession of the youngest son, it is pretty clear that among European peoples it originated in the tribal practice of the elder sons going out of the tribal household to found tribal households of their own, thus leaving the youngest to inherit the original homestead. But among savage peoples where the youngest son inherits the homestead, he does not do so because of a tribal custom such as that to be found in the European evidence. It is because of the conditions of the marriage rites. Thus among the Kafir peoples of South Africa

"the young man of the commonality, who being a young man has had but little or no means of displaying his sagacity—a quality with them most frequently synonymous with cunning—commences for himself in a small way. Hence, too, being polygamous, and his wives being bought with cattle, his first wife is taken from a position accordant with that of a young, untried, and poor or comparatively poor man. Hence also it happens that his wives increase in number, and in—so to speak—position, in accordance with his wealth, and with his reputation for wisdom and sagacity, which may have raised him to the rank of headman of a district, and one of the Chief's counsellors. It is, therefore, only when old in years that he takes to himself his 'great wife,' one of greater social and racial position than were his previous wives, and her son, that is, her eldest son, who is consequently the father's youngest or nearly his youngest, becomes his 'great son,' and par excellence the heir. If the father be a Chief, this son becomes the Chief at his father's death.

"As, however, subordinate heirs, the father after some consultation

130

and ceremony chooses out of his other sons, secondly 'the son of his right hand,' and thirdly, 'the son of his grandfather.' If the father be a Chief, these two are after his death accounted as Chiefs in the tribe, subordinate to the 'great son,' and even if through their superior energy, the size of the tribe requiring emigration to pastures new, or other causes, one or both of them break off, and with their respective inheritance or following form a separate tribe or tribes, yet they are federally bound to their great brother, and their successors to his successors, and recognise him as their supreme or national Chief. Thus Krili, the Chief of the Amagcaleka tribe across the Kei, was also paramount Chief of all the Amaxosas, including his own tribe, and those this side the Kei, who are divided into the two great divisions—each of which includes several tribes—of the Amangquika and Amandhlambi, which latter has among it the Amagqunukwebi, a tribe of Caffre intermingled with Hottentot blood, and therefore rather looked down upon."[225]

Dr. Nicholson, from whom I quote this evidence, goes on to say that the

"custom then of the heirship of the youngest, appears to me to have not unlikely grown up among a polygamous race, and to have arisen both from considerations of self security and from those of race and rank."

Quite independently of Dr. Nicholson I had come to the same conclusion;[226] and Dr. Nicholson, after handsomely acknowledging my priority in the "discovery," very properly alludes to the not unimportant fact of two workers in the same field coming to like conclusions. It is remarkable that the same distinction between the succession of the youngest son and of the son of the youngest wife appears in folk-tales.[227] Now clearly it would be quite wrong to suggest a parallel between the heirship of the youngest among the Kafir peoples of Africa and heirship of the youngest among the tribal people of early Europe. They are not comparable at all points, and it is just where the point of comparison fails that it becomes so important to science.[228]

I will take one other example, and this is the important practice of human sacrifice which looms so largely in anthropological research, and which is considered by so good an authority as Schrader to have taken a prominent place among the Aryans,[229] though he takes his examples, not from language, but from the unexamined customs of the Greeks, Romans, northerns, Indians, and Persians. We know more about the development of sacrifice now that Professor Robertson Smith has dealt with the Semitic part of the evidence. Without resting on the fact that the occurrence of human sacrifice in a country occupied by Aryan-speaking people does not, of itself alone, imply that the rite was Aryan, it is far more important to point out that among the higher races "the feeling that the slaying involves a grave responsibility and must be justified by divine permission" appears, and "care was taken to slay the victim without bloodshed, or to make believe that it had killed itself."[230] This feeling marks distinctly the Greek sacrifice as at Thargelia and in the Leukadian ceremony, the Roman sacrifice at the Tarpeian Rock, the sacrifice at the Valhalla rock of the northerns, while among the Hindus there is much to show that the idea of human sacrifice in some of the early writings is a literary borrowing from the Hebrews; and that if it ever prevailed among the Aryas of India it was very early superseded by the sacrifice of animals.[231] Colonel Dalton has given good reasons for his views "that the Hindus derived from the aboriginal races the practice of human sacrifices."[232] Although, then, Greek ritual and Greek myth are full of legends which tell of sacrifices once human, but afterwards commuted into sacrifices where some other victim is slain or the dummy of a man is destroyed;[233] although the significant Hindu ceremonial of so throwing the limbs of an animal slaughtered to be burnt with the dead that every limb lies upon a corresponding part of the corpse;[234] although Teuton, Celt, and Norse[235] are credited with the practice by authorities not to be questioned, it appears by the evidence that the European form of human sacrifice has little in common with the savage form except in the nature of the victim. It occurred, as Grimm states, when some great disaster, some heinous crime, had to be retrieved or purged, a kind of sacrifice, says Mr. Lang, not necessarily savage except in its cruelty; and the victims were not tribesmen, but captive enemies, purchased slaves, or great criminals.

These two examples will serve as warning against the too general acceptance of the custom and belief of savage and barbaric races, as identical with the custom and belief of early or primitive man. Such identification is in the main correct; but it is correct not because it has been proved by the best methods to be so, but because, of all possible explanations, this is the only one that meets the general position in a satisfactory manner. In many cases, however, it is monstrously incorrect, and it is the incorrect conclusion which weighs far more against the acceptance of the results of folklore than do the correct conclusions in its favour.

The work which has to be accomplished by the comparative method of research is of such magnitude that it needs to be considered. The labour and research might in point of volume be out of proportion to the results, and it may be questioned, as it has already been questioned by inference, whether it is worth the while. The first answer to this objection is that all historical investigation is justified, however much the labour, however extensive the research. Secondly, considering the very few results which the study of folklore has hitherto produced upon the investigations into prehistoric Europe, it must be worth while for the student of custom and belief to conduct his experiments upon a recognised plan in order to get at the secret of man's place in the struggle for existence, which is determined more by psychological than by physical phenomena. Thirdly, if the psychical anthropology of prehistoric times is to be sought for in the customs and beliefs of modern savages, it is of vital importance to anthropological science that this should be established by methods exactly defined. Whatever of traditional custom and belief is capable of bearing the test and of being definitely labelled as belonging to prehistoric man, becomes thereafter the data for the psychical anthropology of civilised man. Edmund Spenser understood this when his official duties took him among the "wild" Irish. "All the customs of the Irish," he says, "which I have often noted and compared with that I have read, would minister occasion of a most ample discourse of the original of them, and the antiquity of that people, which in truth I think to be more ancient than most that I know in this end of the world; so as if it were in the handling of some man of sound judgment and plentiful reading, it would be most pleasant and profitable."[236]

Comparative folklore, then, to be of value must be based upon scientific principles. The unmeaning custom or belief of the peasantry of the Western world of civilisation must not be taken into the domains of savagery or barbarism for an explanation without any thought as to what this action really signifies to the history of the custom or belief in question. No doubt the explanation thus afforded is correct in most cases, and perhaps it was necessary to begin with the comparative method in order to understand the importance and scope of the study of apparently worthless material. A new stage in comparative folklore must now be entered upon. It must be understood what the effective comparison of a traditional peasant custom or belief with a savage custom or belief really amounts to. The process includes the comparison of an isolated custom or belief belonging, perhaps secretly, to a particular place, a particular class of persons, or perhaps a particular family or person, with a custom or belief which is part of a whole system belonging to a savage race or tribe; of a custom or belief whose only sanction is tradition, the conservative instinct to do what has been done by one's ancestors, with a custom or belief whose sanction is the professed and established polity or religion of a people; of a custom or belief which is embedded in a civilisation, of which it is not a part and to which it is antagonistic, with a custom or belief which helps to make up the civilisation of which it is part. In carrying out such a comparison, therefore, a very long journey back into the past of the civilised race has been performed. For unless it be admitted that civilised people consciously borrow from savages and barbaric peoples or constantly revert to a savage original type of mental and social condition, the effect of such a comparison is to take back the custom or belief of the modern peasant to a date when a people of savage or barbaric culture occupied the country now occupied by their descendants, the peasants in question, and to equate the custom or belief of this ancient savage or barbaric culture with the custom or belief of modern savage or barbaric culture. The line of comparison is not therefore simply drawn level from civilisation to savagery; but it consists, first, of two vertical lines from civilisation and savagery respectively, drawn to a height scaled to represent the antiquity of savage culture in modern Europe, and then the level horizontal line drawn to join the two vertical lines. Thus the line of comparison is

Ancient savagery Ancient savagery   Savagery Civilisation

We thus arrive at some conception of the work to be accomplished by and involved in comparative folklore. The results are worth the work. They relate to stages of culture in the countries of civilisation which are recoverable by no other means. The stages of culture are practically lost to history. In ancient Greek and Roman history, and in ancient Scandinavian history, there are priceless fragments of information which tell us much. But these fragments are not the complete story, and they belong to relatively small areas of European history. Every nation has the right to go back as far in its history as it is possible to reach. It can only do this by the help of comparative folklore. In our own country we have seen how history breaks down, and yet historical records in Britain are perhaps the richest in Europe. The traditional materials known to us as folklore are the only means left to us, and we can only properly avail ourselves of these when we have mastered the methods of science which it is necessary to use in their investigation.

FOOTNOTES:

[182] Mr. MacCulloch, in the title of his interesting book, the *Childhood of Fiction*, has emphasised this mischievous idea. I am not convinced to the contrary by the evidence he gives as to the popularity of the folk-tale among all peoples (p. 2). Indeed, the book itself is an emphatic testimony against its title. Mr. MacCulloch evidently began with the idea that the folk-tale belonged to the domain of fiction. Thus the opening words of his book are: "Folk-tales are the earliest form of romantic and imaginative literature—the unwritten fiction of early man and of primitive people in all parts of the world;" whereas as he nears the end of his study he observes: "Thus, in their origin, folk-tales may have had some other purpose than mere amusement; they may have embodied the traditions, histories, beliefs, ideas, and customs of men at an early stage of civilisation" (p. 451). Mr. MacCulloch himself proves this to be the case, and it is therefore all the more unfortunate that he should have stamped his very important study with the word "fiction."

[183] A folk-tale of the Veys, a North African people, explains this view most graphically in its opening sentences. The narrator begins his tale by saying: "I speak of the long time past; hear! It is written in our old-time-palaver-books—I do not say *then*; in old time the Vey people had no books, but the old men told it to their children and they kept it; afterwards it was written" (*Journ. Ethnol. Soc.*, N.S., vi. 354). A parallel to this comes from Ireland: "What I have told your honour is true; and if it stands otherwise in books, it's the books which are wrong. Sure we've better authority than books, for we have it all handed down from generation to generation"

(Kohl's *Travels in Ireland*, 140).

[184] I am the more willing to take this as my illustration of myth because, strangely enough, Mr. MacCulloch has omitted it from the examples he uses in his *Childhood of Fiction*.

[185] *Myth, Ritual, and Religion*, i. 166.

[186] Mr. Jeremiah Curtin has collected and published the *Creation Myths of Primitive America* (London, 1899), and his introduction is a specially valuable study of the subject. I printed the Fijian myth from Williams' *Fiji and Fijians*, i. 204, and the Kumis myth from Lewin's *Wild Races of South-east India*, 225-6, in my *Handbook of Folklore*, 137-139, and Mr. Lang, in cap. vi. of his *Myth, Ritual, and Religion* deals with a sufficient number of examples. *Cf.* also Tylor, *Primitive Culture*, cap. ix.

[187] Grey, *Polynesian Mythology*, 1-15. I have only summarised the full legend on the lines adopted by Dr. Tylor.

[188] On the Kronos myth consult Farnell, *Cults of the Greek States*, i. 23-31, who gives an admirable summary of the evidence as it at present stands; Harrison and Verrall, *Mythology and Monuments of Anc. Athens*, 192; Lang, *Myth, Ritual, and Religion*, i. 295-323.

[189] Mr. Crawley discovered this story in Mr. Bain's *A Digit of the Moon*, 13-15, and printed it in his *Mystic Rose*, 33-34.

[190] "The Interpreters of Genesis and the Interpreters of Nature," and "Mr. Gladstone and Genesis," in *Science and Hebrew Tradition*, cap. iv. and v.

[191] *Adonis, Attis and Osiris*, 4, 25. Mr. Jevons, too, lays stress upon "the source of errors in religion" as human reason gone astray, *Introd. to Hist. of Religion*, 463.

[192] Mr. Jevons practically arrives at this conclusion from a different standpoint. "Beliefs," he says, "are about facts, are statements about facts, statements that certain facts will be found to occur in a certain way or be of a certain kind" (*Introd. to Hist. of Religion*, 402). Mr. Curtin, *Creation Myths of Primitive America* (p. xx), confirms the view I take.

[193] Orpen, *Cape Monthly Magazine*. Quoted in Lang's *Myth, Ritual, and Religion*, i. 71.

[194] This myth is, I think, worth giving, because of its obvious object to account for the difference between white and black races. It is as

follows: "In the beginning of the world God created three white men and three white women, and three black men and three black women. In order that these twelve human souls might not thenceforth complain of Divine partiality and of their separate conditions, God elected that they should determine their own fates by their own choice of good and evil. A large calabash or gourd was placed by God upon the ground, and close to the side of the calabash was also placed a small folded piece of paper. God ruled that the black man should have the first choice. He chose the calabash, because he expected that the calabash, being so large, could not but contain everything needful for himself. He opened the calabash, and found a scrap of gold, a scrap of iron, and several other metals of which he did not understand the use. The white man had no option. He took, of course, the small folded piece of paper, and discovered that, on being unfolded, it revealed a boundless stock of knowledge. God then left the black men and women in the bush, and led the white men and women to the seashore. He did not forsake the white men and women, but communicated with them every night, and taught them how to construct a ship, and how to sail from Africa to another country. After a while they returned to Africa with various kinds of merchandise, which they bartered to the black men and women, who had the opportunity of being greater and wiser than the white men and women, but who, out of sheer avidity, had thrown away their chance."

[195] *Native Tribes of South-east Australia*, cap. viii.

[196] *Northern Tribes of Central Australia*, cap. xxii.; *Native Tribes of Central Australia*, cap. xviii.

[197] Spencer and Gillen, *Northern Tribes*, 624; *cf. Native Tribes of Central Australia*, 564.

[198] Spencer and Gillen, *Native Tribes of Central Australia*, 229.

[199] Grey, *Polynesian Mythology*, p. xi. *Cf.* Taylor, *Te Ika a Maui*, where myths told by the priests are given in cap. vi. and vii., and *Trans. Ethnological Soc.*, new series, i. 45.

[200] White's *Anc. Hist. of the Maori*, i. 8-13.

[201] Curtin, *Creation Myths of Primitive America*, p. xxi.

[202] Im Thurn, *Indians of Guiana*, 335; Landtman, *Origin of Priesthood*, 117.

[203] *Primitive Manners and Customs*, cap. i. "Some Savage Myths and

Beliefs," and cap. viii., "Fairy Lore of Savages."

[204] *Introd. to Hist. of Religion*, 263. Of course I do not accept Mr. J. A. Stewart's "general remarks on the μυθολογία or story-telling myth" in his *Myths of Plato*, 4-17. All Mr. Stewart's research is literary in object and result, though he uses the materials of anthropology.

[205] H. H. Wilson, *Rig Veda Sanhita*, i. p. xvii.

[206] H. H. Wilson, *Vishnu Purana*, i. p. iv; *Rig Veda Sanhita*, i. p. xlv.

[207] *Religion of the Semites*, 19.

[208] Mr. Hartland passes rapidly in his opening chapter from the myth as primitive science to the myth as fairy tale, from the savage to the Celt (*Science of Fairy Tales*, pp. 1-5), and I do not think it is possible to make this leap without using the bridge which is to be constructed out of the differing positions occupied by the myth and the fairy tale.

[209] It will be interesting, I think, to preserve here one or two instances of the actual practice of telling traditional tales in our own country. Mr. Hartland has referred to the subject in his *Science of Fairy Tales*, but the following instances are additional to those he has noted, and they refer directly back to the living custom. They are all from Scotland, and refer to the early part of last century. "In former times, when families, owing to distance and other circumstances, held little intercourse with each other through the day, numbers were in the habit of assembling together in the evening in one house, and spending the time in relating the tales of wonder which had been handed down to them by tradition" (Kiltearn in Ross and Cromarty; Sinclair, *Statistical Account of Scotland*, xiv. 323). "In the last generation every farm and hamlet possessed its oral recorder of tale and song. The pastoral habits of the people led them to seek recreation in listening to, and in rehearsing the tales of other times; and the senachie and the bard were held in high esteem" (Inverness-shire, *ibid.*, xiv. 168). "In the winter months, many of them are in the habit of visiting and spending the evenings in each other's houses in the different hamlets, repeating the songs of their native bard or listening to the legendary tales of some venerable senachie" (Durness in Sutherlandshire, *ibid.*, xv. 95).

[210] W. H. R. Rivers, *The Todas*, 3-4.

[211] Pausanias, viii. cap. xv. § 1.

[212] *Journ. Roy. Asiatic Soc.*, ii. p. 218.

[213] *Hist. of Rome*, i. pp. 177-179. *Cf.* Gunnar Landtman, *Origin of Priesthood*, p. 77.

[214] Perhaps Mr. Lang's study of "Cinderella and the Diffusion of Tales" in *Folklore*, iv. 413 *et seq.*, contains the best summary of the position.

[215] Crawley, *Tree of Life*, 5, 144.

[216] Train, *Hist. of Isle of Man*, ii. 115.

[217] The ceremony is fully described in *Relics for the Curious*, i. 31; *Gentleman's Magazine*, 1784 (see *Gent. Mag. Library*, xxiii. 209), quoting from a tract first published in 1634; and see *Proc. Soc. Antiq. Scot.*, x. 669.

[218] See *Folklore*, iii. 253-264; Rhys, *Celtic Folklore*, i. 337-341.

[219] Couch, *Hist. of Polperro*, 168.

[220] I have investigated the bee cult at some length, and it will form part of my study on *Tribal Custom* which I am now preparing for publication.

[221] Carleton, *Traits and Stories of the Irish Peasantry.*

[222] Mr. Eden Phillpotts mentions in one of his Cornish stories exactly this conception. Rags were offered. "Just a rag tored off a petticoat or some such thing. They hanged 'em up around about on the thorn bushes, to shaw as they'd 'a' done more for the good saint if they'd had the power."—*Lying Prophets*, 60.

[223] I gave an example of this false classification of folklore in accord with its apparent modern association in my preface to *Denham Tracts*, ii. p. ix. The left-leg stocking divination is not associated with dress, but with the left-hand as opposed to the right-hand augury, and I pointed out that the district of the Roman wall, the *locus* of the Denham tracts, thus preserves the luck of the left, believed in by the Romans, in opposition to the luck of the right believed in by the Teutons. See Schrader, *Prehistoric Antiquities of the Aryan Peoples*, 253-7.

[224] I elaborated this plan of comparative analysis in a report to the British Association at Liverpool, in 1896 (see pp. 626-656), illustrating it from the fire customs of Britain.

[225] *Archæological Review*, ii. 163-166; *cf.* the Rev. J. Macdonald in *Folklore*, iii. 338.

[226] *Athenæum*, 29th December, 1883; *Archæologia*, vol. l. p. 213.

[227] See MacCulloch's *Childhood of Fiction*, chap. xiii., where this distinction is noted, though its significance is not pointed out.

[228] Dr. Rivers has dealt with a very similar case of dual origin in connection with bride capture, see *Journ. Roy. Asiatic Soc.*, 1907, p. 624.

[229] Schrader's *Prehistoric Antiquities of the Aryan Peoples*, 422.

[230] Robertson Smith's *Religion of the Semites*, 397.

[231] Monier Williams, *Indian Wisdom*, pp. 29-31. The word-equations for sacrifice are given by Schrader, *op. cit.*, 130, 415.

[232] *Journ. Asiatic Soc. Bengal*, xxxiv. p. 7. On the influence of the aboriginal races *cf.* Monier Williams, *Indian Wisdom*, 312-313; Steel and Temple's *Wide Awake Stories*, 395; Campbell, *Tales of West Highlands*, l. p. xcviii.

[233] Lang, *Myth, Ritual, and Religion*, i. p. 271.

[234] H. H. Wilson, *Religion of the Hindus*, ii. 289. I compare this with the custom of the cow following the coffin mentioned by Mannhardt, *Die Gotterwelt*, 320, and the soul shot or gift of a cow at death recorded by Brand, ii. 248.

[235] *Cf.* Olaus Magnus, pp. 168, 169, for the significant Norse ceremony.

[236] Spenser, *View of the State of Ireland*, 1595 (Morley reprint), 73.

Chapter III

PSYCHOLOGICAL CONDITIONS

Although the great mass of folklore rests upon tradition and tradition alone, an important aid to tradition comes from certain psychological conditions which we must now consider. At an early stage all students of folklore will have discovered that it is not entirely to tradition that folklore is indebted for its material. There are still people capable of thinking, capable of believing, in the primitive way and in the primitive degree. Such people are of course the descendants of long ancestors of such people—people whose minds are not attuned to the civilisation around them; people, perhaps, whose minds have been to an extent stunted and kept back by the civilisation around them. There can be no doubt that civilisation and all it demands of mankind acts as a deterrent upon the minds of some living within the civilisation zone, and belonging apparently to the civilised society. This is the root cause of some of the lunacy and much of the crime which apparently exists as a necessary adjunct of civilisation, and it leads to various forms of thought inconsistent with the knowledge and ideas of the age. When these forms of thought are not concentrated into a new religious sect by the operation of social laws, they become what is sometimes called mere superstition, that kind of superstition which consists of using the same power of logic to a narrow set of facts which primitive man was in the habit of using, and thus repeating in this age the methods of primitive science. We cannot quite understand this in the age of railways and schools and inventions, but it will be understood better if we go back for only a generation or two to those parts of our country which are most remote from civilising influences, and obtain some information as to their condition.

This cannot be better accomplished than by referring to a Scottish author writing, in 1835, of the superstitions then prevailing in Scotland. "Our whole genuine records," says Dalyell,

"teem with the most repulsive pictures of the weakness, bigotry, turbulence, and fierce and treacherous cruelty of the populace. False and

141

corrupt innovations of literature, a compound of facts and fiction, intermingling the old and the new in heterogeneous assemblage, would persuade us to think much more of our forefathers than they thought of themselves. Scotland, until the most modern date, was an utter stranger to civilisation, presenting a sterile country with a famished people, wasted by hordes of mendicants readier to seize than to solicit—void of ingenious arts and useful manufactures, possessed of little skill and learning, plunged in constant war and rapine, full of insubordination, disturbing public rule and private peace. For waving pendants, flowing draperies, brilliant colours, eagles' feathers, herons' plumes, feasts or festivals so splendid in imagination, let naked limbs, scanty, sombre garments to elude discovery by the foe, bits of heath stuck in bonnets if they had them, precarious sustenance, abject humility and all those hardships inseparable from uncultivated tribes and countries be instituted as a juster portrait of earlier generations."[237]

This statement as to Scotland is correctly drawn from social conditions which have now passed away, but which, down to the beginning of last century, belonged to the ordinary life of the people. Thus it is recorded that

"over all the highlands of Scotland, and in this county in common with others, the practice of building what are called head-dykes was of very remote antiquity. The head-dyke was drawn across the head of a farm, when nature had marked the boundary betwixt the green pastures and that portion of hill which was covered totally or partially with heath. Above this fence the young cattle, the horses, the sheep and goats were kept in the summer months. The milch cows were fed below, except during the time the farmer's family removed to the distant grazings called sheilings. Beyond the head-dyke little attention was paid to boundaries. These enclosures exhibit the most evident traces of extreme old age."[238]

Representation of an Irish chieftain seated at dinner (from Derrick's "The Image of Ireland") **REPRESENTATION OF AN IRISH CHIEFTAIN SEATED AT DINNER, 1581 FROM DERRICKE'S "IMAGE OF IRELAND"**

In Ireland the same conditions obtained so late as the sixteenth century; the native Irish retained their wandering habits, tilling a piece of fertile land in the spring, then retiring with their herds to the booleys or dairy habitations, generally in the mountain districts in the summer, and moving about where the herbage afforded sustenance to their cattle.[239] An eighteenth-century traveller in Ireland was assured that the quarter called Connaught was "inhabited by a kind of savages," and there is record of the capture of a hairy dwarf near Longford, who appears hardly to belong to civilisation.[240] Similar conditions obtained in the northern counties of England, and in other parts.[241] Special circumstances kept the borderland outside the influences of ordinary civilised thought and control, and these circumstances have been recorded by an eighteenth-century observer, from whom I will quote one or two facts as to the mode of life of these people: "That they might be more invisible during their outrodes and consequently less liable to the effects of their enemies' vigilance, the colour of their cloathes resembled that of the scenes of their employment or of their season of action, that is, of a brown heath and cloudy evening. Thus examples of what might condemn their conduct were never offered to them, and immemorial custom seemed as it were to sanctify their wildness. Every border-man, almost without exception, was brought up in a state which we would call unhappy, and every circumstance of his life tended to confirm his partiality for an uncertain bed and unprovided diet."[242]

The evidence which this acute observer collected led him to conclude that the "almost uniform train of circumstances which affected these countries from their border situation, and the little difference there was between one of the dark ages and another, strongly induce me to believe that the Northern people were little altered in manners from very remote times to those immediately preceding the reign of Queen Elizabeth," and this is confirmed by what we actually find from the report of the Commissioners appointed to settle the peace of the Marches by fixed and established ordinances, who collected "their ordinances from the traditional accounts of ancient usages that had been sanctified as laws by the length of time which they had endured. These laws were different from most others, nay, almost peculiar to the men to whom they belonged."[243]

I need not continue these notes as to the backwardness of portions of the country compared with its general level of culture, because I have dealt with the evidence elsewhere.[244] What I am anxious to point out here is that the faculty of such people as these to think, not in terms of modern science but in terms of their own psychological conditions, must have been pronounced. If they ever put the question to themselves as to the origin of things, they would answer themselves according to the life impressions they were then receiving, and according to the limited range of their actual knowledge. As with the creators of the traditional myths, the scientific inquirers of primitive times, so with these non-advanced people of later times, they would deal with the problems they did not understand in fashions suitable to their own understanding. It has always appeared to me that the impressions of the surrounding life are not sufficiently regarded in their influence upon primitive thought. They press down upon the mind, and enclose it within barriers so that it can only act through these surroundings. Child-life is, in this respect, much the same as the life of primitive man. A child thinks and acts in terms of his nursery, his school, or his playground. Thus a memory of my own is to the point. When quite a child, probably about eight or nine years old, I was entrusted with the changing of a small cheque drawn by my father in a country town where we were staying. I had never seen a cheque before. I remember the ceremony of writing it and the care with which the necessary instructions were given to me, and I remember the amazement with which I received the golden sovereigns. But my mind dwelt upon this strange thing called a cheque, and after a time I deliberately came to the conclusion that my father was allowed to get money for these cheques on condition only that he wrote them without a mistake and without a blot. The conception is absurd until we come to analyse the cause of it. My young life at that time was receiving its greatest impressions, its all-absorbing impressions, from my school exercises in writing. It was a copybook life for the time being, and when I turned to ask my question as to origins, as every human being has asked himself in turn, I could express myself only in copybook terms. It is so with the primitive mind. It can only express itself in the terms of its greatest impressions, and it is in this way that primitive animism, sympathetic magic and other conceptions obtained from the results

144

of anthropological research, are to be found in much the same degree wherever humanity is found in primitive conditions. As Mr. Hickson puts it so well: "Just as the little black baby of the negro, the brown baby of the Malay, the yellow baby of the Chinaman, are in face and form, in gestures and habits, as well as in the first articulate sound they mutter, very much alike, so the mind of man, whether he be Aryan or Malay, Mongolian or Negrito, has, in the course of its evolution, passed through stages which are practically identical. In the intellectual childhood of mankind natural phenomena, or some other causes, of which we are at present ignorant, have induced thoughts, stories, legends, and myths, that in their essentials are identical among all the races of the world with which we are acquainted;"[245] or to take one other example from the experience of travellers, Mr. Mitchell, speaking of the Australians, says: "I found a native still there, and on my advancing towards him with a twig he shook another twig at me, waving it over his head, and at the same time intimating with it that we must go back. He and the boy then threw up dust at us with their toes (*cf.* 2 Sam. xvi. 13). These various expressions of hostility and defiance were too intelligible to be mistaken. The expressive pantomime of the man showed the identity of the human mind, however distinct the races or different the language."[246]

This identity is shown in many other ways to have been operating, perhaps to be operating still, upon minds not attuned to the civilisation around them. The resistance of agriculturists to change is well known.[247] The crooked ridges of the open-field system were believed to be necessary because they were supposed to deceive the devil,[248] while a superstitious dislike was entertained against winnowing machines, because they were supposed to interfere with the elements.[249] This is nothing but a modern example of sympathetic magic produced by the introduction of the new machine.

I need not go through the researches of the masters of anthropology to explain what the psychological evidence exactly amounts to, and the realms of primitive thought and experience which it connotes.[250] It will, however, be useful for the purpose of our present study, if we can find among the peasantry of our country (perchance from those districts where we have noted conditions under which primitive thought might retain a continuous hold) examples of belief or superstition which belongs rather to psychological than to traditional influences. The interpretation of dreams, the belief in spirit apparitions, the practice of charms, all belong to this branch of our subject, though I shall illustrate the points I wish to bring out by reference to less common departments.

It was only in the seventeenth century that a learned divine of the Church of England was shocked to hear one of his flock repeat the evidence of his pagan beliefs in language which is as explicit as it is amusing; and I shall not be accused of trifling with religious susceptibilities if I quote a passage from a sermon delivered and printed in 1659—a passage which shows not a departure from Christianity either through ignorance or from the result of philosophic study or contemplation, but a sheer non-advance to Christianity, a passage which shows us an English pagan of the seventeenth century.

"Let me tell you a story," says the Reverend Mr. Pemble, "that I have heard from a reverend man out of the pulpit, a place where none should dare to tell a lye, of an old man above sixty, who lived and died in a parish where there had bin preaching almost all his time.... On his deathbed, being questioned by a minister touching his faith and hope in God, you would wonder to hear what answer he made: being demanded what he thought of God, he answers that he was a good old man; and what of Christ, that he was a towardly youth; and of his soule, that it was a great bone in his body; and what should become of his soule after he was dead, that if he had done well he should be put into a pleasant green meadow."[251]

Of the four articles of this singular creed, the first two depict an absence of knowledge about the central features of Christian belief, the latter two denote the existence of knowledge about some belief not known to English scholars of that time. If it had so happened that the Reverend Mr. Pemble had thought fit to tell his audience only of the first two articles of this creed, it would have been difficult to resist the suggestion that they presented us merely with an example of stupid, or, perhaps, impudent, blasphemy caused by the events of the day. But the negative nature of the first two items of the creed is counterbalanced by the positive nature of the second two items; and thus this example shows us the importance of considering evidence as to all phases of non-belief in Christianity.

146

Passing on to the two items of positive belief, it is to be noted that the soul resident in the body in the shape of a bone is no part of the early European belief, but equates rather with the savage idea which identifies the soul with some material part of the body, such as the eyes, the heart, or the liver; and it is interesting to note in this connection that the backbone is considered by some savage races, *e.g.*, the New Zealanders, as especially sacred because the soul or spiritual essence of man resides in the spinal marrow.[252] And there is a well-known incident in folk-tales which seems to owe its origin to this group of ideas. This is where the hero having been killed, one of his bones tells the secret of his death, and thus acts the part of the soul-ghost.

In the pleasant green fields we trace the old faiths of the agricultural peasantry which, put into the words of Hesiod, tell us that "for them earth yields her increase; for them the oaks hold in their summits acorns, and in their midmost branches bees. The flocks bear for them their fleecy burdens ... they live in *unchanged happiness*, and need not fly across the sea in impious ships"—faiths which are in striking contrast to the tribal warrior's conception as set forth by the Saxon thane of King Eadwine of Northumbria. "This life," said this poetical thane, "is like the passage of a bird from the darkness without into a lighted hall where you, O King, are seated at supper, while storms, and rain, and snow rage abroad. The sparrow flying in at our door and straightway out at another is, while within, safe from the storm; but soon it vanishes into the darkness whence it came."

Such faiths as these, indeed, show us primitive ideas at their very roots. This seventeenth-century pagan depended upon himself for his faith. He worked out his own ideas as to the origin of soul and heaven and God and Christ. They were terms that had filtered down to him through the hard surroundings of his life, and he set to work to define them in the fashion of the primitive savage. We meet with other examples. Thus among the superstitions of Lancashire is one which tells us of the lingering belief in a long journey after death, when food is necessary to support the soul. A man having died of apoplexy, near Manchester, at a public dinner, one of the company was heard to remark: "Well, poor Joe, God rest his soul! He has at least gone to his long rest wi' a belly full o' good meat, and that's some consolation," and perhaps a still more remarkable instance is that of the woman buried in Cuxton Church, near Rochester, who directed by her will that the coffin was to have a lock and key, the key being placed in her dead hand, so that she might be able to release herself at pleasure.[253]

These people simply did not understand civilised thought or civilised religion. To escape from the pressure of trying to understand they turned to think for themselves, and thinking for themselves merely brought them back to the standpoint of primitive thought. It could hardly be otherwise. The working of the human mind is on the same plane wherever and whenever it operates or has operated. The difference in results arises from the enlarged field of observation. When the Suffolk peasant set to work to account for the existence of stones on his field by asserting that the fields produced the stones, and for the origin of the so-called "pudding-stone" conglomerate, that it was a mother stone and the parent of the pebbles,[254] he was beginning a first treatise on geology; and when the Hampshire peasant attributes the origin of the tutsan berries to having germinated in the blood of slaughtered Danes,[255] other counties following the same thought, I am not at all sure that he is not beginning all over again the primitive conception of the origin of plants.

Long Meg and her Daughters (from a photograph by Messrs. Frith) **LONG MEG AND HER DAUGHTERS**

Stone circles on Stanton Moor (from Archæologia) **STONE CIRCLES ON STANTON MOOR**

This beginning shows the mark of the primitive mind, and that it was operating in a country dominated by scientific thought is the phenomenon which makes it so important to consider psychological conditions among the problems of folklore. They account for some beliefs which may not contain elements of pure tradition. When the Mishmee Hill people of India affirm of a high white cliff at the foot of one of the hills that approaches the Burhampooter that it is the remains of the "marriage feast of Raja Sisopal with the daughter of the neighbouring king, named Bhismak, but she being stolen away by Krishna before the ceremony was completed, the whole of the viands were left uneaten and have since become consolidated into their present form,"[256] we can understand that the belief is in strict accord with the primitive conditions of thought of the Mishmee people. Can we understand the same conditions of the parallel English belief concerning the stone circle known as "Long Meg and her daughters,"[257] and of that at Stanton Drew;[258] or of the allied beliefs in Scotland that a huge upright stone, Clach Macmeas, in Loth, a parish of Sutherlandshire, was hurled to the bottom of the glen from the top of Ben Uarie by a giant youth when he was only one month old;[259] and in England that "the Hurlers," in Cornwall, were once men engaged in the game of hurling, and were turned into stone for playing on the Lord's Day; that the circle, known as "Nine Maidens," were maidens turned into stone for dancing on the Lord's Day;[260] that the stone circle at Stanton Drew represents serpents converted into stones by Keyna, a holy virgin of the fifth century;[261] and that the so-called snake stones found at Whitby were serpents turned into stones by the prayers of the Abbess Hilda.[262] These are only examples of the kind of beliefs entertained in all parts of the United Kingdom,[263] and they seem based upon psychological, rather than traditional conditions.

The giant and the witch, or wizard, are terms applied to the unknown personal agent. "The two standing stones in the neighbourhood of West Skeld are said to be the metamorphosis of two wizards or giants, who were on their way to plunder and murder the inhabitants of West Skeld; but not having calculated their time with sufficient accuracy, before they could accomplish their purpose, or retrace their steps to their dark abodes, the first rays of the morning sun appeared, and they were immediately transformed, and remain to the present time in the shape of two tall moss-grown stones of ten feet in height."[264] This is paralleled by the Merionethshire example of a large drift of stones about midway up the Moelore in Llan Dwywe, which was believed to be due to a witch who "was carrying her apron full of stones for some purpose to the top of the hill, and the string of the apron broke, and all the stones dropped on the spot, where they still remain under the name of Fedogaid-y-Widdon."[265] Giant and witch in these cases are generic terms by which the popular mind has conveyed a conception of the origin of these strange and remarkable monuments, whether natural or constructed by a long-forgotten people; and we cannot doubt that such beliefs are generated by the peasantry of civilisation from a mental conception not far removed from that of the primitive savage. Neither their religion nor their education was concerned with such things, so the peasants turned to their own realm and created a myth of origins suitable to their limited range of knowledge.

It may perhaps be urged that such beliefs as these are on the borderland of psychological and traditional influences. Witches and giants certainly belong to tradition, but on the other hand they are the common factors of the natural mind which readily attributes personal origins to impersonal objects. I am inclined on the whole to attribute the beliefs attachable to the unexplained boulders or unknown monoliths to the eternal questionings in the minds of the uncultured peasants of uncivilised countries similar to those of the unadvanced savage. That the peasant of civilisation should confine his questionings to the by-products of his surroundings and not to the greater subjects which occupy the minds of savages, is only because the greater subjects have already been answered for him by the Christian Church.[266]

There is a point, however, where psychological and traditional conditions are in natural conjunction, and I will just refer to this. That matters of legal importance should be preserved by the agency of tradition has already been shown to belong to that part of history for which there are no contemporary records, and its importance in this connection has been proved. Equally important from the psychological side is the fact that law is also preserved by tradition where people are unaccustomed to the use of writing, or by reason of their occupation have little use for writing. To illustrate this, I will quote an excellent note preserved by a writer on Cornish superstitions.

"There is an old 'vulgar error'—that no man can swear as a witness in a court of law to any thing he has seen through glass. This is based upon the formerly universal use of blown glass for windows, in which glass the constant recurrence of the greenish, and barely more than semi-transparent bull's eyes, so much distorted the view that it was unsafe for a spectator through glass to pledge his oath to what he saw going on outside. Now, through our present glass, this belief is relegated to the region of forgotten things, but nevertheless it has hold on Westcountry people still. I was, some years since, investigating the case of a derelict ship which had been found off the Scilly Islands, and towed by the pilots into a safe anchorage for the night. Next morning the pilots going out to complete their salvage, saw some men on board the derelict casting off the anchor rope by which they had secured her, but they distinctly declined to swear to the truth of what they had seen, and it turned out that they had seen through glass, by which they meant a telescope. In the same case I found that when these pilots (men intelligent much beyond the average, as all Scillonians are) had, on boarding the derelict (which had, of course, been deserted by her crew), found a living dog, they had deliberately thrown it overboard. They explained this act of cruelty to me by saying that a ship was not derelict if on board of her was found alive 'man, woman, child, dog, or cat.' And it turned out, on after-investigation, that these were the very words used in an obsolete Act of Parliament of one of the early Plantagenet kings, forgotten centuries ago by the English people, but borne in mind as a living fact by the Scillonians."[267]

In some special departments elementary psychological conditions operate in a considerable degree—operate to produce not waifs and strays of primitive thought and belief, but whole classes. Thus in the curious accretion of superstition around the objects connected with church worship, the same agencies are at work. The general characteristic of popular beliefs which originated with, or have grown up around the consecrated objects of the Church, is that such objects are beneficent in their action when employed for any given purpose. Thus, as Henderson says of the North of England, "a belief in the efficacy of the sacred elements in the Eucharist for the cure of bodily disease is widely spread." Silver rings, made from the offertory money, are very generally worn for the cure of epilepsy. Water that had been used in baptism was believed in West Scotland to have virtue to cure many distempers; it was a preventive against witchcraft, and eyes bathed with it would never see a ghost. Dalyell puts the evidence very succinctly. "Everything relative to sanctity was deemed a preservative. Hence the relics of saints, the touch of their clothes, of their tombs, and even portions of structures consecrated to divine offices were a safeguard near the person. A white marble altar in the church of Iona, almost entire towards the close of the seventeenth century, had disappeared late in the eighteenth, from its demolition in fragments to avert shipwreck." And so what has been consecrated, must not be desecrated. In Leicestershire and Northamptonshire there is a superstitious idea that the removal or exhumation of a body after interment bodes death or some terrible calamity to the surviving members of the deceased's family.[268]

In the West of Ireland there were usually found upon the altars of the small missionary churches one or more oval stones, either natural waterwashed pebbles or artificially shaped and very smooth, and these were held in the highest veneration by the peasantry as having belonged to the founders of the churches, and were used for a variety of purposes, as the curing of diseases, taking oaths upon them, etc.[269] Similarly the using of any remains of destroyed churches for profane purposes was believed to bring misfortune,[270] while the land which once belonged to the church of St. Baramedan, in the parish of Kilbarrymeaden, county Waterford, "has long been highly venerated by the common people, who attribute to it many surprising virtues."[271] In 1849 the people of Carrick were in the habit of carrying away from the churchyard portions of the clay of a priest's grave and using it as a cure for several diseases, and they also boiled the clay from the grave of Father O'Connor with milk and drank it.[272] One of the superstitious fancies of the Connemara folk in 1825 was credulity with respect to the gospels, as they are called, which "they wear round their neck as a charm against danger and disease. These are prepared by the priest, and sold by him at the price of two or three tenpennies. It is considered sacrilege in the purchaser to part with them at any time, and it is believed that the charm proves of no efficacy to any but the individual for whose particular benefit the priest has blessed it. The charm is written on a scrap of paper and enclosed in a small cloth bag, marked on one side with the letters I. H. S. On one side of the paper is written the Lord's Prayer, and after it a great number of initial letters."[273]

Such examples could be multiplied indefinitely, but no folklorist has properly classified such beliefs and endeavoured to ascertain their place in the science of folklore.[274] It is clear they have arisen not from tradition, but from a new force acting on minds which were not yet free to receive new influences without going back to old methods of thought.

How completely the sanctity of the church exercises a constant influence upon the minds of men, thus substituting a new form of belief when older forms were thrust on one side by the advance of the new religion, is perhaps best illustrated by a practice in early Christian times for giving sanctity to the oath. Among the Jews the altar in the Temple was resorted to by litigants in order that the oath might be taken in the presence of Yahveh himself, and "so powerful was the impression of this upon the Christian mind, that in the early ages of the Church there was a popular superstition that an oath taken in a Jewish synagogue was more binding and more efficient than anywhere else."[275] In exactly the same way the altar of the Christian Church is used in popular belief after its use in Church ceremonial has been discontinued. Thus, to get in beneath the altar of St. Hilary Church, Anglesey, by means of an open panel and then turn round and come out is to ensure life for the coming year,[276] and the white marble altar in Iona which has been entirely demolished by fragments of it being used to avert shipwreck has already been referred to.[277] These are cases where there has been a throwing back from the new religion to the objects connected with the old religion, and they are paralleled by the practice of Protestants appealing to the Roman Catholic priesthood for protection against witchcraft, and of Nonconformists believing that the clergy of the Episcopal Church possess superior powers over evil spirits.[278]

Psychological evidence is therefore important. One can never be quite sure to what extent civilised man is free from creating fresh myths in place of acquired scientific result, and to what extent this influences the production of primitive beliefs, or allows of the acceptance of traditional belief on new ground. The great mass of traditional belief has come through the ages traditionally, that is, from parent to child, from neighbour to neighbour, from class to class, from locality to locality, generation after generation. Occasionally this main current of the traditional life of a people is swollen by small side streams from fresh psychological sources. Individual examples, such as those I have cited, have perhaps always been present, but their effect must have died away with the passing of those with whom they originated. There are, however, stronger effects than these, coming not from

153

individuals, but from classes. Thus the votaries and enemies of witchcraft produced a more lasting effect. Witchcraft, as Dr. Karl Pearson, I think, conclusively proves, and as I have helped to prove,[279] is founded upon traditional belief and custom, but its remarkable revival in the Middle Ages was in the main a psychological phenomenon. Traditional practices, traditional formulæ, and traditional beliefs are no doubt the elements of witchcraft, but it was not the force of tradition which produced the miserable doings of the Middle Ages and of the seventeenth century against witches. These were due to a psychological force, partly generated by the newly acquired power of the people to read the Bible for themselves, and so to apply the witch stories of the Jews to neighbours of their own who possessed powers or peculiarities which they could not understand, and partly generated by the carrying on of traditional practices by certain families or groups of persons who could only acquire knowledge of such practices by initiation or family teaching. Lawyers, magistrates, judges, nobles, and monarchs are concerned with witchcraft. These are not minds which have been crushed by civilisation, but minds which have misunderstood it or have misused it. It is unnecessary, and it is of course impossible on this occasion to trace out the psychic issues which are contained in the facts of witchcraft, but it may be advisable to illustrate the point by one or two references.

I will note a few modern examples of the belief in witchcraft:—

"In 1879 extraordinary stories were current among the populace of Caergwrle. Mrs. Braithwaite supplied a Mrs. Williams with milk, but afterwards refused to serve her, and the cause was as follows: Mrs. Braithwaite had up to that time been very successful in churning her butter, but about a month ago the butter would not come. She tried every known agency; she washed and dried her bats, but all to no purpose. The milk would not yield an ounce of butter. Under the circumstances she said Mrs. Williams had witched her. The neighbours believed it, and Mrs. Williams was generally called a witch. Hearing these reports, Mrs. Williams went to Mrs. Braithwaite to expostulate with her, when Mrs. Braithwaite said, 'Out, witch! If you don't leave here, I'll shoot you.' Mrs. Williams thereupon applied to the Caergwrle bench of magistrates for a protection order against Mrs. Braithwaite. She assured the Bench she was in danger, as every one believed she was a witch. The Clerk: What do they say is the reason? Applicant: Because she cannot churn the milk. Mr. Kryke: Do they see you riding a broomstick? Applicant (seriously): No, sir. The Bench instructed the police officer to caution Mrs. Braithwaite against repeating the threats."[280]

The next example is from Lancashire:—

"At the East Dereham Petty Sessions, William Bulwer, of Etling Green, was charged with assaulting Christiana Martins, a young girl, who resided near the Etling Green toll-bar. Complainant deposed that she was 18 years of age, and on Wednesday, the 2nd inst., the defendant came to her and abused her. The complainant, who looks scarce more than a child, repeated, despite the efforts of the magistrates' clerk to stop her, and without being in the least abashed, some of the worst language it was possible to conceive—conversation of the most gross description, alleged to have taken place between herself and the defendant. They appeared to have got from words to blows and, while trying to fasten the gate, the defendant hit her across the hand with a stick. She alleged that there was no cause for the abuse and the assault, so far as she knew, and in reply to rigid cross-examination as to the origin of the quarrel, adhered to this statement. Mrs. Susannah Gathercole also corroborated the statement as to the assault, adding that the defendant said the complainant's mother was a witch. Defendant then blazed forth in righteous indignation, and, when the witness said she knew no more about the origin of the quarrel, he said, 'Mrs. Martins is an old witch, gentlemen, that is what she is, and she charmed me, and I got no sleep for her for three nights, and one night at half-past eleven o'clock, I got up because I could not sleep, and went out and found a "walking toad" under a clod that had been dug up with a three-pronged fork. That is why I could not rest; she is a bad old woman; she put this toad under there to charm me, and her daughter is just as bad, gentlemen. She would bewitch any one; she charmed me, and I got no rest day or night for her, till I found this "walking toad" under the turf. She dug a hole and put it there to charm me, gentlemen, that is the truth. I got the toad out and put it in a cloth, and took it upstairs and showed it to my mother, and "throwed" it into the pit in the garden. She went round this here "walking toad" after she had buried it, and I could not rest by day or sleep by night till I found it. The Bench: Do you go to church? Defendant: Sometimes I go to church, and sometimes to chapel, and sometimes I don't go nowhere. Her mother is bad enough to do anything;

155

and to go and put the "walking toad" in the hole like that, for a man which never did nothing to her, she is not fit to live, gentlemen, to go and do such a thing; it is not as if I had done anything to her. She looks at lots of people, and I know she will do some one harm. The Chairman: Do you know this man, Superintendent Symons? Is he sane? Superintendent Symons: Yes, sir; perfectly."[281]

In Somerset belief in witchcraft still lingers in nooks and corners of the west, as appears from a case brought before the magistrates of the Wiveliscombe division.

"Sarah Smith, the wife of a marine store dealer, residing at Golden Hill, was for some time ill and confined to her bed. Finding that the local doctor could not cure her, she sent for a witch doctor of Taunton. He duly arrived by train on St. Thomas's day. Smith inquired his charge, and was informed he usually charged 11s., remarking that unless he took it from the person affected his incantation would be of no avail. Smith then handed it to his wife, who gave it to the witch doctor, and he returned 1s. to her. He then proceeded to foil the witch's power over his patient by tapping her several times on the palm of her hand with his finger, telling her that every tap was a stab on the witch's heart. This was followed by an incantation. He then gave her a parcel of herbs (which evidently consisted of dried bay leaves and peppermint), which she was to steep and drink. She was to send to a blacksmith's shop and get a donkey's shoe made, and nail it on her front door. He then departed."[282]

Such examples as these may be added to from various parts of the country, but they do not compare with the terrible case at Clonmel, in county Tipperary, which occurred in 1895. The evidence showed that the husband, father, and mother of the victim, together with several other persons, were concerned in this matter, and one of the witnesses, Mary Simpson, stated "that on the night of March 14th she saw Cleary forcibly administer herbs to his wife, and when the woman did not answer when called upon in the name of the Trinity to say who she was, she was placed on the fire by Cleary and the others. Mrs. Cleary did not appear to be in her right senses. She was raving."[283] The whole record of the trial is of the most amazing description, pointing back to a system of belief which, if based upon traditional practices, has been fed by entirely modern influences. Such

156

records as these stretch back through the ages, and almost every village, certainly every county in the United Kingdom, has its records of trials for witchcraft, in which clergy and layman, judge, jury, and victim play strange parts, if we consider them as members of a civilised community. Superstition which has been preserved by the folk as sacred to their old faiths, preserved by tradition, has remained the cherished possession, generally in secret, of those who practise it. The belief in witchcraft is a different matter. Though it has traditional rites and practices it has been kept alive by a cruel and crude interpretation of its position among the faiths of the Bible, and it has thus received fresh life.

The miserable records of witchcraft illustrate in a way no other subject can how the human mind, when untouched by the influences of advanced culture, has the tendency to revert to traditional culture, and they demonstrate how strongly embedded in human memory is the great mass of traditional culture. The outside civilisation, religious or scientific, has not penetrated far. Science has only just begun her great work, and religion has been spending most of her efforts in endeavouring to displace a set of beliefs which she calls superstition, by a set of superstitions which she calls revelation. Not only have the older faiths not been eradicated by this, but the older psychological conditions have not been made to disappear. The folklorist has to make note of this obviously significant fact, and must therefore deal with both sides of the question, the traditional and the psychological, and because by far the greater importance belongs to the former it does not do to neglect the importance, though the lesser importance, of the latter.

It assists the student of tradition in many ways. People who will still explain for themselves in primitive fashion phenomena which they do not understand, and who remain content with such primitive explanations instead of relying upon the discoveries of science, are just the people to retain with strong persistence the traditional beliefs and ideas which they obtained from their fathers, and to acquire other traditional beliefs and ideas which they obtain from neighbours. One often wonders at the "amazing toughness" of tradition, and in the psychological conditions which have been indicated will be found one of the necessary explanations.

FOOTNOTES:

[237] Dalyell, *Darker Superstitions of Scotland*, 197-198.

[238] Robertson, *Agriculture of Inverness-shire*. For Argyllshire see *New Stat. Account of Scotland*, vii. 346; Brown, *Early Descriptions of Scotland*, 12, 49, 99.

[239] Wilde, *Catalogue of Museum of Royal Irish Academy*, 99; Joyce, *Social Hist. of Anc. Ireland*, ii. 27.

[240] *Tour in Ireland*, 1775, p. 144; *Gent. Mag.*, v. 680.

[241] Hutchinson, *Hist. of Cumberland*, i. 216.

[242] James Clarke, *Survey of the Lakes*, 1789, p. xiii; *Berwickshire Nat. Field Club*, ix. 512.

[243] Clarke, *Survey of the Lakes*, pp. x, xv. Referring to the statutes enacted as a result of the Commissioners' work the facts are as follows: There were certain franchises in North and South Tynedale and Hexhamshire, by virtue of which the King's writ did not run there. [Tynedale, though on the English side of the border, was an ancient franchise of the Kings of Scotland.] In 1293 Edward I. confirmed this grant in favour of John of Balliol (1 Rot. Parl., 114-16), and the inhabitants took advantage of this immunity to make forays and commit outrages in neighbouring counties. In the year 1414, at the Parliament holden at Leicester, "grievous complaints" of these outrages were made "by the Commons of the County of Northumberland." It was accordingly provided (2 Henry V., cap. 5) that process should be taken against such offenders under the common law until they were outlawed; and that then, upon a certificate of outlawry made to lords of franchises in North and South Tynedale and Hexhamshire, the offender's lands and goods should be forfeited. In 1421 the provisions of this statute were extended to like offenders in Rydesdale, where also the King's writ did not run (9 Henry V., cap. 7). Still these excesses continued in Tynedale. By an enactment of Henry VII. (2 Henry VII., cap. 9) this "lordship and bounds" were annexed to the county of Northumberland. "Forasmuch," the preamble sets forth, "as the inhabitants and dwellers within the lordships and bounds of North and South Tyndale, not only in their own persons, but also oftentimes accompanied and confedered with Scottish ancient enemies to this realm, have at many seasons in time past committed

158

and done, and yet daily and nightly commit and do, great and heinous murders, robberies, felonies, depredations, riots and other great trespasses upon the King our Sovereign lord's true and faithful liege people and subjects, inhabiters and dwellers within the shires of Northumberland, Cumberland, and Westmoreland, Exhamshire [*sic*], the bishopric of Durham and in a part of Yorkshire, in which treasons, murders, robberies, felonies, and other the premises, have not in time past in any manner of form been punished after the order and course of the common law, by reason of such franchise as was used within the same while it was in the possession of any other lord or lords than our Sovereign lord, and thus for lack of punishment of these treasons, murders, robberies and felonies, the King's true and faithful liege people and subjects, inhabiters and dwellers within the shires and places before rehearsed, cannot be in any manner of surety of their bodies or goods, neither yet lie in their own houses, but either to be murdered or taken or carried into Scotland and there ransomed, to their great destruction of body and goods, and utter impoverishing for ever, unless due and hasty remedy be had and found," it is therefore provided that North and South Tynedale shall from thenceforth be gildable, and part of the shire of Northumberland, that no franchise shall stand good there, and the King's writ shall run, and his officers and all their warrants be obeyed there as in every other part of that shire. Further, lessees of lands within the bounds are to enter into recognisances in two sureties to appear and answer all charges.

[244] See my *Ethnology in Folklore*, cap. vi.

[245] Hickson, *North Celebes*, 240.

[246] Mitchell's *Australian Expeditions*, i. 246.

[247] See my *Village Community*, 18; Stewart's *Highlanders of Scotland*, i. 147, 228.

[248] *Notes and Queries*, second series, iv. 487.

[249] Wild, *Highlands, Orcadia and Skye*, 196.

[250] The psychology of primitive races is now receiving scientific attention, thanks chiefly to Dr. Haddon and the scholars who accompanied him upon his Torres Straits expedition in 1898. The volume of the memoirs of this expedition which relates to psychology has already been published, and students should consult it as an example of scientific method.

[251] One is reminded of the famous Shakespearian emendation

159

whereby Falstaff on his death-bed "babbled o' green fields."

[252] Shortland, *New Zealanders*, 107. An Algonquin backbone story is quoted by MacCulloch, *Childhood of Fiction*, 92, and he says, "the spine is held by many people to be the seat of life," 93 and *cf.* III. *Cf.* Frazer, *Adonis, Attis, and Osiris*, 277.

[253] *Gent. Mag. Lib., Popular Superstitions*, 122.

[254] *County Folklore, Suffolk*, 2.

[255] *Hardwick's Science Gossip*, vi. 281; *cf.* Worsaae, *Danes and Norwegians*, 25.

[256] *Journ. Asiatic Soc., Bengal*, xiv. 479.

[257] King, *Munimenta Antiqua*, i. 195-6; *Gent. Mag. Lib., Archæology*, i. 319-321; Hutchinson, *Hist. Cumberland*, i. 226.

[258] *Arch. Journ.*, xv. 204.

[259] Sinclair, *Stat. Acct. of Scotland*, xv. 191.

[260] *Journ. Anthrop. Inst.*, i. 2; *Gent. Mag. Lib., Archæology*, i. 21.

[261] *Archæologia*, xxv. 198.

[262] *Gent. Mag.*, 1751, pp. 110, 182.

[263] Some Irish examples are collected in *Folklore Record*, v. 169-172.

[264] Sinclair, *Stat. Acct. of Scotland*, xv. 111.

[265] *Trans. Cymmrodorion Soc.* (1822), i. 170.

[266] It is not worth while, perhaps, to pursue this part of our subject into further regions. It is to be sought for in innumerable pamphlets, such, for instance, as those relating to the Civil War. Beesley, *Hist. of Banbury*, 334, mentions one, the title of which I will quote: "A great Wonder in Heaven shewing the late Apparitions and prodigious noyses of War and Battels seen on Edge Hill neere Keinton," and the contents are "Certified under the hands of William Wood Esq and Justice for the Peace in the said Countie, Samuel Marshall, Preacher of God's Word in Keinton, and other Persons of Qualitie." The date is exactly three months after the battle of Edgehill, "London, printed for Thomas Jackson, January 23rd, 1642-3."

[267] *West of England Magazine*, February, 1888.

[268] Henderson, *Folklore of the Northern Counties*, 146; Napier, *Folklore of West of Scotland*, 140; Dalyell, *Darker Superstitions of Scotland*, 142; *Choice Notes (Folklore)*, 8; Brand, iii. 300; Dyer, *English Folklore*, 146, 153 (Hereford, Lincoln, and Yorks).

[269] Wilde, *Catalogue of Royal Irish Academy*, 131.

[270] *Folklore Record*, iv. 105.

[271] Rev. R. H. Ryland, *Hist. of Waterford*, 271.

[272] Wilde, *Beauties of the Boyne*, 45; Croker, *Researches in South of Ireland*, 170; *Revue Celtique*, v. 358.

[273] Blake, *Letters from the Irish Highlands*, 130-131.

[274] *Church Folklore*, by Rev. J. E. Vaux, is a collection of material, and does not attempt to give any indication of its value.

[275] Lea, *Superstition and Force*, 28.

[276] *Journ. Brit. Arch. Assoc.*, xxv. 142; Rev. W. Bingley, *North Wales*, 216-217.

[277] Sacheverell, *Voyage to Isle of Man*, 132.

[278] Tylor, *Primitive Culture*, i. 115; Landt, *Origin of the Priesthood*, 85; Henderson, *Folklore of Northern Counties*, 32-33; *Folklore Record*, i. 46.

[279] Pearson's *Chances of Death*, ii. cap. ix., "Woman as Witch;" Gomme, *Ethnology in Folklore*, 48-62.

[280] *Daily Chronicle*, 15th February, 1879.

[281] *Leigh Chronicle*, 19th April, 1879.

[282] *Somerset County Gazette*, 22nd January, 1881.

[283] *Standard*, 3rd April, 1895. The full details are reprinted in *Folklore*, vi. 373-384.

Chapter IV

ANTHROPOLOGICAL CONDITIONS

In dealing with the folklore of any country, it is important to note the general bearing of anthropological conditions. The earliest inhabitants, to whom part of the folklore belonged, and the later peoples, to whom part belonged, have both arrived at their ultimate point of settlement in the country where we discover their folklore after being in touch with many points of the world's surface. They are both world-people as well as national people—they belonged to anthropology before they came under the dominion of history. This important fact is often or nearly always neglected. We are apt to treat of Greek and Roman and Briton, of Cretan, Scandinavian, and Russian, as bounded by the few thousands of years of life which have fixed them with their territorial names, and to ignore all that lies behind this historic period. There is, as a matter of fact, an immense period behind it, reckoned according to geological time in millions of years, and this period, longer in duration, more strenuous in its influences upon character and mind, containing more representatives in peoples, societies, and races than the later period, has affected the later period to a far greater extent than is generally conceded or understood. We cannot understand the later period without knowing something of the earlier period.

There is more than this; for the dominating political races occupying European countries to-day were, in most cases, preceded by a non-political people. Thus, if we turn to Britain for illustration, we find evidence of a people physically allied with a race which cannot be identified with Celt or Teuton,[284] philologically allied with a people which spoke a non-Aryan language,[285] archæologically allied with the prehistoric stone-circle and monolith builders,[286] and we find custom, belief, and myth in Britain retaining traces of a culture which is not Celtic and not Teutonic, and which contains survivals of the primitive system of totemism.[287] These four independent classes of evidence have to be combined if we would ascertain the true position they occupy in the history of Britain, and it is perfectly clear that, apart from general considerations, a direct appeal to anthropology is necessary to help out the deficiencies of both history and folklore. The questions involved in totemism alone compel us to this course. It is questionable whether there is any existing savage or barbaric people who are non-totemic in the sense of either not possessing the rudimentary beginnings of totemism, or not having once possessed a full system of totemism. Totemism, at one stage or another of its development, is, in fact, one of the universal elements of man's life, and all consideration of its traces in civilised countries must begin with some conception of its origin. Its origin must refer back to conditions of human life which are also universal. Special circumstances, special peoples, special areas could not have produced totemism unless we proceed to the somewhat violent conclusion that beginning in one area it has spread therefrom to all areas. I know of no authority who advocates such a theory and no evidence in its favour. We are left therefore with the proposition that the origin of totemism must be sought for in some universal condition of human life at one of its very early stages, which would have produced a state of things from which would inevitably arise the beliefs, customs, and social organisations which are included under the term totemism.

There is therefore ample ground for a consideration of anthropological conditions as part of the necessary equipment of the study of folklore as an historical science. Unfortunately, authorities are now greatly divided on several important questions in anthropology, and it is not possible to speak with even a reasonable degree of certainty on many things. This compels further research than the mere statement of the present position, and I find myself obliged even for my present limited purpose to suggest many new points beyond the stage reached by present research. There is one advantage in this. It allows of a hypothesis by which to present the subject to the student, and a working hypothesis is always a great advantage where research is not founded entirely on actual observation by trained experts in the field. Where, therefore, I depart from the guidance of conclusions already arrived at by scholars in this department of research, it will be in order to substitute an opinion of my own which I think it is necessary to consider, and the whole study of the anthropological problems in their relation to folklore will assume the shape of a restatement of the entire case.

I am aware that a subject of this magnitude is too weighty and far-reaching to be properly considered in a chapter of a book not devoted to the single purpose, but it is necessary to attempt a rough statement of the evidence, though it will take us somewhat beyond the ordinary domain of folklore; but, while dealing with the anthropological position at sufficient length to make a complicated subject clear, if I can do so, I shall limit both my arguments and the evidence in support of them to the narrowest limits.

I

Mr. Wallace, I think, supplies the dominant note of the anthropological position when he suggests, though in a strangely unsatisfactory terminology, that it is the conscious use by man of his experience which causes his superior mental endowments, and his superior range of development.[288] We must lay stress upon the important qualification "conscious." It is conscious use of experience which is the great factor in man's progress. It is the greatest possession of man in his beginning, and has remained his greatest possession ever since. His experience did not always lead him to the best paths of progress, but it has led him to progress.

Even Mr. Wallace did not appreciate the full significance of this principle. The conscious adoption of a natural fact, of an observation from nature, or an assumed observation from nature, for social purposes, is an altogether different thing from the unconscious knowledge which man might have been possessed of, but which he never put to any use in his social development. Anthropologists must note not the natural facts known to later man or known to science, but the facts, or assumed facts, which early man consciously adopted for his purpose during the long period of his development from savage to civilised forms of life. The unconscious acts of mankind are of no use, or of very little use. It is only the conscious acts that will lead us along the lines of man's development. Man did not begin to build up his social system with the scientific fact of blood kinship through father and mother, but he evolved a theory of social relationship which served his purpose until the fact of blood kinship supplied a better basis. At almost the first point of origin in savage society we see man acting consciously, and it is amongst his conscious acts that we must place those traces of a sort of primitive legislation which have been found.[289]

Now this being the basis of anthropological observation, we have to apply it to the question of man's earliest progress. It is at its base an economic question. Primitive economics dominated the movements and condition of early man in a far more thorough manner than modern economics affect civilisation, and between the two systems lies the whole history of man. It reveals man adapting the social unit to the productive powers of its food supply, and developing towards the adaptation of the productive powers of food supply to the social unit. In the various stages that accompany this great change, there is no defined separation of peoples according to stages of culture, savage, barbaric, or civilised. There is nothing to suggest that all peoples do not come from one centre of human life. On the contrary, the evidence is strong that the primal stages in human evolution are traceable in all the culture stages, and, therefore, that they fit in with the general conclusions of anthropologists and naturalists as to man's origin in one definite centre, and his gradual spreading out from that centre.

I will take the chief conclusions arrived at in respect of this condition of birth at one centre and subsequent spreading out. Darwin has summarised the problem between the monogenists and polygenists in a manner which still ranks as a sufficient statement of the case, and his conclusion that "all the races of man are descended from a single primitive stock"[290] is accepted by the most prominent naturalists,[291] and confirmed by recent discoveries, which go to prove that this primitive stock began in miocene or pliocene times in the Indo-Malaysian intertropical lands.[292]

Anthropologists, who have been deeply interested in the controversy ranging round the origin of man, have in a remarkable manner neglected to take into full account the most significant phenomenon of spreading out.[293] They either neglect it altogether, or they relegate it to so small a place in their argument as to become a practical neglect. They treat of man as if he were always in a stationary condition, and exclude the important condition of movement as an element in his development. Mr. Spencer's general dictum that geological changes and meteorological changes, as well as the consequent changes of flora and fauna, must have been causing over all parts of the earth perpetual emigrations and immigrations,[294] does not help much, because it refers to special and cataclysmic events. Lord Avebury, though stating the true case, unfortunately contents himself at the end of his book on prehistoric man with a short summary of the evidence as to the equipment of primitive man in mental and social qualities when he began the great movement, and gives only a few lines to his conclusion that "there can be no doubt that he originally crept over the earth's surface little by little, year by year, just, for instance, as the weeds of Europe are now gradually but surely creeping over the surface of Australia."[295]

Mr. Keane is the first authority who thinks it appropriate to commence his treatise on man with an examination of the facts which show that "the world was peopled by migration from one centre by pleistocene man ... who moved about like other migrating faunas, unconsciously, everywhere following the lines of least resistance, advancing or receding, and acting generally on blind impulse rather than of set purpose;"[296] and it still remains with Dr. Latham to have formulated some fixed principles of the migratory movement in his admirable though, of course, wholly inadequate summary of man and his migrations. I will quote the passage in full: "So long as any continental extremities of the earth's surface remained unoccupied—the stream (or rather the enlarging circle of migration) not having yet reached them—the *primary* migration is going on; and when all have got their complement, the primary migration is over. During this primary migration, the relations of man, thus placed in movement and in the full, early and guiltless exercise of his high function of subduing the earth, are in conflict with physical obstacles and with the resistance of the lower animals only. Unless, like Lot's wife, he turn back upon the peopled parts behind him, he has no relations with his fellow-men—at least none arising out of the claim of previous occupancy. In other words, during the primary migration, the world that lay before our progenitors was either brute or inanimate. But before many generations have passed away, all becomes full to overflowing, so that men must enlarge their boundaries at the expense of their fellows. The migrations that now take place are *secondary*. They differ from the primary in many respects. They are slower, because the resistance is that of humanity to humanity, and they are violent, because dispossession is the object. They are partial, abortive, followed by the fusion of different populations, or followed by their extermination as the case may be."[297] This passage, written so long ago as 1841, is still applicable to the facts of

166

modern science, and there is only to add to it that the migration of man from a common centre, where life was easy, to all parts of the world, where life has been difficult, must have been undertaken in order to meet some great necessity, and must have become possible by reason of some great force which man alone possessed. The necessity was economic; the force was social development. If the movement has not been geographically ever forward, it has been ethnographically constant.[298] Movement always; sometimes the pressure has come from one direction, sometimes from another; sometimes it has caused compression and at other times expansion; sometimes it has sent humanity to inhabit regions that required generations of victims before it could hold its own. At all times the essential condition of life has been that of constant movement in face of antagonistic forces.[299] In whatever form the movement has come about, movement of a very definite character has taken place over an immense period of time, and sufficient to cover practically the whole earth with descendants from the original human stock. This conclusion is enormously strengthened by the accumulating evidence for the world-wide area covered by the remains of man's earliest weapon, the worked stone implement. It is everywhere. It is practically co-extensive with man's wanderings, and the greatness of the territory it covers marks it off as another of the universal relics of man's primitive life. Of no other weapon or instrument or associated object can this be said. The bow and arrow are unknown to the Australians and other peoples; pottery is unknown to the Bushmen and other peoples; the use of fire in cookery is not found among the South Sea Islanders, and is not claimed for other peoples.[300] We can get behind the development of these and other arts and come upon the ruder people who had not arrived at the stage they represent. But we cannot get behind the worked flint. It must have been the chief material cause of man's success in the migratory movement, and with the social development accompanying it must have made migration not only possible, but the only true method of meeting the earliest economic difficulties. It also provides us with the elements of a chronological basis. Behind palæolithic times there is an immensity of time when man struggled with his economic difficulties and spread out slowly and painfully. During palæolithic times the movement was more rapid and more general. Obstacles were overcome by palæolithic man becoming superior to his enemies by the use of weapons, and use of weapons caused, or at all events aided, the development of social institutions capable of bearing the new force of movement.

These two factors of economic necessity and social development are of equal importance in man's history, and they interlace at all points. They lead straight to the necessity for always taking count of the fact that man is primarily a migratory being, and that he has spread over the earth. Everywhere we find man. There is no habitable part of the world where he has not found a home. But we do not find him under equal conditions everywhere, and the different conditions afford evidence of the main lines of development. Roughly speaking, it may be put in this way. In the savage world the people appear as aborigines, that is to say, the first and only occupiers of the territory where they are located. In the barbaric world the condition of aboriginal settlement is tinged with the result of conquest, namely, the pushing out or absorption of the aboriginal folk in favour of a more powerful and conquering folk. In the political world, and in the political world only, there is not only the element of conquest, but the definite aim of conquest, which is to retain the aboriginal or conquered people as part of the political fabric necessary to the settlement of the conqueror, and at the same time to keep intact the superior position of the conqueror. In the savage world, society and religion are based upon locality; in the barbaric world there is the first sign of the element of kinship consciously used in the effort of conquest, which dies away gradually as successful settlement, by which conqueror and conquered become merged in one people, follows conquest; in the political world, and in the political world only, kinship is elevated into a necessary institution, is made sacred to the minds of tribesmen, and becomes an essential part of the religion of the tribe in order to keep the organisation of the tribal conquerors intact and free from the perils of dissolution when conquerors and conquered become members of one political unit. The savage and barbaric worlds are the homes of the backward peoples, the non-advanced or fossilised types of early humanity. The political world is the domain for the most part of the Aryan-speaking people, and of the Semitic people, and of those people who in Egypt within the Mediterranean area, and in China in the eastern Asian area, have built up civilisations which have only recently come under scientific observation.

These distinctions are not made by anthropologists as a rule, yet I

168

cannot but think they are in the main the true distinctions which must be made if we are to arrive at any general conception of the progress of man from savagery to civilisation. The distinctions which seem to hold the field against those I have suggested, are those of hunter, pastoral, and agricultural. I say seem to hold the field, because they have never been scientifically worked out. They are stated in textbooks and research work almost as an axiom of anthropology, but their claim to this position is singularly weak and unsatisfactory, and has never been scientifically established. They are only economical distinctions, not social, and they do not properly express related stages. Hunting, cattle keeping, and agriculture are found in almost all stages of social evolution, and I, for one, deny that in the order they are generally given, they express anything approaching to accurate indication of the line of human progress. The distinctions I have suggested do not, of course, contain everything indicative of human progress. They are the first broad outlines to be filled up by the details of special peoples, special areas, and special ages. They involve many sub-stages which need to be properly worked out, and for which a satisfactory terminology is required. In the meantime, as measuring-posts of man's line of progress, they express the most important fact about man, namely, that his present enforced stationary condition has followed upon an enormous period of enforced movement. That movement has finally resulted in the presence of man everywhere on the earth's surface. This has been followed by the continued moving of savage man within the limited areas to which he has been finally pushed; by the movement of barbaric man from one place of settlement to another place of settlement, again within limited areas; and by the movement of political man through countries and continents of vast extent, and the final overlordship of political man over savage and barbaric man whom he has subjected and used for his purpose of final settlement in the civilised form of settlement. It will be apparent from the terms I have used to express the three chief stages in man's progress, that I give a special significance to the use of blood kinship as a social force, and in the sequel I think this special significance will be justified.[301]

No one can properly estimate the tremendous amount of movement which preceded these later limitations to movement. Savage and barbaric races are now hemmed in by the forces of modern civilisation. This was not the case even a few hundred years ago, and though we cannot say when constant movement all over the world was stayed, we can form some idea of the comparatively late period when this took place by a contemplation of the very recent growth of the political civilisations known to history. At the most, this can only be reckoned at some ten thousand years. At the back of this short stretch of time, or of the successive periods at which the new civilisations have arisen, there are recollections of great movements and great migrations. Egypt, Babylonia, India, Persia, Greece, and Rome have preserved these recollections by tradition, and tradition has been largely confirmed by archæology. Celts and Teutons have preserved parallel traditions which are confirmed by history observed from without. These traditions and memorials of the migration period have not been scientifically examined in each case, but where scholars have touched upon them, great and unexpected results have been produced.[302]

There was time enough, before these late and special movements which led to civilisation, for man, in the course of peopling the earth, to be brought at various stages to a standstill, and such a change in his life-history would have its own special results. One of the most momentous of these results is the fossilisation of social and mental conditions. Man stationary, or movable by custom within restricted areas, would live under conditions which must have produced forms of culture different from those under which man lived when he was always able to penetrate, not by custom but by the force of circumstances, into the unknown domain of unoccupied territory; and the fossilisation of his culture at various stages of development, in accord with the various periods of his being brought to a standstill, would be the most important result.[303] Whenever man was compelled to move onward the social forces which were demanded of him, as he proceeded from point to point, must have been quite different from those which he could have adopted if he had been allowed to stay in areas which suited him, if he could have selected his settlement grounds and awaited events. The calmness of the latter methods would perhaps have led to the unconscious development of social forms; the roughness of the actual method of constant movement led to the conscious adoption of social forms which has altered man's history. These considerations bring us to the conclusion that it is during the period of migratory movement that man has developed the social

170

and religious elements with which the anthropologist finds him endowed, when at last in modern days he has been brought within the ken of scientific observation, and that therefore it is as a migratory not a stationary organism that the evolution of human society has to be studied, aided by the fact that enforced stationary conditions have produced in the savage world examples of perhaps the most remote as well as the more recent types of primitive humanity.

This last possibility, however, is not admitted by the best authorities. They endeavour to use biological methods in order to get behind existing savagery for the earliest period of human savagery. Darwin is not satisfied with the evidence as to promiscuity, strong as it appeared to him to be, and he pronounced it to be "extremely improbable" in a state of nature, and falls back upon the evidence of the rudimentary stages of human existence, there being, as among the gorillas, but one adult male in the band, and "when the young male grows up, a contest takes place for the mastery, and the strongest, by killing and driving out the others, establishes himself as the head of the community."[304] Mr. McLennan nowhere states the evidence for his first stage of human society—the primitive horde without any ideas of kinship, and based upon a fellowship of common interests and dangers[305]—but arrives at it by argument deduced from the conditions of later stages of development, and from the necessary suppositions as to the pre-existing stage which must have led to the later. Mr. Westermarck leads us straight to the evidence of the lower animals, from which he arrives at the small groups of humans headed by the male, and provides us with the theory of a human pairing season.[306] Mr. Morgan claims that no exemplification of mankind in his assumed lower status of savagery remained to the historical period,[307] presumably meaning the anthropo-historical period. And finally, Mr. Lang definitely claims that conjecture, and conjecture alone, remains as the means of getting back to the earliest human origins.[308]

There is great danger in relying too closely upon conjecture. We shall be repeating in anthropology what the analytical jurists accomplished in law and jurisprudence, and it will then soon become necessary to do for anthropology what Sir Henry Maine did for comparative jurisprudence, namely, demonstrate that the analytical method does not take us back to human origins, but to highly developed systems of society. Law, in the hands of the analytical jurists, is merely one part of the machinery of modern government. Social beginnings in the hands of conjectural anthropologists are merely abstractions with the whole history of man put on one side. Mr. Lang in leading the way towards the analytical method in anthropology has avoided many of its pitfalls, but his disciples are not so successful. Thus, when Mr. Thomas declares that "custom which has among them [primitive peoples] far more power than law among us, determines whether a man is of kin to his mother and her relatives alone, or to his father and father's relatives, or whether both sets of relatives are alike of kin to them,"[309] he is neglecting the whole significance and range of custom. His statement is true analytically, but it is not true anthropologically until we have ascertained what this custom to which he refers really is, whence it is derived, how it has obtained its force, what is its range of action, how it operates in differentiating among the various groups of mankind—in a word, what is the human history associated with this custom.

We must, however, at certain points in anthropological inquiry have recourse to the conjectural method. Its value lies in the fact that it states, and states clearly, the issue which is before us, and it is always possible to take up the conjectural position and endeavour to ascertain whether the neglected facts of human history which it expresses can be recovered. Its danger lies in the neglect of certain anthropological principles which can only be noted from definite examples, and the significance of which can only be discovered by the handling of definite examples. I will refer to one or two of the principles which I have in mind. Thus, it is necessary to distinguish between what is a practice and what is a rule. A practice precedes a rule. A practice incidental to one stage of society must not be confused with a rule, similar to the practice, obtaining in a different stage of society. Again, it must be borne in mind that identity of practice is no certain evidence of parallel stages of culture, and already it has been pointed out that identical practices do not always come from the same causes. Thirdly, it has to be borne in mind that primitive peoples specialise in certain directions to an extreme extent, and correspondingly cause neglect in other directions. The normal, therefore, has to give way to the special, and it is the degree of specialisation and the degree of neglect which are measuring factors of progress; in other words, it is the conscious adoption of certain rules of life with which we alone have to do.

These principles are apt to be wholly neglected, and, indeed, the last-mentioned element in the evolution of human society does not enter into the calculations of analytical anthropologists. They provide for the normal according to scientific ideas of what the normal is. They either neglect or openly reject what cannot be called abnormal, because it appears everywhere, but which they are inclined to treat as abnormal because it does not fit into their accepted lines of development. That which I have ventured to term specialisation and neglect is a great and important feature in anthropology. It obtains everywhere in more or less degree, and accounts for some of the apparently unaccountable facts in savage society, where we are frequently encountered by a comparatively high degree of culture associated with a cruel and debasing system of rites and practices which belong to the lowest savagery. Dr. Haddon has usefully suggested the term "differential evolution" for this phenomenon in the culture history of man,[310] and as I find myself in entire agreement with this distinguished anthropologist as to the facts[311] which call for a special terminology, I gladly adopt his valuable suggestion.

It is advisable to explain this phenomenon by reference to examples, and I will take the point of specialisation first. Even where industrial arts have advanced far beyond the primitive stage we are considering, we have the case of the Ahts, with whom "though living only a few miles apart, the tribes practise different arts and have apparently distinct tribal characteristics. One tribe is skilful in shaping canoes, another in painting boards for ornamental work, or making ornaments for the person, or instruments for hunting and fishing. Individuals as a rule keep to the arts for which their tribe has some repute, and do not care to acquire those arts in which other tribes excel. There seems to be among all the tribes in the island a sort of recognised tribal monopoly in certain articles produced, or that have been long manufactured in their own district. For instance, a tribe that does not grow potatoes, or make a particular kind of mat, will go a long way year after year to barter for those articles, which if they liked they themselves could easily produce or manufacture."[312] The remarkable case of the Todas specialising in cattle rearing and dairy farming is another example. Other people, both higher and lower in civilisation than the Todas, keep cattle and know the value of milk, but it is reserved for the Todas alone to have used this particular economic basis of their existence as the basis also of their social formation and their religious life.[313] The result is that they neglect other forms of social existence. They are not totemists, though perhaps they have the undeveloped germs of totemistic beliefs.[314] Their classificatory system of relationship makes their actual kinship scarcely recognisable; they "have very definite restrictions on the freedom of individuals to marry," and have a two-class endogamous division, but their marriage rite is merely the selection of nominal fathers for their children.[315] Throughout the careful study which we now possess, thanks to Dr. Rivers, of this people, there is the dominant note of dairy economy superimposing itself upon all else, and even religion seems to be in a state of decadence.[316] I do not know that anywhere else could be found a stronger example of the results of extreme specialisation upon the social and mental condition of a people. As a rule such specialisation does not extend to a whole people, but rather to sections, as, for instance, among the Gold Coast tribes of Africa who "transmit the secret of their skill from father to son and keep the corporation to which they belong up to a due degree of closeness by avoiding intermarriage with any of the more unskilled labourers,"[317] and Dr. Bucher, who has worked out many of the earliest conditions of primitive economics, concludes that it may be safely claimed that every "tribe displays some favourite form of industrial activity in which its members surpass the other tribes."[318] This rule extends to the lowest type of man, as, for instance, among the Australians. Each tribe of the Narrinyeri, says Taplin, have been accustomed to make those articles which their tract of country enabled them to produce most easily; one tribe will make weapons, another mats, and a third nets, and then they barter them one with another.[319]

The evidence for industrial evolution is full of cases such as these, and they are extremely important to note, because it is not the mere existence of particular customs or particular beliefs among different peoples which is the factor to take into account, but the use or non-use, and the extent of the use or non-use, to which the particular customs or beliefs are put in each case.[320] Let me turn from the phenomenon of over-specialisation to that of neglect, and for this purpose I will take the simple fact of blood kinship. Existing obviously everywhere through the mother, and not obviously but admittedly through the father among most primitive peoples, there are examples where both maternal kinship and paternal kinship are neglected factors in the construction of the social group. The Nahals of Khandesh, for instance, neglect kinship altogether, and exist perfectly wild among the mountains, subsisting chiefly on roots, fruits, and berries, though the children during infancy accompany the mother in her unattached freedom from male control,[321] just as Herodotos describes the condition of the Auseans "before the Hellenes were settled near them."[322] Similarly, among many primitive peoples, kinship with the mother is recognised while kinship with the father is purposely neglected as a social factor. Thus, among the Khasia Hill people, the husband visits his wife occasionally in her own home, where "he seems merely entertained to continue the family to which his wife belongs."[323] This statement, so peculiarly appropriate to my purpose, is not merely an accident of language. With the people allied to the Khasis, namely, the Syntengs and the people of Maoshai, "the husband does not go and live in his mother-in-law's house; he only visits her there. In Jowai, the husband came to his mother-in-law's house only after dark," and the explanation of the latest authority is that among these people "the man is nobody ... if he be a husband he is looked upon merely as *u shong kha*, a begetter."[324]

The neglect of maternal and paternal kinship respectively in these two cases is obvious. They are recognised physically. But they are not used as part of the fabric of social institutions. Physical motherhood or fatherhood is nothing to these people, and one must learn to understand that there is wide difference between the mere physical fact of having a mother and father, and the political fact of using this kinship for social organisation. Savages who have not learnt the political significance have but the scantiest appreciation of the physical fact. The Australians, for instance, have no term to express the relationship between mother and child. This is because the physical fact is of no significance, and not as Mr. Thomas thinks because of the meagreness of the language.[325] Our field anthropologists do not quite understand the savage in this respect. It is of no use preparing a genealogical tree on the basis of civilised knowledge of genealogy if such a document is beyond the ken of the people to whom it relates. The information for it may be correctly collected, but if the whole structure is not within the compass of savage thought it is a misleading anthropological document. It is of no use translating a native term as "father," if father did not mean to the savage what it means to us. It might mean something so very different. With us, fatherhood connotes a definite individual with all sorts of social, economical, and political associations, but what does it mean to the savage? It may mean physical fatherhood and nothing more, and physical fatherhood may be a fact of the veriest insignificance. It may mean social fatherhood, where all men of a certain status are fathers to all children of the complementary status, and social fatherhood thus becomes much more than we can understand by the term father.

We cannot ignore the evidence which over-specialisation in one direction and neglect in other directions supply to anthropology. It shows us that human societies cannot always be measured in the scale of culture by the most apparent of the social elements contained in them. The cannibalism of the Fijians, the art products of the Maori, the totemism of the Australian blacks, do not express all that makes up the culture of these people, although it too often happens that they are made to do duty for the several estimates of culture progress. It follows that a survey of the different human societies might reveal examples of the possible lowest in the scale as well as various advances from the lowest; or in lieu of whole societies in the lowest scale, there might be revealed unexceptional examples of the possible lowest elements of culture within societies not wholly in the lowest scale. It will be seen how valuable an asset this must be in anthropological research. It justifies those who assert that existing savagery or existing survival will supply evidence of man at the very earliest stages of existence. It is the root idea of Dr. Tylor's method of research, and it is an essential feature in the science of folklore.

Evidence of this nature, however, needs to be exhaustively collected, and to be subjected to the most careful examination, as otherwise it may be used for the merest *a priori* argument of the most mischievous and inconclusive description. It involves consideration of whole human groups rather than of particular sections of each human group, of the whole corpus of social, religious, and economical elements residing in each human group rather than of the separated items. Each human group, having its specialised and dormant elements, must be treated as an organism and not as a bundle of separable items, each one of which the student may use or let alone as he desires. That which is anthropological evidence is the indivisible organism, and whenever, for convenience of treatment and considerations of space, particular elements only are used in evidence, they must be qualified, and the use to which they are provisionally put for scientific purposes must be checked, by the associated elements with which the particular elements are connected.

The human groups thus called upon to surrender their contributions to the history of man are of various formations, and consist of various kinds of social units. There is no one term which can properly be applied to all, and it will have been noted that I have carefully avoided giving the human groups hitherto dealt with any particular name, and only under protest have I admitted the terms used by the authorities I have quoted. I think the term "tribe" is not applicable to savage society, for it is used to denote peoples in all degrees of social evolution, and merely stands for the group which is known by a given name, or roams over a given district. But the use of this term is not so productive of harm as the use of the term "family," because of the universal application of this term to the smallest social unit of the civilised world, and because of the fundamental difference of structure of the units which roughly answer to the definition of family in various parts of the world. It is no use in scientific matters to use terms of inexact reference. As much as almost anything else it has led to false conclusions as to the evolution of the family, conclusions which seem to entangle even the best authorities in a mass of contradictions. I cannot think of a family group in savagery with father, mother, sons, and daughters, all delightfully known to each other, in terms which also belong to the civilised family, and still less can I think of these terms being used to take in the extended grouping of local kinships. One of our greatest difficulties, indeed, is the indiscriminate use of kinship terms by our descriptive authorities. We are never quite sure whether the physical relationships included in them convey anything whatever to the savage. If he knows of the physical fact, he does not use it politically, for blood kinship as a political force is late, not early, and the early tie was dependent upon quite other circumstances. Over and over again it will be found stated by established authorities that the family was the primal unit, the grouped families forming the larger clan, the grouped clans forming the larger tribe. This is Sir Henry Maine's famous formula, and it is the basis of his investigation into early law and custom.[326] It is founded upon the false conception of the family in early history, and upon a too narrow interpretation of the stages of evolution. When we are dealing with savage society, the terms family and tribe do not connote the same institution as when we are dealing with higher forms of civilisation. There is something roughly corresponding to these groupings in both systems, but they do not actually equate. When we pass to the Semitic and the Aryan-speaking peoples, both the family and tribe have assumed a definite place in the polity of the races which is not to be found outside these peoples.

So strongly has the family impressed itself upon the thought of the age that students of man in his earliest ages are found stating that "the family is the most ancient and the most sacred of human institutions."[327] This proposition, however, is not only denied by other authorities, as, for instance, Mr. Jevons, who affirms that "the family is a comparatively late institution in the history of society,"[328] but it rests upon the merely analytical basis of research, separated entirely from those facts of man's history which are discoverable by the means just now suggested. One is, of course, quite prepared to find the family among civilisations older than the Indo-European, and yet to find that it is a comparatively late institution among Indo-European peoples. As a matter of fact, this is the case; for the two kinds of family, the family as seen in savage society and the family as it appears among the antiquities of the Indo-European people, are totally distinct in origin, in compass, and in force; while welded between the two kinds of family is the whole institution of the tribe. It is no use introducing the theory adopted by Grote, Niebuhr, Mommsen, Thirlwall, Maine, and other authorities who have studied the legal antiquities of classical times, that the tribe is the aggregate of original family units. Later on I shall show that this cannot be the case. The larger kinship of the tribe is a primary unit of ancient society, which thrusts itself between the savage family and the civilised family, showing that the two types are separated by a long period of history during which the family did not exist.

It has taken me some time to explain these points in anthropological science, which appear to me not to have received proper consideration at the hands of the masters of the science, but which are essential factors in the history of man and are necessary to a due consideration of the position occupied by folklore. The chief results obtained are:—

(1) Migratory man would deposit his most rudimentary social type

not at the point of starting his migration, but at the furthest point therefrom.

(2) Custom due to the migratory period would continue after real migratory movement had ceased, and from this body of custom would be derived all later forms of social custom.

(3) Non-kinship groups are more rudimentary than kinship groups, and are still observable in savage anthropology.

(4) Anthropological evidence must be based upon the whole of the characteristics of human groups, not upon special characteristics singled out for the purpose of research.

It is with these results we have to work. They will help us to see how far the facts of anthropology, which begin far behind the historical world, have to do with the problems presented by folklore as a science having to deal with the historical world.

II

We may now inquire where anthropology and folklore meet. It is significant in this connection that in order to reach back to the earliest ages of man, our first appeal seems to be to folklore. The appeal at present does not lead us far perhaps, but it certainly acts as a finger post in the inquiry, for Dr. Kollmann, rejecting the evidence of the Java *Pithecanthropus erectus* as the earliest palæontological evidence of man, advances the opinion that the direct antecedents of man should not be sought among the species of anthropoid apes of great height and with flat skulls, but much further back in the zoological scale, in the small monkeys with pointed skulls; from which, he believes, were developed the human pygmy races of prehistoric ages with pointed skulls, and from these pygmy races finally developed the human race of historic times. And he relies upon folklore for one part of his evidence, for it is this descent of man, he thinks, which explains the persistency with which mythology and folklore allude to the subject of pygmy people, as well as the relative frequency with which recently the fossils of small human beings belonging to prehistoric times have been discovered.[329] It must not be forgotten, too, that this remote period is found in another class of tradition, namely, that to which Dr. Tylor refers as containing the memory of the huge animals of the quaternary period.[330]

It must be confessed that we do not get far with this evidence alone. If it proves that the true starting point is to be found in folklore, it also proves that folklore alone is not capable of working through the problem. Anthropology must aid here, and I will suggest the lines on which it appears to me it does this.

Our first effort must be made by the evidence suggested by the conjectural method. This leads us to small human groups, each headed by a male who drives out all other males and himself remains with his females and his children. Sexual selection thus acts with primitive economics[331] in keeping the earliest groups small in numbers, and creating a spreading out from these groups of the males cast out. We have male supremacy in its crudest form accompanied by an enforced male celibacy, so far as the group in which the males are born is concerned, on the part of those who survive the struggle for supremacy and wander forth on their own account. Marking the stages from point to point, in order to arrive at a systematic method of stating the complex problem presented by the subject we are investigating, we can project from this earliest condition of man's life two important elements of social evolution, namely—

(*a*) Younger men are celibate within the natural groups of human society, or are driven out therefrom.

(*b*) Men thus driven out will seek mates on their own account, and will secure them partly from the original group as far as they are permitted or are successful in their attempts, and partly by capture from other local groups.

The first of these elements strongly emphasises the migratory character of the earliest human groups. The second shows how each group is relieved of the incubus of too great a number for the economic conditions by the double process of sending forth its young males, and of its younger females being captured by successful marauders.

Let us take a fuller note of what the conditions of such a life might be. There is no tie of kinship operating as a social force within the groups; there is the unquestioned condition of hostility surrounding each group, and there is the enforced practice of providing mates by capture. Of these three conditions the most significant is undoubtedly the absence of the kinship tie. If then we use this as the basis for grouping the earliest examples of social organisation, we proceed to inquire whether there are any examples of kinless society in anthropological evidence.

Following up the clue supplied by folklore, we may see whether the pygmy people of anthropological observation answer in any way to those conjectural conditions.[332] I think they do. Thus, we find that the pygmy people are in all cases on the extreme confines of the world's occupation ground; that they occupy the territory to which they have been pushed, not that which they have chosen. As the most primitive representatives, they are the last outposts of the migratory movements. Dr. Beke has preserved an account of the pygmies which even in its terminology assists in their identification as a type of the remotest stages of social existence. Dr. Beke obtained certain information about the countries south-west of Abyssinia, from which Latham quotes the following:—

"The people of Doko, both men and women, are said to be no taller than boys nine or ten years old. They never exceed that height even in the most advanced age. They go quite naked; their principal foods are ants, snakes, mice, and other things which commonly are not used as food.... They also climb trees with great skill to fetch down the fruits, and in doing this they stretch their hands downwards and their legs upwards.... They live mixed together; men and women unite and separate as they please.... The mother suckles the child only as long as she is unable to find ants and snakes for its food; she abandons it as soon as it can get its food by itself. No rank or order exists among the Dokos. Nobody orders, nobody obeys, nobody defends the country, nobody cares for the welfare of the nation."[333]

This evidence is confirmed in many directions. It coincides with the account by Herodotos of the expedition from Libya which met with a pygmy race,[334] and with a seventeenth-century account of a Dutch expedition to the north from the south, who "found a tribe of people very low in stature and very lean, entirely savage, without huts, cattle, or anything in the world except their lands and wild game."[335] Captain Burrows' account of the Congoland pygmies agrees in all essentials, and he particularly notes that they "have no ties of family affection such as those of mother to son or sister to brother, and seem to be wanting in all social qualities;" they have no religion and no fetich rites; no burial ceremony and no mourning for the dead; in short, he adds, "they are to my thinking the closest link with the original

Darwinian anthropoid ape extant."[336] The evidence of the African pygmy people everywhere confirms these views, and differences of detail do not alter the general results.[337]

Chinese representation of pygmies going about arm-in-arm for mutual protection (from Moseley's "Note by a Naturalist on H.M.S. Challenger") **CHINESE REPRESENTATION OF PYGMIES GOING ABOUT ARM-IN-ARM FOR MUTUAL PROTECTION**

Semang of Kuala Kenering, Ulu Perak (from Skeat and Blagden's "Pagan Races of the Malay Peninsula") **SEMANG OF KUALA KENERING, ULU PERAK**

Negrito type: Semang of Perak (from Skeat and Blagden's "Pagan Races of the Malay Peninsula") **NEGRITO TYPE: SEMANG OF PERAK**

Following this up we get the greatest assistance from Asia.[338] The Semang people of the Malay Peninsula are a short race, the male being four feet nine inches in height, with woolly and tufted hair, thick lips and flat nose, and their language is connected with the group of which the Khasi people is a member.[339] They subsist upon the birds and beasts of the forest, and roots, eating elephants, rhinoceros, monkeys, and rats. They are said to have chiefs among them, but all property is common. Their huts or temporary dwellings, for they have no fixed habitations but rove about like the beasts of the forest, consist of two posts stuck in the ground with a small cross-piece and a few leaves or branches of trees laid over to secure them from the weather, and their clothing consists chiefly of the inner bark of trees.[340] They use stone or slate implements. The authority for this information does not directly state their social formation, but in a footnote he compares them to the Negritos of the Philippine Islands, "who are divided into very small societies very little connected with each other." This is confirmed by Mr. Hugh Clifford, who relates a story told to him in the camp of the Semangs, which tells how these people were driven to their present resting-place, "not for love of these poor hunting grounds," but because they were thrust there by the Malays who stole their women. One further point is interesting; they have a legend of a people in their old home, composed of women only. "These women know not men, but but when the moon is at the full, they dance naked in the grassy places near the salt-licks; the evening wind is their only spouse, and through him they conceive and bear children."[341] All this has been confirmed and more than confirmed by the important researches of Messrs. Skeat and Blagden in their recently published work on these people. There is no necessity to do more than refer to the principal features brought out by these authorities. In the valuable notes on environment, we have the actual facts of the migratory movement drawn clearly for us;[342] their nomadic habits, rude nature-derived clothing, forest habitations and natural sources of food are described;[343] the evolution of their habitations from the natural shelters, rock shelters, caves, tree buttresses, branches, etc., is to be traced;[344] they belong to the old Stone Age, if not to a previous Wood and Bone Age;[345] they have no organised body of chiefs, and there is no formal recognition of kinship; marital relationship is preceded by great ante-nuptial freedom;[346] the name of every child is taken "from some tree which stands near the prospective birthplace of the child; as soon as the child is born, this name is shouted aloud by the *sage femme*, who then hands over the child to another woman, and buries the after-birth underneath the birth-tree or name-tree of the child; as soon as this has been done, the father cuts a series of notches in the tree, starting from the ground and terminating at the height of the breast;"[347] the child must not in later life injure any tree which belongs to the species of his birth-tree, and must not eat of its fruit. There is a theory to accompany this practice, for birds are believed to be vehicles for the introduction of the soul into the newborn child, and all human souls grow upon a soul-tree in the other world, whence they are fetched by a bird which is killed and eaten by the expectant mother;[348] but there seems to be no evidence of any religious cult or rite, and what there is of mythology or legend is probably borrowed.[349] The details in this case are of special importance, as they form a complete set of associated culture elements, and I shall have to return to them later on.

Semang of Kedah having a meal (from Skeat and Blagden's "Pagan Races of the Malay Peninsula") **SEMANG OF KEDAH HAVING A MEAL**

I shall not attempt to exhaust the evidence to be derived from the pygmy people. What has been said of the examples I have chosen may in all essentials be said of the remaining examples. But it is perhaps advisable to be assured that the evidence of kinless people is not confined to the stunted and dwarfed races, for it has been argued that the pygmies are nothing but the ne'er-do-wells of the stronger races, and may not therefore be taken as true racial types. This may be true, but it does not affect my case, because I am not depending so much upon the physical characteristics of these people as upon their culture characteristics. These are definite and conclusive, and they are repeated among people of higher physical type. Thus the Jolas of the Gambia district have practically no government and no law; every man does as he chooses, and the most successful thief is considered the greatest man. There is no recognised punishment for murder or any other crime. Individual settlement is the only remedy, and the fittest survives. There is no formality in regard to marriage, or what passes for marriage, amongst them. Natural selection is observed on both sides, and the pair, after having ascertained a reciprocity of sentiment, at once cohabit. They do not intermarry with any other race.[350]

It is possible to proceed from this to other regions of man's occupation ground. In America, the evidence of the modern savage is preceded by most interesting facts. If we compare Dr. Brinton's conclusions as to the spread of the American Indians from the north to the south, and as to the development of culture in the favoured districts being of the same origin as the undeveloped culture of the less favoured and of absolutely sterile districts, with Mr. Curtin's altogether independent conclusions as to the growth of the American creation myth with its cycle of first people peaceful and migratory, and its cycle of second people "containing accounts of conflicts which are ever recurrent," we are conscious that mythic and material remains of great movements of people are in absolute accord,[351] an accord which leads us to expect that the peoples who were pushed ever forward into the most desolate and most sterile districts of southern America would be the most nearly savage of all the American peoples. This is in agreement with Darwin's estimate of the Fuegians who wander about in groups of kinless society,[352] and it is in accord with other evidence. Thus the Zaparos, belonging to the great division of unchristianised Indians of the oriental province of Ecuador, have the fame of being most expert woodsmen and hunters. To communicate with one another in the wood, they generally imitate the whistle of the toman or partridge. They believe that they partake of the nature of the animals they devour. They are very disunited, and wander about in separate hordes. The stealing of women is much carried on even amongst themselves. A man runs away with his neighbour's wife or one of them, and secretes himself in some out of the way spot until he gathers information that she is replaced, when he can again make his appearance, finding the whole difficulty smoothed over. In their matrimonial relations they are very loose—monogamy, polygamy, communism, and promiscuity all apparently existing amongst them. They allow the women great liberty and frequently change their mates or simply discard them when they are perhaps taken up by another. They believe in a devil or evil spirit which haunts the woods, and call him Zamáro.[353]

In all these cases, and I do not, of course, exhaust the evidence, there is enough to suggest that the social forms presented are of the most rudimentary kind. Conjecture has not and, I think, cannot get further back than such evidence as this. The social grouping is supported by outside influences rather than internal organisation; neither blood kinship nor marital kinship is recognised; hostility to all other groups and from other groups is the basis of inter-groupal life. To these significant characteristics has to be added the special birth custom and belief of the Semang pygmies. It is clear that the soul-bird belief and the tree-naming custom are different phases of one conception of social life, a conception definitely excluding recognition of blood kinship, and derived from the conscious adoption of an experience

185

which has not reached the stage of blood kinship, but which includes a close association with natural objects. All this makes it advisable to take fuller count of pygmy culture than has hitherto been given to it. The pygmies have in truth always been a problem in man's history. From the time of Homer, Herodotos, and Aristotle, the pygmies have had their place among the observable types of man, or among the traditions to which observers have given credence. In modern times they have been accounted for either as peoples degraded from a higher level of culture, or as peoples who have never advanced. But whether we look upon these people as the last remnants of the primitive condition of hostility or whether they are reversions to that condition by reason of like causes, they bring before us what conjectural research has prepared us for. The first supposition is neither impossible nor incredible. The slow spreading-out in hostile regions would allow of the preservation of some examples of preference for unrestrained licence at the expense of constant hostility, in place of a modified peacefulness at the expense of restricted freedom in matters so dear to the human animal as sexual choice and power. The second supposition contains an element of human history which must find a place in anthropological research. The possible phases of social formation are very limited. If any section of mankind cannot develop in one direction, they will stagnate at the stage they have reached, or they will retrograde to one of the stages from which in times past they have proceeded. There is no other course, and the very limitations of primitive life prevent us from considering the possibility of any other course. Either of these alternatives allows us to consider the examples of hostile inter-grouping as sufficient to supply us with the vantage ground for observation of man in his earliest stages of existence. Perhaps each of them may contain somewhat of the truth. But whatever may be considered as the true cause of the pygmy level of culture, there is an underlying factor which must count most strongly in its determination, namely, that these people are the people who in the process of migration have been pushed out to the last strongholds of man. Whether they could not or would not conform to the newer condition of stationary or comparatively stationary society is not much to the point in presence of the fact that nowhere have they conformed to this standard of existence. Moreover we are entitled to the argument, which has been the main point advanced in connection with the anthropological

186

problems we are discussing, that the most primitive type of man must of necessity be sought for, and can only be found at the extremes of the migration movement wherever that is discernible.[354]

The question now becomes, can we by means of recognisable links proceed from the rudimentary kinless stage of society to the earliest stage of kinship society? This is a most difficult problem, but it must be solved. If the rudimentary kinless groups do indeed constitute a factor in human evolution, they are a most important factor. If they do not constitute such a factor, they can only be accidental productions, the sport of exceptional circumstances not in the line of evolution, and as such they are not of much use in anthropology. It will be seen, therefore, that the connection between rudimentary kinless society and the earliest, or representatives of the earliest, kinship society, is an essential part of an inquiry into origins.

It may be approached first from the conjectural basis. On this basis it may be asserted that the victorious male of the primary groups would remain victorious only just so long as he could continue to adjust the conditions on the primary basis, and preserve his females to himself. New conditions would arise whenever the limitation of the food lands produced a degree of localisation of the hitherto movable groups. There would then have crept into human experience the necessity for something of common action among a wider range than the simple group. This is a new force, and social evolution is henceforth going to operate in addition to, perhaps to a limited extent in substitution of, the constant movement towards new food lands. The single male would no longer be the victorious male by himself; and sharing his power with other males meant the reduction of his power in his own group. Called away for something more than the defence of his own primary group of females, he would leave the females with the practical governance of the primary groups. This tendency would develop. Wherever the constant movement outwards became stayed by geographical or other influences, the groups which experienced the shock of stoppage would undergo change. The female in the various primary groups would become a static element, and the male alone would follow out in the more restricted area the older force of movement which he had learned during the period of unrestricted scope.[355] He would have to find his mates during his roamings, instead of the former condition of fighting for them during the group movements; and his relationship to the primary groups would be therefore fundamentally changed. From being the central dominant head, he would become a constantly shifting unit. The female under these conditions would become the centre of the new social unit, and the male would become the hunter for food and the fighter against enemies. The new social forces would thus consist of local units commanded by the female, and revolving units composed of the males, and there would arise therefrom cleavage between the economic conditions of the two sexes.

That primitive economics bear the impress of sex cleavage is borne out by every class of evidence, and it is in this circumstance that we first come upon societies distinguished by containing two of the most important social elements, exogamy and totemism. Before, however, examining examples of societies containing the two elements of exogamy and totemism, it will be necessary to say something by way of preliminaries on these two elements themselves. They have rightly been made the subject of important special inquiry by anthropological scholars, as being in fact the key to the question of social evolution, and we shall clear the ground considerably by first of all turning to the principal authorities on the subject, and ascertaining the present position of the inquiry.

I must however note, in the first place, that as I have stated the case, exogamy and totemism appear as two separate and distinct elements, whereas it is usual to consider exogamy as an essential part of totemism. I cannot, however, see that this is so. In advanced totemism, it is true, they are found as inseparable parts of one system, but they may well have started separately and coalesced later. In point of fact, all the evidence points in this direction, and if we cease to consider exogamy as a necessary element of totemism, we can advance investigation more rapidly and with greater accuracy.

We come very quickly upon what may be termed natural exogamy. Male working with male outside the groups formed by women and the younger offspring would produce a natural exogamy, which would have followed upon the exogamy produced by hostile capture of women, and two streams of influence would thus tell in favour of the evolution of a system of formal exogamy, and Dr. Westermarck's theory of a natural avoidance of housemates, with all its wealth of evidence, helps us at this point.

The position is not so clear as to totemism. If we begin, however, with a clear understanding that it is not a part of the machinery of exogamous grouping, but an independent growth of its own, we shall have gained an important point, for the contrary opinion has very often obscured the issue and prevented research in the right direction.

It will be advisable to have before us the principal theories as to the origin of totemism. There are practically three—Mr. Frazer's, Mr. Lang's, and Mr. Baldwin Spencer's. Mr. Frazer considers totemism to be "in its essence nothing more or less than an early theory of conception, which presented itself to savage man at a time when he was still ignorant of the true cause of the propagation of the species." Mr. Frazer explains this theory further by saying that "naturally enough, when she is first aware of the mysterious movement within her, the mother fancies that something has that very moment passed into her body, and it is equally natural that in her attempt to ascertain what the thing is, she should fix upon some object that happened to be near her, or to engage her attention at the critical moment."[356]

Mr. Lang rejects Mr. Frazer's theory *in toto*, and propounds his own as due to the naming of savage societies, and to a sort of natural exogamy produced by practically the same set of conditions as I have already described. Mr. Lang's totemism began in the primary groups, and began with exogamy as a necessary part of it. "Unessential to my system," says Mr. Lang, "is the question how the groups got animal names, as long as they got them, and did not remember how they got them, and as long as the names according to their way of thinking indicated an essential and mystic rapport between each group and its name-giving animal. No more than these three things—a group animal name of unknown origin; belief in a transcendental connection between all bearers human and bestial of the same name; and belief in the blood superstitions (the mystically sacred quality of the blood as life)—was needed to give rise to all the totemic creeds and practices including exogamy," and further, "we guess that for the sake of distinction, groups gave each other animal and plant names. These became stereotyped we conjecture, and their origin was forgotten. The belief that there must necessarily be some connection between animals and men of the same names led to speculation about the nature of the connection. The usual reply to the question was that the men and animals of the same name were akin by blood. The kinship *with animals* being particularly mysterious was peculiarly sacred. From these ideas arose tabus, and among others that of totemic exogamy."[357]

Mr. Baldwin Spencer, and with him Dr. Haddon, consider totemism to have arisen from economic conditions. Primitive human groups, says Dr. Haddon, "could never have been large, and the individuals comprising each group must have been closely related. In favourable areas each group would have a tendency to occupy a restricted range, owing to the disagreeable results which arose from encroaching on the territory over which another group wandered. Thus, it would inevitably come about that a certain animal or plant, or group of animals or plants, would be more abundant in the territory of one group than in that of another."[358]

These theories are not necessarily mutually destructive, though they seem to me even collectively not to contain the full case for totemism. Mr. Frazer does not account for woman's isolation at the time of conceptual quickening, for the closeness of her observation of local phenomena, and for the separateness of her ideas from the actual facts of procreation. Mr. Lang overloads his case. He is accounting not for the origin of totemism, but for the origin of all, or almost all, that totemism contains in its most developed forms—"all the totemic creeds and practices including exogamy" as he says. He postulates a name-giving process by drawing upon the conceptions as to names by advanced savage thought, and he does not account for the fact that according to his theory, animals and plants must not only have been named, but named upon some sort of system known to a wide area of peoples, before totemistic names for the groups could have been given to them. Mr. Spencer's and Dr. Haddon's theory is perhaps open to the doubts caused by Mr. Lang's criticism of it that there is only one case of a known economic cause for totemism—an Australian case where two totem kins are said to have been so called "from having in former times principally subsisted on a small fish and a very small opossum;"[359] but on the other hand it does supply a *vera causa*, the actual evidence for which may well have passed away with the development of totemism, without leaving survivals.

All these theories, however, are the result of considerable research and experience, and it is more than probable that they may each contain fragments of the truth which need the touch of combination to show how they stand in relation to the problem which they are propounded to solve. There are features of totemism which are not noticed by any of these distinguished authorities. By using the hitherto unnoticed features, I think it possible to produce a theory as to the origin of totemism, which will contain the essential features of those theories now prominently before the world.

I will set down the order in which the problem can be approached from the standpoint already reached, and we may afterwards try to ascertain what proof is to be derived from totemic societies of the rudest type.

Now totemism is essentially a system of social grouping, whose chief characteristic is that it is kinless—that is to say, the tie of totemism is not the tie of blood kinship, but the artificially created association with natural objects or animals. It takes no count of fatherhood, and only reckons with the physical fact of motherhood. It is not the actual fatherhood or the actual motherhood which is the fundamental basis of totemism, but the association with animal, plant, or other natural object. This is evidently the fact, whatever view is taken of totemism, and that totemism is, in its origin and principle, a kinless, not a kinship system, is the first fact of importance to bear in mind throughout all inquiry. Thus Messrs. Spencer and Gillen say "the identity of the human individual is often sunk in that of the animal or plant from which he is supposed to have originated."[360]

The next fact of importance is that as it commences at birth time, it must be closely associated with the mother and her actions as mother. This leads us to the observation that it is through the agency of the mother that the totem name is conferred upon their children, and to the necessary antecedent fact that women must have themselves possessed the name they conferred—possessed, that is, either the name as a personal attribute and valued as such, or else the power of evolving the name and the capacity of using it with totemic significance. I conclude from this, therefore, that the search for the origin of totemism must be made from the women's side of the social group. Such a search would lead straight to the industrialism of early woman, from which originated the domestication of animals, the cultivation of fruits and cereals, and the appropriation of such trees and shrubs as were necessary to primitive economics.[361] The close and intimate relationship with human life which such animals, plants, and trees would assume under the social conditions which have been postulated as belonging to this earliest stage of evolution, and the aid which these friendly and always present companions would render at all times and under most circumstances, would generate and develop many of those savage conceptions which have become known to research. As human friends they would become part of humanity, just as Livingstone notes of an African people that they did not eat the beef which he offered to them because "they looked upon cattle as human and living at home like men,"[362] an idea which is also the basis of the custom in India not to taste fruit of a newly planted mangrove tree until it is formally "married" to some other tree.[363] These are but the fortunate instances where definite record in set terms has been made. At the back of them lies a whole collection of anthropomorphic conceptions, indulged in by man at all stages of his career.[364] As superhuman agencies for pregnancy and birth, they would do what the human father in the society we are contemplating could not be expected to do, for he would be seldom present during the long period of pregnancy; he would have shared with other males the privileges of sexual intercourse, and he would therefore not be so closely in companionship with the women of the local groups as the friendly animal, plant, or tree who did so much for the mothers. There would thus be formed the groundwork for the fashioning of that most incredible of all beliefs, well founded, as Mr. Hartland has proved both from tradition and belief,[365] that the human father was not father, and that other agencies were responsible for the birth of children.

Gathering up the several threads of this argument, it seems to me that there is within this sphere of primitive thought and within these conditions of primitive life, ample room for the growth of all the main conceptions belonging to totemism; and it will be seen how necessary it is to separate totemism at its beginning from totemism in its most advanced stages. Totemism has not come to man fully equipped in all its parts. It is like every other human institution, the result of a long process of development, and the various stages of development are important parts of the evidence as to origins. At the beginning, it was clearly not connected with blood kinship and descent; it was as clearly not connected with any class system of marriage. But its beginnings would allow of these later growths, would perhaps almost engender these later growths.

Thus, the primary notion of the totem birth of children would, when blood kinship and descent became a consciously accepted element in social development, easily slide into the belief of a totemic ancestor and kinship

192

with the totem; the protection and assistance afforded by the totem to the women of the primary groups who became the mothers of new generations, would easily grow into a sort of worship of the totem; the adoption of the totem name from the circumstances of birth implying the origin of the name from within the group and not from without would, as aggregation took the place of segregation, give way before the association of groups of persons with common interests; the aggregate totem name would come to the separate local totems as soon as, but not before, aggregation had taken the place of segregation in the formation of the social system, and this was not at the earliest stage; the close association of the totems with groups of mothers who always took the fathers of their children from without the mother group, would readily develop into differentiating the mother totems within the group from the totems of the fathers without the group, and this differentiation would produce a special relationship between the sexes based upon the difference of totems instead of upon the sameness of them; and finally there would be produced first a two-class division founded on sex—all the mothers and all the fathers—and, only in a developed form, a two-class division founded on the accepted totem name.

If this is a probable view of the course of totemic evolution, we may more confidently refer to its final stages for further evidence. Advanced totemic society shows a constant tendency to substitute blood kinship for the association with natural objects: first, blood kinship with the mother, then with the mother and the father, finally recognised through the father only. At this last stage, blood kinship has practically succeeded in expelling totemic association altogether in favour of tribal kinship by blood descent, for totemism with male descent as the basis of the social group is totemism in name only; the names of totemism remain but they are applied to kinship tribes or sections of tribes, and they do duty therefore as a convenient name-system without reference to their origin in definite association with the naming animal or plant; and it is already in position to surrender also the names and outward signs. Blood kinship is therefore the destroyer, not the generator, of totemism, and we are therefore compelled to get at the back of blood kinship if we want to find totem beginnings.

This is an important aspect of the case, and it is one which, I think, cannot be ignored. We have found that rudimentary totemism was the basis of a social system founded on artificial associations with animal or plant, was therefore kinless in character; and we have found that when totemism has been carried on into a society developed upon the recognition of blood kinship, blood kinship became antagonistic to totemism, and ultimately displaced it. These two facts point to the rudimentary kinless system as the true origin of totemism.

III

Now we may test these conclusions by applying the theory they contain to an actual case of totemic society. It would be well to choose for this purpose a people who had specialised their totemic organisation, and there are only two supreme instances of this among the races of the world—the North American Indians and the Australians. Everywhere else, where totemism exists, it is not the dominant feature of the social organisation. In Asia and in Africa totemism is subordinate to, or at all events in close or equal association with, other elements, and we cannot be quite sure that we have in these cases pure totemism. North American totemism is in the most advanced stage. Australian totemism is to a very considerable degree less advanced, and it is therefore to Australian totemism I shall turn for evidence.

But even here it is necessary to bear in mind that primitive as the Australians are, they are not so primitive as to be in the primary stages of totemic society. They have developed, and developed strongly along totemic lines, and we know that such development once started has the capacity to proceed far. What we have to do, therefore, is to attempt to penetrate beneath the range of development, to search for the social group at the farthest from the centre point from which migration started, to discover, if we can, relics of group hostility, hostile capture of women and of kinless society, all of which belong to the primary stage from which totemic development has taken place. If we can do this, we may hope to arrive at the origin of totemism, and we are more likely to accomplish it in the case of the Australians than with any other people. If we cannot, as Mr. Lang alleges, anywhere see "absolutely primitive man and a totemic system in the making,"[366] we may go back along the lines from which totemism has developed in Australian society and see somewhat of the process of the making.

We may commence with evidence of the survival of the most primitive human trait, the condition of hostility among the local groups produced by the struggle for women. "The possession of a girl appears to be connected with all their ideas of fighting ... after a battle the girls do not always follow their fugitive husbands from the field, but frequently go over as a matter of course to the victors, even with young children on their backs."[367] Mr. Curr puts the evidence even more definitely in a primitive setting when he informs us of "the young bachelors of the tribe carrying off some of the girl wives of the grey-beards," leaving the old territory and settling at the first convenient place within thirty or forty miles of the old territory. I call this state of things "survival,"[368] because it is the existence in totemic society of the fundamental basis of pre-totemic society. It is checked in Australian totemic society by rules which show a strong development from the primitive. Thus the successful warrior may not take any of his captives to himself; "if a warrior took to himself a captive who belonged to a forbidden class, he would be hunted down like a wild beast," is the evidence of Mr. Fison, who allows it to be "a strong statement, but it rests upon strong evidence."[369] This is the exogamous class system operating even in the case of conflict, when men have resorted to their primitive instincts and their primitive methods.

This discovery of primitive hostility accompanying the obtaining of wives leads us to look for other survivals of the earliest conditions, and we come upon mother-right groups in which the females in each local group are the sexual companions of males from outside their own social group. This is shown by the Kamilaroi organisation, where "a woman is married to a thousand miles of husbands."[370] This phrase may be textually an exaggeration of actual fact, but it undoubtedly expresses a condition of things which actually existed. Women in Australian society must look outside their class, and in general outside their totem, for their sexual mates, and they must expect to be claimed as rightful sexual mates by men whom they have never seen and who live at great distances. Carry this state of things but a few steps back, and we must come to a condition of localised female groups with males moving from group to group. Surely there is something more here than savage organisation. The something more is the development into a system of one of the results of the enforced migratory conditions of early man, namely, the migratory instincts of the males moving outside the female local groups and thus producing natural exogamy. This is what appears to me to be clearly a distinct element in the Australian system. But there is a new element in juxtaposition with it. The new element is the organisation into marriage classes—not every man from without, but only special men from without, are allowed the sexual companionship.

Now in both these cases, where we have apparently penetrated to the most primitive conditions, we are also brought up abruptly against conditions which are not primitive, namely, the exogamous class system, and we are bound to conclude that this class system thus shows itself to be an intruding force which has not, however, been strong enough to quite obliterate the older forces of hostile marriage-capture and mother-right society.

Our next quest is therefore to find out, if we can, an explanation of these two contrasted elements in Australian totemic society, and for this purpose it is advisable to still further narrow down the range of inquiry to one special section of the Australian peoples. For this purpose I shall take the Arunta. There has been much controversy about this people. Mr. Lang argues that the presence of exogamous classes and male descent shows the Arunta to be more advanced than other Australian peoples;[371] Messrs. Spencer and Gillen that the survival of totem beliefs, which are local and unconnected with the class system, proves them to be the least advanced. In this country Mr. Hartland and Mr. Thomas side with Mr. Lang; Mr. Frazer with Messrs. Spencer and Gillen.

The first point of importance to note about the Arunta people is that they occupy the least favourable districts for food supply.[372] This means that they have been pushed there. They did not choose such a location—in other words, they are among the last units of the migration movements which peopled Australia; they are among the last people to have become stationary as a group, and to have been compelled to resort to the development of social organisation in lieu of constantly swarming off from the centre or from the last stopping place to the ends. This tells for primitive, not advanced, conditions.

The next point is the totem system. Messrs. Spencer and Gillen, describing one special case as an example of the rest, give us the following particulars. The Arunta believe that the most marked features of the district they inhabit, the gaps and the gorges, were formed by their Alcheringa ancestors. These Alcheringa are represented as collected together in companies, each of which consisted of a certain number of individuals belonging to one particular totem. Each of these Alcheringa ancestors carried about with him or her one or more of the sacred stones called churinga. These are the general traditions related by the Arunta of to-day to explain their own customs, and let it be noted that the explanation does not necessarily lead us to the primitive conceptions of the Arunta people, but to their present conceptions as to unknown facts. The local example is found close to Alice Springs, where there are deposited a large number of churinga carried by the witchetty grub men and women. A large number of prominent rocks and boulders, and certain ancient gum trees, are the nanja trees and rocks of these spirits. If a woman conceives a child after having been near to this gap, it is one of these spirit individuals which has entered her body, and when born must of necessity be of the witchetty grub totem; "it is, in fact, nothing else but the reincarnation of one of the witchetty grub people of the Alcheringa;" the nanja tree, or stone, ever afterwards is the nanja of the child, and there is special connection between it and the child, injury to the nanja object meaning injury to the nanja man.[373] There is evidence that the reincarnation theory is not admissible,[374] and, indeed, it does not seem warranted on the facts presented by the authors. With this unnecessary element out of the way, then, there is left a system of local totemism, arising at birth and depending upon the mother, without reference in any way to the father, associated with natural features, rocks and trees, and showing in a special way a curious system of sex cleavage by the men of the group being the exclusive guardians of the sacred churinga, and the women the active power by which the churinga becomes connected with the newly-born member of the totem group.[375]

Now at this point we may surely refer back to the custom and belief of the Semang people of the Malay Peninsula, and I suggest that we have the closest parallel between Semang belief and custom and Arunta totemism, not quite the same formula perhaps, but assuredly the same fundamental conception of every child at birth being in intimate association with objects of nature, and this association being the determining force of the newly-born man's social status and class, lasting all through life. In each case the kinless basis of totemism is thus fully shown. The totem names given by women, or assumed on account of the conditions attachable to women as mothers, did not extend to the human fathers. The fathers may be known or unknown to the mothers, but they did not become associated with the totems which the mothers associated with their children. To the extent of fatherhood, therefore, totemism of this type was clearly not based upon the natural fact of blood kinship, but upon the conscious adoption of a non-kinship form of society. To the extent of motherhood also it was not based upon blood kinship, for it was the local totem, not the mother's totem, which became the totem of the newly-born member of the group. We thus have an entirely non-kinship form of society to deal with, a kinless society, "where there is no necessary relationship of any kind between that of children and parents."[376] Primitive man consciously adapted certain of his observations of nature to his social needs, and among these observations the fact of actual blood kinship with father and mother played no part. It would appear therefore that totemism at its foundation was based upon a theoretical conception of relationship between man and animal or plant. Place of birth, association with natural objects, not motherhood and not fatherhood, are the determining factors.

We may proceed to inquire as to the social form which has become evolved from this kinless system.

In the case of the Semangs we have the kinless totemic belief and custom existing within a kinless society. In the case of the Arunta we have the kinless totemism existing in a society based on a kinless organisation still, but containing also full recognition of motherhood,[377] and perhaps recognition of physical fatherhood.[378] There is, therefore, an important distinction in the social position of the two parallel systems. Among the Semang people, their totemic belief and custom do not carry with them a superstructure of society. They form the substantive cult of the scattered social groups, which are kinless groups dependent upon ties local in character and derived from the conscious use of the facts of nature surrounding them. Among the Arunta people, on the contrary, the totem belief and custom are

198

contained within a social system of extraordinary dimensions and proportions. Of course, the obvious questions to raise are—have the Semang people lost a once existing social system connected with their totemic cult? Have the Arunta people had imposed upon them a social system which has not destroyed their primitive totemic cult?

To answer these questions I can only deal with the Semang evidence as it appears in researches of great authority and weight, and there is undoubtedly in all the evidence produced by Messrs. Skeat and Blagden, and the authorities they use, nothing whatever to suggest that Semang totemism once possessed above it an elaborate social organisation of the usual totemic type. There is indeed, the myth which points to a two-class exogamous division for marital purposes,[379] but there is more than myth for the unrestricted intercourse of the sexes both before and after marital rights.[380] In every other direction we get simple groups fashioned on no larger basis than nomadic roaming and journeying to fresh food grounds. On the other hand, there is much to suggest that the Arunta have a dual system of organisation; one, in which the primitive types are still surviving, the second, a more advanced type which covers but does not crush out the first. If this is so, it is clear that the parallel between Semang and Arunta totemism is considerably closer than at first appears.

It will be necessary, therefore, to deal with the two principal signs of alleged Arunta progress, male descent and the exogamous classes. I see no evidence whatever of male descent; male ascendancy, a very different thing, appears, but there cannot strictly be male descent where fatherhood is unrecognised. And here I would interpose the remark that the use of the term descent, male descent and female descent, in these studies is far too indiscriminate.[381] Descent means succession by blood kinship by acknowledged sons or daughters, and this is exactly what does not always occur. Sonship and daughtership in our sense of the term are not always known to savagery. They were not known to the Arunta males, for fatherhood was not recognised by them and motherhood was not definitely used in the social sense. All that the Arunta can be said to have developed is a mother-right society with male ascendancy in the group.[382] Group sons succeeded to group fathers, but individual descent from father to son there is not.

There remain the exogamous classes. In the first place, it is necessary to get rid of a difficulty raised by Mr. Lang. "In no tribe with female descent can a district have its local totem as among the Arunta.... This can only occur under male reckoning of descent."[383] But surely so acute an observer as Mr. Lang would see that with female descent right through, as it exists among the Khasia and Kocch people of Assam, local totem centres are just as possible as with male descent. Mr. Lang is conscious of some discrepancy here, for a little later on he repeats the statement that local totem centres "can only occur and exist under male reckoning of descent," but adds the significant qualification "in cases where the husbands do not go to the wives' region of abode."[384] This is the whole point. Where husbands do go to the wives' region of abode, as they do among the Khasis and the Kocch, female descent would allow of the formation of local totem centres. This is not far from the position of the Arunta. They are mother-right societies. The mother secures the totem name. The father, *de facto*, is not father according to the ideas of the Arunta people, is at best only one of a group of possible fathers according to the practices of the Arunta people. Therefore, the local totem centre is formed out of a system which may be called a mother-right system for the purpose of scientific description, but which is not even a mother-right system to the natives, because motherhood is not the foundation of the local group.

Secondly, we have the important fact, which Mr. Lang has duly noted, though he does not apparently see its significance in the argument as to origins, that the class system "arose in a given centre and was propagated by emigrants and was borrowed by distant tribes."[385] Messrs. Spencer and Gillen distinctly affirm that the "division into eight has been adopted (or rather the names for the four new divisions have been) in recent times by the Arunta tribe from the Ilpirra tribe which adjoins the former on the north, and the use of them is at the present time spreading southwards."[386] This view is supported by the widespread organisation of eaglehawk and crow, and by the general homogeneity of Australian social forms. It is clear, therefore, that room is made for the external organisation of the class system and the consequent production of the dual characteristics of the Arunta—the joint product of the fossilisation of mother-right society at the end of the migration movement, and the superimposing upon this fossilisation, with its tendency towards the class system, of the fully organised class system. The two systems are not now fully welded in the Arunta group. Whatever view is taken of these, whether they be considered advanced or primal, the undoubted dualism has to be accounted for, and the best way of accounting for this dualism is, I submit, that of differential evolution. Further study of Messrs. Spencer and Gillen's work, together with the criticisms of various scholars, Mr. Lang, Mr. Hartland, Mr. Frazer, Mr. Thomas, and others, convinces me that the extreme artificiality of the class system is due partly to a want of understanding of the entire facts, and partly to the *ad hoc* adoption by the natives themselves of new plans to meet difficulties which must arise out of a too close adhesion to their rules. Mr. Lang has allowed me to see a manuscript note of his, in which he points out that the inevitable result of the one totem to the one totem rule of marital relationship,—that is, totem A always intermarrying with totem B, males and females from both totems, and with no others,—is the consanguineous relationship of all the members of the two totems. The rule for non-consanguineous marriage has therefore broken down, and when it breaks down the Australian introduces a new rule which satisfies immediate necessities. When this in turn breaks down a further new rule is made, and this is the way I think the differing rules resulted. They represent, therefore, not varying degrees of culture progress, but only varying degrees of artificial social changes, and they spring from the oldest conditions of all where there is no class system at all.[387] Arunta society is not a "sport" under this view, but a product—a product to be accounted for and explained by anthropological rules, derived not only from Australian society but from the general facts of human society which have remained for observation by the science of to-day. The parallel between Semang and Arunta, therefore, helps us in two ways. It enables us to go back to Semang totemism as an example of primitive kinless society, and forward to Arunta totemism as an example of early development therefrom. We have, in point of fact, discovered the datum line of totemism. Upon this may be constructed the various examples according to their degrees of development, and we may thus see in detail the commencing elements of totemism as well as the means by which we may proceed from the commencing elements to the more advanced elements, and finally to the last stages of totemic society where blood kinship is fully recognised and used, where, in fact, totemic tribes as distinct from totemic peoples take their place in the world's history.

IV

I do not propose in this chapter to proceed further with this inquiry. It will not advance my object, nor is it absolutely necessary. Totemism in the full has been described adequately by Mr. Frazer in his valuable abstract of the evidence supplied from all parts of the world, and there is not much in dispute among the authorities when once the stage of origin is passed. There is danger, however, at the other extreme, namely, the attempt to discover totemism in impossible places in civilisation. Mr. Morgan has shown us totemic society in its highest form of development, untouched by other influences of sufficient consequence to divert its natural evolution. This, I think, is the merit of Mr. Morgan's great work, and not his attempt, his futile attempt as I think, to apply the principles of totemic society to the elucidation of societies that have long passed the stage of totemism. In particular, the great European civilisations are not totemic, nor are they to be seen passing from totemism. It is true that Mr. Lang, Mr. Grant Allen, and others have attempted to trace in certain features of Greek ritual and belief, and in certain tribal formations discoverable in Anglo-Saxon Britain, the relics of a living totemism in the civilised races of Europe;[388] but I do not believe either of these scholars would have endorsed his early conclusions in later studies. Mr. Grant Allen did not, so far as I know, repeat this theory after its first publication, and Mr. Lang has given many signs of being willing to withdraw it. The fact is, there is no necessity to think of Greek or English totem society because in Greece and England there are traces of totem beliefs. We may disengage them from their national position and put them back to the position they occupied before the coming of Greek or Englishman into the countries they have made their own.

In that position there may well have been totemic peoples in Britain of the type we have been considering from Australia. I have already indicated that totemic survivals in folklore have been the subject of a special study of my own which still in the main stands good, and for which I have collected very many additional illustrations and proofs. I discovered that folklore contained some remarkably perfect examples of totemic belief and custom,

202

and also a considerable array of scattered belief and custom connected with animals and plants which, unclassified, seemed to lead to no definite stage of culture history, yet when classified, undoubtedly led to totemism. The result was somewhat remarkable. At many points there are direct parallels to savage totemism, and the whole associated group of customs received adequate explanation only on the theory that it represented the detritus of a once existing totemic system of belief.

The present study enables me to take the parallel to primitive totemism much closer. One of the perfect examples was of a local character. This was found in Ossory. Giraldus Cambrensis tells an extraordinary legend to the following effect: "A priest benighted in a wood on the borders of Meath was confronted by a wolf, who after some preliminary explanations gave this account of himself: There are two of us, a man and a woman, natives of Ossory, who through the curse of one Natalis, saint and abbot, are compelled every seven years to put off the human form and depart from the dwellings of men. Quitting entirely the human form, we assume that of wolves. At the end of the seven years, if they chance to survive, two others being substituted in their places, they return to their country and their former shape."[389] Here is a saintly legend introduced to explain the current tradition of the men of Ossory, that they periodically turned into wolves. Fynes Moryson, in 1603, ridiculed the beliefs of "some Irish who will be believed as men of credit," that men in Ossory were "yearly turned into wolves."[390] But an ancient Irish MS. puts the matter much more clearly in the statement that the "descendants of the wolf are in Ossory,"[391] while the evidence of Spenser and Camden explains the popular beliefs upon even more exact lines. Spenser says "that some of the Irish doe use to make the wolf their gossip;"[392] and Camden adds that they term them "Chari Christi, praying for them and wishing them well, and having contracted this intimacy, professed to have no fear from their four-footed allies." Fynes Moryson expressly mentions the popular dislike to killing wolves, and they were not extirpated until the eighteenth century.[393] Aubrey adds that "in Ireland they value the fang-tooth of an wolfe, which they set in silver and gold as we doe ye Coralls;"[394] and Camden notes the similar use of a bit of wolf's skin.[395]

In the local superstitions of Ossory, therefore, we have several of the cardinal features of savage totemism, the descent from the totem-animal, the ascription to the totem of a sacred character, the belief in its protection, and a taboo against killing it. I will venture to suggest, however, that to these important features there is to be added a parallel in survival to the Semang and Arunta features where the local circumstances of birth are the determining forces which supply the totem name, for the relationship of "gossip," "god-sib," is clearly of the same character as that of the soul-tree of the Semang and the alcheringa of the Australian.[396] The condition of survival has altered the detail of the parallel, but the parallel is on the same plane.

The wolf as gossip to the men of Ossory leads us on to inquire whether any other animal had such close connections with human beings. In Erris, a part of Connaught, "the people consider that foxes perfectly understand human language, that they can be propitiated by kindness, and even moved by flattery. They not only make mittens for Reynard's feet to keep him warm in winter, and deposit these articles carefully near their holes, but they make them sponsors for their children, supposing that under the close and long-established relationship of Gossipred they will be induced to befriend them."[397] Thus it appears that the selfsame conception which the men of Ossory had in the thirteenth century for the wolf, the men of Erris had for the fox in the nineteenth century. No explanation from the dry details of the natural history of these animals is sufficient to account for this curious parallel, and we must turn to ancient beliefs for the explanation.

The general attitude of the men of Erris towards the fox is confirmed as an attribute of totemism when we come to examine a special local form of it. This we can do by turning to Galway. The Claddagh fishermen in Galway would not go out to fish if they saw a fox: their rivals of a neighbouring village, not believing in the fox, do all they can to introduce a fox into the Claddagh village.[398] These people are peculiar in many respects, and are distinctively clannish. They retain their old clan-dress—blue cloaks and red petticoats—which distinguishes them from the rest of the county of Galway, and it may be conjectured that the present-day custom of naming from the names of fish—thus, Jack the hake, Bill the cod, Joe the eel, Pat the trout, Mat the turbot, etc.[399]—may be a remnant of the mental attitude of the folk towards that belief in kinship between men and animals which is at the basis of totemism. But, returning to the fox, we have in the belief that meeting this animal would prevent them from going out to fish, a parallel to the prohibition against looking at the totem which is to be found among savage people, and we have in the neighbours' disbelief in the fox and a corresponding belief in the hare,[400] that local distribution of different totems which is also found in savagery. But all these particulars about the relationship of the fox to the Claddagh fishermen receive unexpected light when we inquire into the biography of their local saint, named MacDara. This saint is the patron saint of the fishermen who, when passing MacDara's island, always dip their sails thrice to avoid being shipwrecked. But then, in the folk-belief, we have this remarkable fact, that MacDara's real name was Sinach, a fox[401]—an instance, it would seem, of a totem cult being transferred to a Christian saint. Thus, then, in the superstitions of these Claddagh fisherfolk we can trace the elements of totemism, the root of which is contained, first, in the nominal worship of a Christian saint, and second, in the actual worship of an animal, the fox.

These examples of local totemism may be followed by a remarkable example of tribal or kinship totemism. It was noted by Mr. G. H. Kinahan in his researches for Irish folklore, and is mentioned quite incidentally among other items, the collector himself not fully perceiving the importance of his "find." This really enhances the value of the evidence, because it destroys any possibility of an objection to its validity—a really important matter, considering the remarkable character of this survival of totem-stocks in Western Europe. The exact words of Mr. Kinahan are as follows:—

"In very ancient times some of the clan Coneely, one of the early septs of the county, were changed by 'art magick' into seals; since then no Coneely can kill a seal without afterwards having bad luck. Seals are called Coneelys, and on this account many of the name changed it to Connolly."[402] The same local tradition is mentioned by Hardiman in one of his notes to O'Flaherty's *Description of West or H-iar Connaught*,[403] but the note is equally significant of genuineness from the fact that the tradition is styled "a ridiculous story." It strengthens Mr. Kinahan's note in the following passage: "In some places the story has its believers, who would no more kill a seal, or eat of a slaughtered one, than they would of a human Coneely."

The clan Coneely is mentioned both by Mr. Kinahan and by Mr.

Hardiman as one of the oldest Irish septs; and that it is widely spread, and not congregated into one locality, is to be inferred from the description of the tradition as prevalent in Connaught, especially from Mr. Hardiman's words, describing that "in some places" the story has its believers now; and hence we may conclude that wherever the clan Coneely are situated there would exist this totem belief.

The full significance of these facts may best be tested by reference to the conditions laid down by Dr. Robertson Smith for the discovery of the survivals of totemism among the Semitic races. These conditions are as follows:—

"'(1) The existence of stocks named after plants and animals'—such stocks, it is necessary to add, being scattered through many local tribes; (2) the prevalence of the conception that the members of the stock are of the blood of the eponym animal, or are sprung from a plant of the species chosen as totem; (3) the ascription to the totem of a sacred character which may result in its being regarded as the god of the stock, but at any rate makes it be regarded with veneration, so that, for example, a totem animal is not used as ordinary food. If we can find all these things together in the same tribe, the proof of totemism is complete; but even when this cannot be done, the proof may be morally complete if all the three marks of totemism are found well developed within the same race. In many cases, however, we can hardly expect to find all the marks of totemism in its primitive form; the totem, for example, may have become first an animal god, and then an anthropomorphic god, with animal attributes or associations merely."[404]

Now in the Irish case all three of these conditions are found together in the same tribe, the clan Coneely, and it is impossible to overlook the importance of such a discovery. It proves from survivals in folklore that totemistic people once lived in ancient Ireland, just as the corresponding evidence proved that the ancient Semitic stock possessed the totemic organisation.

We have now examined the most archaic forms of the survival of totemism in Britain. If we pass on to inquire whether we can detect the more scattered and decayed remnants of totem beliefs and customs, we turn to Mr. Frazer as our guide. From Mr. Frazer's review of the beliefs and customs incidental to the totemistic organisation of savage people, it is possible to extract a formula for ascertaining the classification of savage beliefs and practices incidental to totemism. This formula appears to me to properly fall into the following groups:—

(*a*) Descent from the totem.

(*b*) Restrictions against injuring the totem.

(*c*) Restrictions against using the totem for food.

(*d*) The petting and preservation of totems.

(*e*) The mourning for and burying of totems.

(*f*) Penalties for non-respect of totem.

(*g*) Assistance by the totem to his kin.

(*h*) Assumption of totem marks.

 (*i*) Assumption of totem dress.

(*j*) Assumption of totem names.

My suggestion is that if a reasonable proportion of the superstitions and customs attaching to animals and plants, preserved to us as folklore, can be classified under these heads this is exactly what might be expected if the origin of such superstitions and customs is to be sought for in a primitive system of totemism which prevailed amongst the people once occupying these islands. The clan Coneely and the Ossory wolves are proofs that such a system existed, and if such perfect survivals have been able to descend to modern times, in spite of the influences of civilisation, there is no *primâ facie* reason why the beliefs and customs incidental to such a system should not have survived, even though they are no longer to be identified with special clans. When once a primitive belief or custom becomes separated from its original surroundings, it would be liable to change. Thus, when the wolf totem of Ossory passes into a local cultus, we meet with the belief that human beings may be transformed into animal forms, as the derivative from the totem belief in descent from the wolf. Fortunately, the process by which this change took place is discernible in the Ossory example; but it will not be so in other examples, and we may therefore assume that the Ossory example represents the transitional form and apply it as a key to the origin of similar beliefs elsewhere.

Again, if we endeavour to discover how the associated totem-beliefs of the clan Coneely would appear in folklore supposing they had been scattered by the influences of civilisation, we can see that at the various places where members of the clan had resided for some time there would be preserved fragments of the once perfect totem-belief. Thus, one place would retain traditions about a fabulous animal who could change into human form;

another place would preserve beliefs about its being unlucky to kill a seal (or some other animal specially connected with the locality); another place would preserve a superstitious regard for the seal (or some other local animal) as an augury; and thus the process of transference of beliefs into folklore, from one form into other related forms, from one particular object connected with the clan to several objects connected with the localities, would go on from time to time, until the difficulty of tracing the original of the scattered beliefs and customs would be well-nigh insurmountable without some key. But having once proved the existence of such examples as the clan Coneely and the Ossory wolves, this difficulty, though still great, is very much lessened. Our method would be as follows. We first of all postulate that totem peoples did actually exist in ancient Britain, or whence such extraordinary survivals? We next examine and classify the beliefs and customs which are incidental to totemism in savage society, and having set these forth by the aid of Mr. Frazer's admirable study on the subject, we ascertain what parallels to these beliefs and customs may be found in the folklore of Britain. And then our position seems to be very clearly defined. We prove that in folklore certain customs and superstitions are identical, or nearly so, with the beliefs and customs of totemism among savage tribes, and we conclude that this identity in form proves an identity in origin, and therefore that this section of folklore originated from the totemistic people of early Britain.

I shall not take up all these points on the present occasion, especially as they have in all essentials appeared in the study to which I have referred; but as an example of the scattering of totem beliefs I will refer to the well-known passage in Cæsar (lib. v. cap. xii.), from which we learn that certain people in Britain were forbidden to eat the hare, the cock, or the goose, and see whether this does not receive its only explanation by reference to the totemic restriction against using the totem for food. Mr. Elton, with this passage in his mind, notices that "there were certain restrictions among the Britons and ancient Irish, by which particular nations or tribes were forbidden to kill or eat certain kinds of animals;" and he goes on to suggest that "it seems reasonable to connect the rule of abstaining from certain kinds of food with the superstitious belief that the tribes were descended from the animals from which their names and crests or badges were derived."[405]

Let us see whether this reasonable conjecture holds good. The most famous example is that of Cuchulainn, the celebrated Irish chieftain, whose name means the hound of Culain. It is said that he might not eat of the flesh of the dog, and he came by his death after transgressing this totemistic taboo. The words of the manuscript known as the Book of Leinster are singularly significant in their illustration of this view. "And one of the things that Cúchulainn was bound not to do was going to a cooking hearth and consuming the food [*i.e.* the dog]; and another of the things that he must not do was eating his namesake's flesh."[406] Diarmaid, whose name seems to be continued in the current popular Irish name for pig (Darby), was intimately associated with that animal, and his life depended on the life of the boar.[407] These examples are so much to the point that we may examine the cases mentioned by Cæsar from the same standard.

Mr. Frazer points out that even among existing totem-tribes the respect for the totem has lessened or disappeared, and among the results of this he notes instances where, if any one kills his totem, he apologises to the animal. Under such an interpretation as this, we may surely classify a "memorandum" made by Bishop White-Kennett about the hare, the first of the British totems mentioned by Cæsar: "When one keepes a hare alive and feedeth him till he have occasion to eat him, if he telles before he kills him that he will doe so, the hare will thereupon be found dead, having killed himself."[408] But respect for the hare, in accordance with totem ideas, was carried further than this at Biddenham, where, on the 22nd September, a little procession of villagers carried a white rabbit [a substitute for hare] decorated with scarlet ribbons through the village, singing a hymn in honour of St. Agatha. All the young unmarried women who chanced to meet the procession extended the first two fingers of the left hand pointing towards the rabbit, at the same time repeating the following doggerel:—
 Gustin, Gustin, lacks a bier, Maidens, maidens, bury him here.[409]

This points to a very ancient custom, not yet fully explained, but which clearly had for its object the reverential burying of a rabbit or hare. It is characteristic of the totem animal that it serves as an omen to its clansmen, and we find that the hare is an omen in Britain. Boudicca is said to have drawn an augury from a hare, taken from her bosom, and which when released pursued a course that was deemed fortunate for her attack upon the Roman army;[410] and in modern south Northamptonshire the running of a hare along the street or mainway of a village portends fire to some house in the immediate vicinity.[411] In 1648 Sir Thomas Browne tells us that in his time there were few above three-score years that were not perplexed when a hare crossed their path.[412] In Wilts and in Scotland it was unlucky to meet a hare, but the evil influence did not extend after the next meal had been taken.[413] Then, too, the prohibition against naming the totem object is found in north-east Scotland attached to the hare, whose name may not be pronounced at sea, and Mr. Gregor adds the significant fact that some animal names and certain family names were never pronounced by the inhabitants of some of the villages, each village having an aversion to one or more of the words.[414] A classification of the beliefs and customs connected with the hare takes us, indeed, to almost every phase of totemistic belief, and it is impossible to reject such a mass of cumulative evidence.

Of the second of the British food taboos mentioned by Cæsar we have the most perfect illustration in the instance of the Irish chieftain, Conaire, who, descended from a fowl, was interdicted from eating its flesh.[415]

Turning next to the goose, we find that at Great Crosby, in Lancashire, there is held an annual festival which is called the "Goose Fair," and although it is accompanied by great feasting, the singular fact remains that the goose itself, in whose honour the feast seems to have been held, is considered too sacred to eat, and is never touched by the villagers.[416] In Scotland also the goose was never eaten, being too sacred for food.[417]

Thus the hare, the fowl, and the goose have retained their sacred character in a special manner in various parts of the country, and I may add a further note of more general significance. In Scotland there exists a prejudice against eating hares and cocks and hens.[418] In the south-western parts of England the peasant would not eat hares, rabbits, wild-fowl, or poultry, and when asked whence this dislike proceeds, he asserts that it was derived from his father[419]—the traditional sanction which is so essential to folklore.[420]

The ideas surrounding these three special animals might be easily extended to others, but I will only observe that Mr. Elton, noting both the classical and modern accounts of certain districts in Scotland and Ireland where fish, though abundant, is tabooed as food, quotes with approval a modern suggestion that this abstinence was a religious observance.[421] That fish are carved on numerous stones is a curious commentary on this assertion, while another point to be noted is that the inhabitants of the various islands have each their peculiar notions as to what fish are good for food. Some will eat skate, some dog-fish, some eat limpets and razor-fish, and as a matter of course, says Miss Gordon Cumming, those who do not, despise those who do.[422] A prejudice also existed against white cows in Scotland, and Dalyell ventures upon the acute supposition that this was on account of the unlawfulness of consuming the product of a consecrated animal.[423] These are not stray notes of inexperienced observers, and with two centuries between them it must be that they contain the essence of the people's conception—a conception which leads us back to totemism for its explanation.

I do not think we could get closer to totemic beliefs and ideas than this, nor could we have a better example of the necessity of examining early historical data by anthropological tests and by folklore parallels. Cæsar's words are unimportant by themselves. They convey nothing of any significance to the modern reader—a mere dietetic peculiarity which means nothing and counts for nothing. And yet it might be considered certain that Cæsar knew that the details he recorded were of importance in the historical sense. He did not indicate what the importance was, probably because he was not aware of it; but because he was conscious that among the influences which counted with these people were the food taboos, he rightly recorded the facts. They have remained unconsidered trifles until now, when anthropology has brought them within the range of scientific observation, and they are now to be reckoned with as part of the material which tells of the culture conditions of a section of the early British peoples.

I must here interpose a remark with reference to this grouping of the evidence. Apart from the significance of the superstitions as they are recorded in their bare condition among the peasantry, there is the additional fact to note that the superstition against eating or killing certain animals or birds, or against looking at them or naming them, etc., is not universal. It obtains in one place and not in another. If the injunction not to kill, injure, or eat a certain animal were simply the reflection of a universal practice, such a practice might originate in some attribute of the animal itself which characteristically would produce or tend to produce superstition. But the spread of this class of superstition in certain districts, and not in others, is indicative of an ancient origin, and it is exactly what might be expected to have been produced from totem-peoples. Unfortunately, neither the negative evidence of superstitious beliefs nor the local distribution of superstitious beliefs has ever been considered worthy of attention. But some little evidence is incidentally forthcoming, and I would submit that this may be taken as indicative of what might be obtained more fully by further research into this neglected aspect of folklore. I drew Miss Burne's attention to this subject, and she has noted some particulars in her valuable *Shropshire Folklore*.[424] But for the most part this portion of our evidence wants picking out by a long and tedious process from the mass of badly recorded facts about popular superstitions. I do not believe in the generally stated opinion that certain superstitions are universally believed or practised. It is difficult to prove a negative, and such evidence is not absolutely scientific, but when it comes in direct antithesis to positive, there does not seem any harm in accepting it. Every class of superstition wants tracing out geographically, and local variants want careful noting. I cannot doubt if this were properly done that many so-called universal superstitions would be found to be distinctly local. In the meantime, it is not with universal superstitions that we have to deal. It is primarily with those local variants which show us side by side the differences of belief. It is thus that we can afford evidence of that intermixture of totem-objects which is to be expected from the known facts of totem-beliefs and customs. Indeed, Mr. McLennan has laid it down that "we might expect that while here and there perhaps a tribe might appear with a single animal god, as a general rule tribes and nations should have as many animal and vegetable gods as there were distinct stocks in the population ... we should not expect to find the same animal dominant in all quarters, or worshipped even everywhere within the same nation."[425]

It is important that we should thoroughly understand what these survivals of totemism in the British isles really mean. On the extreme west coast of Ireland, farthest away from the centres of civilisation, there are found these unique examples of a savage institution. The argument that they might have been transplanted thither by travellers from the far west, where totemism has developed to its highest form, cannot seriously be advanced. The argument that they might be the accidental form into which some merely

213

superstitious fancies of ignorant peasants happened to have ultimately shaped themselves, is met by the mathematical demonstration that the ratio of chance against such a development would be well-nigh incalculable. The remaining argument is that they indicate the last outpost, or perhaps one of the last outposts, of a primitive savage organisation which once existed throughout these lands. This is the view that appears to me to be the only possible one to meet all the conditions of the case; one proof in support of this view being the discovery of evidence in other parts of the country which shows that totemism has left its stamp in more or less perfect form upon the traditional beliefs and practices of the nation. Though we are not able to identify further complete examples of the same type as the seal clan of Western Ireland, or the wolf people of Ossory, we should be able, if the explanation I have advanced of their origin be the correct one, to produce examples of the varying forms which such an institution as totemism must have assumed when it had been broken up by the advance of civilising influences. If the seal clan, or the wolf clan, is in truth the last outpost of a savage organisation, there will be in the lands less remote from the centres of civilisation some evidences of the break-up of savagery as it has been driven westward. Somewhere in tradition, somewhere in local observances of beliefs or superstition, there must still be echoes, more or less faint, but still echoes, from totemism. Having discovered these undoubted examples of totemism, the argument shifts its ground. We can no longer say that the theory of totemism may possibly explain some of the customs and traditions of the people. We are, by the logic of the position, compelled to say that custom and tradition must have preserved many relics of totemism, and that so far from seeking to explain custom and tradition by the theory of totemism, we must seek to explain the survival of totemism by custom and tradition. I lay stress on this view of the case because it is hard to combat the views of those who look upon "mere superstition" as no explanation of primitive originals. To us of the present day the beliefs of the peasantry are no doubt properly definable as "mere superstition." But when we examine it as folklore we are seeking for its origin, not for its modern aspect; we are asking how "mere superstition" first arose, and in what forms, not how it exists; we are pushing back the inquiry from to-day when it exists side by side with a philosophical and moral religion to the time when it existed as the sole substitute for

214

philosophy and morals. Even if it is "mere superstition" it has a dateless history. It is not conceivable that it suddenly arose at a particular period before which "mere superstition" did not exist, and all, both peasant and chief, were philosophical and moral. It is not conceivable that the mere superstition of to-day has replaced bodily the mere superstition of other ages. Every succeeding age of progress has influenced it, no doubt, but not eradicated it, and hence the mere superstition of to-day has just such an unbroken continuity of history as language or institutions. That we are able to pick out from among its items undoubted forms of totemism, and that we may add to these complete examples a classified grouping of customs and beliefs in survival parallel to the customs and beliefs of savage totemism, affords proof that at least we may carry back that history to the era of totemism, at whatever point that era may cross the line of, or come into contact with, political history.

This is the definite conclusion to be drawn from the anthropological interpretation of the presence of totemic beliefs among the survivals of folklore. The study of the anthropological conditions has occupied a wide range of thought and inquiry, but it leads us back to a safe basis for research, for it brings definitely within touch of that realm of man which lies outside the civilisation wherein folklore is embedded, the peoples who have made, and the peoples who are dominated by, that civilisation. The savage of Britain cannot with this evidence before us be considered as the mere product of the literature of Greece and Rome. He is part and parcel of the savagery of the human race. Anthropology has shown us that savagery reached the land we now call Britain as part of the general movement of people which has caused the whole earth to become a dwelling-place for man, and now that we know this we must appeal to anthropology whenever we find that the problems of folklore take us out of the culture period of a civilisation known to history.[426]

APPENDIX

I append a synopsis of the culture-structure of the Semangs of the Malay Peninsula (references are to Skeat and Blagden's *Pagan Races of the Malay*

Peninsula where not otherwise specified), in order that the position claimed for the one section of totemic belief may be tested by the remaining characteristics of Semang culture. I claim that there is nothing that remains which is inconsistent with the interpretation given of the totemic items.

Physical:—

(*a*). Live exclusively in the forest surrounded by hostile fauna (i. 13).

(*b*). Food consists of such wild vegetable food as may happen to fall from time to time in season (i. 109, 341, 525), together with small mammals and birds (i. 112), fish (i. 113).

(*c*). As soon as they have exhausted the sources of food in one neighbourhood they move on to the next (i. 109).

(*d*). Fire obtained by friction (i. 111, 113), but meat is eaten raw (i. 112).

(*e*). Nudity is alleged (*Journ. Indian Archipelago*, i. 252; ii. 258); no satisfactory proof (i. 137); do not use skins of animals nor feathers of birds (i. 138); a girdle of fungus string (i. 138, 142, 380); fringe of leaves suspended from a string (i. 139, 142); necklaces and ligatures of jungle fibre (i. 144, 145); women wear a comb made of bamboo as a charm against diseases (i. 149).

(*f*). Habitations are rock shelters (i. 173), tree shelters afforded by branches of trees improved by construction of a weather screen (i. 174); ground screen of palm leaves (i. 175).

(*g*). Hunt successfully the largest animals, escaping easily up the trees (i. 202-204).

(*h*). Knives made of bamboo, flakes and chips of stone, knives of bone (i. 249, 269); bow and arrow (i. 251, 255); not sufficiently advanced to have produced neolithic implements (i. 268); wooden spear (i. 270).

(*i*). Ignorant of pottery, vessels made from big stems of bamboo (i. 383).

Social:—

(*j*). Chief of the group is the principal medicine man, but is on an equal footing with his men, no caste and property is in common (i. 497, 499).

(*k*). Marriage rights are secured by the presentation of a jungle knife to the bride's parents and a girdle to the bride, and the bride never lets the girdle part from her for fear of its being used to her prejudice in some magic ceremony; adultery is punishable by death (ii. 58, 59) [but this information

216

was not obtained from the most primitive of the Semang people].

(*l*). Semang women are common to all men (Newbold, *Political and Stat. Acc. of Settlements in Straits of Malacca*, ii. 379). Great ante-nuptial freedom (ii. 56, 218); "Of the Semang I have not had an opportunity of personally judging" (ii. 377, Newbold).

Tree hut, Ulu Batu, about twelve miles from Kuala Lumpur, Selangor (from Skeat and Blagden's "Pagan Races of the Malay Peninsula") **TREE HUT, ULU BATU, ABOUT 12 MILES FROM KUALA LUMPUR, SELANGOR**

(*m*). Eat dead kindred except head (Newbold, ii. 379); burial takes place in the ground, and the older practice was exposure in trees; the Semang have no dread of ghosts of the deceased (ii. 89, 91).

(*n*). No sacred shrines or places (ii. 197).

(*o*). Avoidance of mother-in-law (ii. 204).

(*p*). Myth of the ringdove informing the children of the first woman that they had married within prohibited degrees of consanguinity, and advising them to separate and marry "other people" (ii. 218).

(*q*). Myth as to ignorance of cause of birth being dispelled by the cocoanut monkey informing the first man and woman (ii. 218).

(*r*). The Semang are almost ineradicably nomadic, have no fixed habitation, and rove about like the beasts of the forest (i. 172; ii. 470).

(*s*). Women and girls are not allowed to eat until the men and boys have finished their repast (i. 116); the men do most of the hunting and trapping, and the women take a large share in the collecting of roots and fruits; all the cooking is performed by the women and girls (i. 375).

(*t*). They are split up into a large number of dialects, each of which is confined to a relatively small area, and it often happens that a little [clan] or even a single family uses a form of speech which is differentiated from other dialects to be practically unintelligible to all except the members of the little community itself (ii. 379).

217

(*u*). Natural segregation of the [tribes] into small [clans] to some extent cut off from one another and surrounded by settled Malay communities (ii. 379).

(*v*). The most thoroughly wild and uncivilised members of our race, regarded by the Malays as little better than brute beasts, with no recorded history (ii. 384).

(*w*). Nomadic life of the Semang leads them over a considerable tract of country (ii. 388).

Psychical:—

(*x*). Decorative patterns on quivers representing natural objects, and possessing magical virtue to bring down various species of monkeys and apes and other small mammals (i. 417), and as charms for the men (i. 423).

(*y*). Decorative pattern on magic comb worn by women to serve as a charm against venomous reptiles and insects, similar design for similar reason sometimes painted on the breast (i. 41, 420-436).

(*z*). Child's name is taken from some tree which stands near the prospective birthplace of the child. As soon as the child is born this name is shouted aloud by the *sage femme*, who then hands over the child to another woman, who buries the afterbirth underneath the birth-tree or name-tree of the child. As soon as this is done the father cuts a series of notches in the tree, starting from the ground and terminating at the height of the breast. The cutting of these notches is intended to signalise the arrival on earth of a new human being, since it thus shows that Kari registers the souls that he has sent forth by notching the tree against which he leans. Trees thus "blazed" are never felled. The child must not in later life injure any tree which belongs to the species of his tree; for him all such trees are taboo, and he must not even eat their fruit, the only exception being when an expectant mother revisits her birth-tree. Every tree of its species is regarded as identical with the birth-tree (ii. 3, 4). When an East Semang dies his birth-tree dies too (ii. 5).

(*aa*). The child's soul is conveyed in a bird, which always inhabits a tree of the species to which the birth-tree belongs. It flies from one tree of the species to another, following the as yet unborn body. The souls of first-born children are always young birds newly hatched, the offspring of the bird which contained the soul of the mother. If the mother does not eat the soul-bird during her accouchement the child will be stillborn or will die

218

shortly after birth (ii. 4, 192, 194, 216). She keeps the soul-bird within the birth-bamboo, and does not eat it all at once, but piecemeal (ii. 6). All human souls grow upon a soul-tree in the other world, whence they are fetched by a bird which was killed and eaten by the expectant mother (ii. 194).

(*bb*). Semang religion, in spite of its recognition of a thunder-god (Kari) and certain minor deities (so called), has very little indeed in the way of ceremonial, and appears to consist mainly of mythology and legend. It shows remarkably few traces of demon worship, very little fear of ghosts of the deceased, and still less of any sort of animistic beliefs (ii. 174). [As the Kari is the deity common to the Semang and the people higher in culture than the Semang, it is difficult to trace out the primitive idea. The myths also show a common impress, "which is probably mainly due to the same savage Malay element" (ii. 183).]

(*cc*). During a storm of thunder and lightning the Semang draw a few drops of blood from the region of the shin bone, mix it with a little water in a bamboo receptacle, and throw it up to the angry skies (ii. 204).

(*dd*). Pretend entire ignorance of a supreme being, but on pressure confessed to a very powerful yet benevolent being, the maker of the world (ii. 209).

FOOTNOTES:

[284] Beddoe, *Races of Britain*, cap. ii., and *Journ. Anthrop. Inst.*, xxxv. 236-7; Boyd-Dawkins, *Early Man in Britain*, cap. vii. viii. and ix.; Ripley, *Races of Europe*, cap. xii.

[285] Rhys, *Celtic Britain*, 271; Rhys, *Celtic Heathendom*, *passim*; Rhys and Jones, *Welsh People*, cap. i. and Appendix B on "Pre-Aryan Syntax in Insular Celtic," by Professor Morris Jones.

[286] Barrows, mounds, tumuli, stone circles, monoliths are generally admitted to belong to the Stone Age people before the Celts arrived, and when they are adequately investigated, as Mr. Arthur Evans has investigated Stonehenge (*Archæological Review*, vol. ii. pp. 312-330), and the Rollright Stones (*Folklore*, vol. vi. pp. 5-51), the evidence of a prehistoric origin is unquestioned.

[287] I have worked out the evidence for this in the *Archæological*

Review, vol. iii. pp. 217-242, 350-375, and though I do not endorse all I have written there, the main points are still, I think, good.

[288] Wallace, *Darwinism*, cap. xv.

[289] Spencer and Gillen, *Central Tribes of Australia*, 12, 272, 324, 368, 420.

[290] *Descent of Man*, i. cap. vii. 176.

[291] *Cf.* Topinard's *Anthropology*, part iii., "On the Origin of Man," pp. 515-535, for the details of the various authorities ranged on the sides of monogenists and polygenists.

[292] Keane, *Man, Past and Present*, discusses the important evidence obtained by Dr. Dubois from Java, and Dr. Noetling from Upper Burma, pp. 5-8. It is only fair to that brilliant scholar, Dr. Latham, to point out that without the evidence before him to prove the point, he came to the same conclusion that the original home of man was "somewhere in intra-tropical Asia, and that it was the single locality of a single pair."—Latham, *Man and his Migrations*, 248.

[293] The most recent example of this is Mr. Thomas's extraordinary treatment of the evidence of migration in Australia. It produces in his mind "novel conditions," but has effects which he cannot neglect, but which he strangely misinterprets. N. W. Thomas, *Kinship Organisations in Australia*, 27-28.

[294] Spencer, *Principles of Sociology*, i. 18.

[295] Lord Avebury, *Prehistoric Times*, 586.

[296] *Man, Past and Present*, pp. 1, 8.

[297] Latham, *Man and his Migrations*, 155-6.

[298] The ethnographic movement is a very definite fact in anthropological evidence, though it has been little noted. Thus "the Coles are evidently a good pioneering race, fond of new clearings and the luxuriant and easily raised crops of the virgin soil, and have constitutions that thrive on malaria, so it is perhaps in the best interest of humanity and cause of civilisation that they be kept moving by continued Aryan propulsion. Ever armed with bow, arrows, and pole-axe, they are prepared to do battle with the beasts of the forest, holding even the king of the forest, the 'Bun Rajah,' that is, the tiger, in little fear."—Col. Dalton in *Journ. Asiatic Soc., Bengal*, xxxiv. 9.

[299] Traditions of great migrations exist among most primitive races. Some of these contain unexpected corroboration from actual discoveries. Thus the natives of New Zealand had a tradition that their ancestors, when they arrived in their canoes some four centuries ago, buried some sacred things under a large tree. It is said that the tree was blown down in recent times and that the sacred things were discovered. Taplin records "a good specimen of the kind of migration which has taken place among the aborigines all over the continent" (*The Narrinyeri*, p. 4); and similar evidence could be produced in almost every direction. Mr. Mathew in *Eaglehawk and Crow* deals with "the argument from mythology and tradition" as to the origin of the Australians in a very suggestive fashion (pp. 14-22). Stanley has preserved an African native tradition of local groups spreading out from the parent home *(Through the Dark Continent*, i. 346).

[300] I am aware this is disputed by O. Peschel—*Races of Man*, 137 *et seq.*—but I think the evidence is sufficient; and it must be remembered that there is direct evidence of the most backward races not using the fire they possess for cooking, but always eating their animal food raw, as, for instance, the Semang people of the Malay Peninsula. (See Skeat and Blagden, *Pagan Races of the Malay Peninsula*, i. 112.) The Andaman Islanders could not make fire, though they possessed and kept it alive. This shows that they must have borrowed it and did not previously possess it.—Quatrefages, *The Pygmies*, 108. Tylor, *Early History of Mankind*, cap. ix., should be consulted.

[301] The term political is, I confess, a little awkward, owing to its specially modern use, but it is the only term which, in its early sense, expresses the stage of social development represented by a polity as distinct from a mere localisation.

[302] It was one of the first efforts of the science of language to endeavour to trace out the original home of the so-called Aryas and their subsequent migrations. "Emigration," said Bunsen, "is the great agent in forming nations and languages" (*Philosophy of Hist.*, i. 56); and Niebuhr, who has traced out most of the migrations of the Greek tribes, observes that "this migration of nations was formerly not mentioned anywhere" (*Anc. Hist.*, ii. 212). Quite recently, Professor Flinders Petrie has worked at the question of European migrations in the Huxley lecture of 1907 (*Journ. Anthrop. Inst.*, xxxvi. 189-232), his valuable maps showing "the movements of twenty of the

221

principal peoples that entered Europe during the centuries of great movements that are best known to us" (204). In the meantime, the folklorist has much to do in this direction, and up to the present he has almost entirely ignored or misread the evidence. I do not know whether Mr. Nutt would still adhere to his conclusion that the myth embodied in the Celtic expulsion-and-return formula is undoubtedly solar (*Folklore Record*, iv. 42), but a restatement of Mr. Nutt's careful and elaborate analysis would lead me to trace the myth to the migration period of Aryan history, just as I agree with von Ihering that the *ver sacrum* of the Romans is a rite continued from the migration period to express in religious formulæ, and on emergency to again carry out, the ancient practice of sending forth from an overstocked centre sufficient of the tribesmen and tribeswomen to leave those who remained economically well-conditioned (*The Evolution of the Aryan*, 249-290). Pheidon's law at Corinth, alluded to by Aristotle (*Pol.*, ii. cap. vi.), could only be carried out by a sending out of the surplus. See also Aristotle, *Pol.*, ii. cap. xii.; and Newman's note to the first reference, quoting similar laws elsewhere. Both the "junior-right" traditions and customs take us back to the same conditions. The occupation of fresh territories is an observable feature of the Russian mir (Wallace, *Russia*, i. 255; Laveleye *Primitive Property*, 34), and Mr. Chadwick has recently called attention to the corresponding Scandinavian evidence (*Origin of the English Nation*, 334).

[303] Mr. J. R. Logan long ago pointed out that "the further we go back, we find ethnic characteristics more uniform," and further concluded that certain facts observed by himself "lead to the inference that the Archaic world was connected."—*Journ. Indian Archipelago*, iv. 290, 291.

[304] *Descent of Man*, pp. 590, 591.

[305] *Studies in Ancient History*, i. 84.

[306] *History of Human Marriage*, cap. ii.

[307] *Ancient Society*, p. 10.

[308] *Secret of the Totem*, p. 32.

[309] N. W. Thomas, *Kinship Organisation in Australia*, 4.

[310] *Folklore*, xii. 232.

[311] Both Dr. Haddon and myself made the same point on a criticism of Mr. Fraser's *Golden Bough*, mine being from the Aricia rites, and Dr. Haddon's from the savage parallels thereto. See *Folklore*, xii. 223, 224,

232.

[312] Sproat's *Scenes and Studies of Savage Life*, 19. The use of the term "tribe" in this quotation is, of course, descriptive only. There is no tribal constitution among the Ahts, and "group" would have been the preferable term.

[313] Dr. W. H. Rivers' recently published work on the Todas is the best authority.

[314] Rivers, *op. cit.*, 432, 455.

[315] Rivers, *op. cit.*, cap. xxi. 504, 517.

[316] Rivers, *op. cit.*, 452-456.

[317] Latham, *Descriptive Ethnology*, ii, 137.

[318] Bucher, *Industrial Evolution*, 56.

[319] Rev. George Taplin, *The Narrinyeri; South Australian Aborigines*, 40. *Cf.* Howitt, *Native Tribes of South-east Australia*, 710-720; Grierson, *The Silent Trade*, 22.

[320] *Cf.* Skeat and Blagden, *Pagan Tribes of Malay Peninsula*, i, 10.

[321] Graham, *Bheel Tribes of Khandesh*, 3.

[322] Herodotos, iv. 180.

[323] *Journ. Asiatic Soc., Bengal*, xiii. 625.

[324] Major Gurdon, *The Khasis*, 76, 82.

[325] N. W. Thomas, *Kinship Organisations in Australia*, 124.

[326] Fustel de Coulange's *Cité Antique*, cap. xiv. and xv., is, however, the most exaggerated example of this point of view.

[327] Lang, *Social Origins*, 1. The latest exponent of anthropological principles affirms that "the family which exists in the lower stages of culture, though it is overshadowed by the other social phenomena, has persisted through all the manifold revolutions of society."—N. W. Thomas, *Kinship Organisations in Australia*, 1.

[328] Jevons' *Introd. to Hist. of Religion*, 195.

[329] See also Prof. Geikie in *Scottish Geographical Mag.* (Sept. 1897).

[330] *Early Hist. of Mankind*, 303; MacCulloch, *Childhood of Fiction*, 396; Gould, *Mythical Monsters*.

[331] Mr. Westermarck has collected excellent evidence as to the economic influences upon savage society (*Hist. of Human Marriage*, 39-49), and we may quite properly assume the same conditions for earliest man.

[332] A very good summary of the pygmy peoples in all parts of the world is given by Mr. W. A. Reed in his useful *Negritos of Zambales*, 13-22. *Cf.* Keane, *Man, Past and Present*, 118-121; Keane, *Ethnology*, 246-248; and Sir W. H. Flower, *Essays on Museums*, cap. xix.

[333] Latham, *Man and his Migrations*, 55, 56. Dr. Beke was a most cautious observer, and I have consulted all his contributions to the *Journal of the Geographical Society* (vol. xiii.) and have found no sign of his retraction of the evidence. His correspondence in the *Literary Gazette* of 1843, p. 852, discusses the question of the Dokos being pygmies, but he adheres to his information as to the absence of social structure being correct.

[334] Lib. ii. 32, 8; *cf.* Quatrefages, *The Pygmies*, cap. 1, "The Pygmies of the Ancients."

[335] Lieut.-Col. Sutherland, *Memoir respecting the Kaffirs, Hottentots, and Bosjemans*, i. 67 (Cape Town, 1846).

[336] Burrows, *The Land of Pygmies*, 182.

[337] Mr. A. B. Lloyd's volume *In Dwarfland and Cannibal Country*, p. 96, is the most recent evidence.

[338] It is worth noting here that the Chinese traditions of the pygmies are exceedingly suggestive and curious. See Moseley, *Notes by a Naturalist*, 369.

[339] Skeat and Blagden, *Malay Peninsula*, ii. 443.

[340] *Journ. Indian Archipelago*, iv. 425-427; *cf. Journ. Anthrop. Inst.*, xvi. 228; Wallace, *Malay Archipelago*, 452.

[341] Clifford, *In Court and Kampong*, 171-181.

[342] Skeat and Blagden, *Pagan Races of Malay Peninsula*, i. 13.

[343] *Op. cit.*, i. 53-4, 139, 169, 172, 341.

[344] *Op. cit.*, i. 170.

[345] *Op. cit.*, i. 243-248, 268.

[346] *Op. cit.*, i. 494; ii. 56, 218.

[347] *Op. cit.*, ii. 3. Compare *Journ. Indian Archipelago*, iv. 427, "they are called after particular trees, that is, if a child is born under or near a cocoanut or durian, or any particular tree in the forest, it is named accordingly," and John Anderson, *Considerations relative to Malayan Peninsula*, 1824, p. xli.

[348] *Op. cit.*, ii. 4, 192, 194.

[349] *Op. cit.*, ii. 174, 209.

[350] *Archæological Review*, i. 13, from an official report published in a Government Blue Book.

[351] Brinton, *The American Race*; Curtin, *Creation Myths of Primitive America*.

[352] Darwin, *Journal of Researches*, 228.

[353] *Anthropological Inst.*, vii. 502-510.

[354] Quatrefages, *The Pygmies*, 24, 48, 69.

[355] There is ample evidence of this characteristic. Thus, of the Australians of Port Lincoln district, it is said that "the habit of constantly changing their place of rest is so great that they cannot overcome it even if staying where all their wants can be abundantly supplied."—*Trans. Roy. Soc., Victoria*, v. 178.

[356] *Fortnightly Review*, lxxviii. 455.

[357] *Secret of the Totem*, 125, 140.

[358] *British Association Report*, 1902, p. 745. *Cf.* Spencer and Gillen, *Northern Tribes of Central Australia*, 160.

[359] Lang, *Secret of the Totem*, 140, quoting Grey, *Vocabulary of the Dialects of South-west Australia*.

[360] Spencer and Gillen, *Tribes of Central Australia*, 119.

[361] The reader should consult Mason's *Women's Share in Primitive Culture*, and Bucher's *Industrial Evolution*, for evidence on this point.

[362] Livingstone, *South Africa*, 462.

[363] Sleeman, *Rambles of an Indian Official*, i. 43. "Banotsarg is the name given to the marriage ceremony performed in honour of a newly planted orchard, without which preliminary observance it is not proper to partake of its fruit. A man holding the Salagram personates the bridegroom, and another holding the sacred Tulsi personates the bride. After burning a hom or sacrificial fire, the officiating Brahmin puts the usual questions to the couple about to be united. The bride then perambulates a small spot marked out in the centre of the orchard. Proceeding from the south towards the west, she makes the circuit three times, followed at a short distance by the bridegroom holding in his hand a strip of her chadar of garment. After this, the bridegroom takes precedence, making his three circuits, and followed in like manner by his bride. The ceremony concludes with the usual offerings" (Elliot, *Folklore of North-west Provinces of India*, i. 234).

[364] Myths explaining the domestication of animals belong to this stage of culture. The dog is a sacred animal among the Khasis, with certain totemic associations, and there is a very realistic and humanising myth relating how the dog came to be regarded as the friend of man (Gurdon, *The Khasis*, 51, 172-3). The Kyeng creation legend includes a good example of animal friendship with man (Lewin, *Wild Races of South-east India*, 238-9). The American creation myths afford remarkable testimony to this view of the case. "Game and fish of all sorts were under direct divine supervision ... maize or Indian corn is a transformed god who gave himself to be eaten to save men from hunger and death" (Curtin, *Creation Myths of Primitive America*, pp. xxvi, xxxviii). The Narrinyeri Australians "do not appear to have any story of the origin of the world, but nearly all animals they suppose anciently to have been men who performed great prodigies, and at last transformed themselves into different kinds of animals and stones" (Taplin, *The Narrinyeri*, 59).

[365] *Legend of Perseus*, i. cap. vi.

[366] *Secret of the Totem*, 29.

[367] Mitchell, *Australian Expeditions*, i. 307; *cf.* Fison and Howitt, *Kamilaroi and Kurnai*, 200, 224; Taplin, *The Narrinyeri*, 10.

[368] Curr, *Australian Race*, i. p. 193; *cf.* Smyth, *Aborigines of Victoria*, ii. p. 316.

[369] Fison and Howitt, *Kamilaroi and Kurnai*, 66, 285, 289.

[370] Fison and Howitt, *op. cit.*, 68, 73.

[371] Lang, *Secret of the Totem*, 64.

[372] Spencer and Gillen, *Central Tribes*, 7.

[373] Spencer and Gillen, *Central Tribes*, 120, 124, 133.

[374] *Globus*, xci, a very important criticism of Spencer and Gillen's work.

[375] Spencer and Gillen, *op. cit.*, 139, 154.

[376] Spencer and Gillen, *Northern Tribes*, 144.

[377] *Globus*, xci, gives important evidence of traces of female descent among the Arunta.

[378] There is conflict of testimony on this point. Spencer and Gillen deny that the Arunta recognise the fact of paternity in any way (see *Northern Tribes*, pp. xiii, 145, 330), and yet talk of the "actual father" in ceremonial

226

functions (p. 361).

[379] Skeat and Blagden, *Malay Peninsula*, ii. 218.

[380] Newbold, *Political and State Acc. of Malacca*, ii.; Skeat and Blagden, *op. cit.*, ii. 56.

[381] Messrs. Spencer and Gillen, *Central Tribes*, 36, give a useful note on this point.

[382] In this they are exactly paralleled by the Khasi people of Assam, among whom we find a limited sort of male chiefship by succession through females, and an absolute succession to property by females by succession through females (Gurdon, *The Khasis*, 68, 88). Descent from the female is absolute in both cases, and all we get is male ascendancy.

[383] *Secret of the Totem*, 73.

[384] *Op. cit.*, 79.

[385] Lang, *Secret of the Totem*, 148.

[386] *Central Tribes*, 72. Mrs. Langloh Parker's information as to the origin of the Euahlayi two-class division having arisen from an amalgamation of two distinct tribes, points to the same facts.—*Euahlayi Tribe*, 12.

[387] Spencer and Gillen, *Tribes of Central Australia*, 96, 99, 106.

[388] Lang's Introd. to Bolland's *Aristotle's Politics* (1877), p. 104; Grant Allen's *Anglo-Saxon Britain* (1888), pp. 79-83.

[389] *Topography of Ireland*, lib. ii. cap. 19.

[390] *Hist. of Ireland*, ii. 361.

[391] *Irish Nennius*, p. 205; Lang, *Custom and Myth*, p. 265; *Revue Celtique*, ii. 202.

[392] *View of the State of Ireland*, p. 99.

[393] Moryson, *Hist. of Ireland*, ii. 367.

[394] Aubrey, *Remaines of Gentilisme*, 204.

[395] Camden, *Britannia*, iii. 455; iv. 459.

[396] The significance of the word "gossip" is worth noting. Halliwell says it "signified a *relation* or sponsor in baptism, all of whom were to each other and to the parents *God-sibs*, that is, *sib*, or related by means of religion." This meaning does not seem to have died out in the days of Spenser, and his use of the word to describe the relationship of the men of Ossory to wolves is very significant. For the history of this important word see Hearn's *Aryan Household*, 290.

[397] Otway, *Sketches in Erris*, 383-4.

[398] *Folklore Record*, iv. 98.

[399] *Ulster Journ. Arch.*, ii. 161, 162. They have also another primitive trait. Their trade emblems are carved on their tombstones. *Roy. Irish Acad.*, vii. 260.

[400] This I gather from *Ulster Journ. Arch.*, ii. 164, where it is stated that the hare is unpropitious.

[401] *Folklore Journal*, ii. 259.

[402] *Folklore Journal*, ii. 259; *Folklore Record*, iv. 104. Miss Ffennell kindly informed me at the meeting of the Folklore Society where I read a paper on the subject, that she had frequently heard the islanders of Achill, off the coast of Ireland, state their belief that they were descended from seals.

[403] Published by the *Irish Archæological Society*, p. 27; there is a Seal Island off the coast of Donegal (Joyce, *Irish Place-Names*, ii. 282); and some Shetland legends of the seal will be found in *Soc. Antiq. Scot.*, i. 86-89. Seals are eaten for food in the island of Harris (see Martin, *Western Islands*, 36), and one called the Virgin Mary's Seal is offered to the minister (Reeves, *Adamnan Vita. Columb.*, 78, note *g*). The attitude of the Irish to seals is shown by the two following notes:— "At Erris, in Ireland, seals are considered to be human beings under enchantment, and they consider it unlucky to have anything to do with seals, and to have one live near their dwelling is considered as productive of evil to life and property. A story current, in 1841, describes how a young fisherman came in a fog upon an island whereon lived these enchanted men in their human form, but when they quitted it they turned to seals again" (Otway, *Sketches of Erris*, 398, 403). Off Downpatrick Head they used to take seals, but have given up the practice, because once two young fellows had urged their curraghs into a cave where the seals were known to breed, and they were killing them right and left when, in the farthest end of the cave and sitting up on its bent tail in a corner, there sat an old seal. One of the boys was just making ready to strike him, when the seal cried out, "Och, boys! och, ma bouchals, spare your old grandfather, Darby O'Dowd." He then proceeded to tell the boys his story. "It's true I was dead and dacently buried, but here I am for my sins turned into a sale as other sinners are and will be, and if you put an end to me and skin me maybe it's worser I'll be, and go into a shark or a porpoise. Lave your ould forefather

where he is, to live out his time as a sale. Maybe for your own sakes you will ever hereafter leave off following and parsecuting and murthering sales who may be nearer to yourselves nor you think." The story is universally believed, and on the strength of it the people have given up seal hunting (Otway, *Sketches of Erris*, 230).

[404] *Kinship and Marriage in Arabia*, 188. *Cf.* Mr. Jacobs' articles in *Archæological Review*, "Are there totem clans in the Old Testament?" vol. iii. pp. 145-164.

[405] *Origins of English History*, 297.

[406] *Proc. Roy. Irish Acad.*, x. 436; Lang's *Custom and Myth*, 265; Elton's *Origins of English History*, 299-300; *Revue Celtique*, i. 50; iii. 176.

[407] *Rev. Celtique*, vi. 232.

[408] Aubrey's *Remaines of Gentilisme*, 102.

[409] *Folklore Record*, i. 243.

[410] Xiphilinus in *Mon. Hist. Brit.*, p. lvii.

[411] *Choice Notes, Folklore*, p. 16.

[412] *Vulgar Errors*, p. 320.

[413] Aubrey, *Gentilisme and Judaisme*, 109; Napier, *Folklore of West of Scotland*, 26. Consult Mr. Billson's valuable paper on "The Easter Hare" in *Folklore*, iii. 441-466.

[414] Gregor, *Folklore of North-East Scotland*, 129, 199.

[415] O'Curry, *Manners of the Anc. Irish*, i. p. ccclxx.

[416] *Notes and Queries*, 3rd ser. iv. 82, 158; Dyer's *Popular Customs*, 384.

[417] Gordon Cumming, *Hebrides*, 369.

[418] Gordon Cumming, *Hebrides*, 369.

[419] *Gentleman's Magazine Library, Pop. Sup.*, 216.

[420] It will be useful to refer to Mr. Thrupp's paper on "British Superstition as to Hares, Geese, and Poultry" in *Trans. Ethnological Society of London*, new ser. vol. v. pp. 162-167.

[421] *Origins of English History*, 170.

[422] Gordon Cumming, *Hebrides*, 365.

[423] Dalyell's *Darker Superstitions of Scotland*, 431. It should be noted that Dalyell wrote before the age of scientific folklore, and therefore his observations are founded more upon conjectures derived from the practices and beliefs themselves than from any theory as to origins.

[424] White horse, p. 208; black cat, p. 211, note 3; two magpies, p. 224; crickets, p. 238; hawthorn, p. 244.

[425] *Fortnightly Review*, xii. 562.

[426] It is just possible that the value of investigating Australian totemism may prove to have a still more direct bearing upon British folklore, for Huxley's opinion as to the Australoid race is not entirely to be neglected. He argued that "The Australoid race are dark complexion, ranging through various shades of light and dark chocolate colour; dark or black eyes; the hair of the scalp black and soft, silky and wavy; the skull dolichocephalic. The great continent of Australia is the headquarters of the Australoid race.... The Dekkan, which is so remarkably isolated on the north by the valleys of the Ganges and Indus, beyond these by the Himalaya Mountains, and on the east and west by the sea, was originally inhabited, and is still largely peopled by men who completely come under the definition of the Australoid race given above. In Abyssinia and Egypt there is a smooth-haired, dark-complexioned, long-headed stock which I am strongly inclined to regard as a westward extension of the Australoid race. I would venture to suggest that the dark whites who stretch from Northern Hindostan through Western Asia, skirt both shores of the Mediterranean, and extend through Western Europe to Ireland, may have had their origin in a prolongation of the Australoid race, which has become modified by selection or intermixture" (Huxley in *Prehistoric Congress, 1868*, pp. 92-94). This point of view is confirmed by Mr. Mathew's conclusions, *Eaglehawk and Crow*, cap. iii.

Chapter V

SOCIOLOGICAL CONDITIONS

Perhaps the most important part of the anthropological aspect of custom, rite, and belief in tradition is sociological. Perhaps, too, it is the most neglected. Inquirers into the origin of religion proceed one after the other to investigate the phenomena of early beliefs as they interpret the origin of religion, without one thought of the sociological conditions of the problem. They interpose, as I have already pointed out, the theory of a state religion, when such a foundation is incidentally found to be necessary to carry the imposing superstructure of Celtic mythology, but they do not pause to inquire whether the state, suddenly introduced into the argument, is a discoverable factor; or they proceed to erect their superstructure of religious origins without any social foundation whatever, and we are left with a great concept of abstract thought having no roots in the source from which it is supposed to be drawn. The sun-god and the dawn-god, even the All-father, are traced in the most primitive thought of man, but it is not deemed necessary to show in what relation these concepts stand to practical life. It is here I must refer back to Robertson-Smith's dictum on mythology, for it is the necessary preliminary to showing that belief cannot enter into life except through the sociological units into which all humanity fits itself; or rather, I would prefer Robertson-Smith's way of putting it, "the circle into which a man was born was not simply a human society, a circle of kinfolk and fellow-citizens, but embraced also certain divine beings, the gods of the family and the state, which to the ancient mind were as much a part of the particular community with which they stood connected as the human members of the social group."[427] Any proposal to examine a group of customs, beliefs, and rites which at their origin take us back to the earliest history of a country must, therefore, be considered from the sociological side. The great mass of the material to be used in such an inquiry is not ancient so far as its date of record is a test of antiquity, but it is ancient as traditional survival, and it is not possible to trace back custom and belief surviving in modern times to the earliest times, except through the medium of the institutions which formed the social basis of the peoples to whom such custom and belief belonged. A custom or belief exists as a living force before it sinks back into the position of a survival. It is the lingering effect of this living force which helps to preserve it for so many ages, and in the midst of such adverse circumstances, as a survival among other customs and beliefs existing under a different living force. It is not possible, therefore, to ascertain the origin of custom or belief in survival, except as a fragment of the social institution to which it originally belonged. No custom or belief has a life of its own separate from all other. It is joined to other customs and beliefs in indissoluble co-partnership, the whole group making up the institutions under which the race or people to whom they belong live and flourish. This, as we have already seen, is a most important principle in the study of survivals. Not only is it strictly true of all primitive peoples, but it is true of the early stages of more advanced communities.[428] Indeed it has been put into a phrase used long ago by an English writer on the manorial tenant, "His religion is a part of his copyhold,"[429] and when the jurist talks to us in highly technical language of lords, freeholders, villans, and serfs, we must bear in mind that at any rate these villans and serfs belonged to a social institution, one element of which was religion. So, too, must the folklorist bear in mind that it is not the individual belief he is concerned with, but with the belief that belongs to a community. It must be assumed that the true test of the antiquity of every custom or belief is its natural and easy assimilation with other customs and beliefs, equally with itself in the position of a survival, and the recognition of the whole group thus brought into relationship as belonging to the institutions of the people from whom it is derived.

It is well to understand what this condition of things exactly means as an element in the study of early beliefs. It will be dealing with beliefs from their place in the social habitat; housing them, so to speak, within the groups of human beings with which they are connected. It will be considering them as part of the living organism which the social units of man have created. All this indicates a method of treating the subject entirely different from what has hitherto obtained. Students of early English institutions are content to construct elaborate arguments from the often conflicting testimony of historical authorities; students of early beliefs construct elaborate systems of religious thought far above the custom and rite with which they are dealing. The two branches of the same subject are never brought together to illustrate each other. Early institutions cannot be separated from early beliefs. Early beliefs cannot properly be separated from the society of which they form a component part. We require to know not only what beliefs a particular people possess, but in what manner these beliefs generate custom and rite and take their place among the influences which affect the social organism. Early man does not live individually. His life is part of a collective group. The group worships collectively as it lives collectively, and it is extremely important to work out the dual conditions. If the several items of custom and belief preserved by tradition are really ancient in their origin, they must be floating fragments, as it were, of an ancient *system* of custom and belief—the cultus of the people among whom they originated. This cultus has been destroyed, struggling unsuccessfully against foreign and more vigorous systems of religion and society. To be of service to history each floating fragment of ancient custom and belief must not only be labelled "ancient," but it must be placed back in the system from which it has been torn away. To do this is to a great extent to restore the ancient system; and to restore an ancient system of culture, even if the restoration be only a mosaic and a shattered mosaic, is to bring into evidence the people to which it belongs.

In the previous chapter it was necessary to lay somewhat special stress upon the system of social organisation known as totemism, which was not founded upon kinship. This was traced in survival among the pre-Celtic peoples of Britain. If we now turn to the Celts and Teutons of Britain we shall find that we have to deal with a social organisation founded definitely upon kinship; and if there are survivals of belief, custom, and rite, derived from this kinship system, existing side by side in the same culture area with survivals from the kinless system, it will be necessary to explain how two such opposite streams can have been kept flowing.

It is not difficult in the case of countries occupied by Celtic or Teutonic peoples to ascertain what the particular institution was which linked together the beliefs of the people, though it is not easy to trace out all the phases of it. It is the tribe—that system of society which appears as the means by which Greek and Roman, Celt and Teuton, Scandinavian and Slav,

233

Hindu and Persian, were able to conquer, overrun, and finally to settle in the lands which they have made their own. We know something of the Celtic tribe, less of the Teutonic tribe, but all we know is that it possesses features in common with the tribe of its kindred. There is no fact more certainly true as a result of comparative research than that the tribe is the common heritage of those people who have become the dominant rulers of the Indo-European world. I use this term "tribe" in no formal sense, not in the sense of its Roman derivation and use, which shows it quite as a secondary institution, but as the most convenient term to define that grouping of men with wives, families, and descendants, and all the essentials of independent life, which is found as a primal unit of European society in a state of unsettlement as regards land or country. The tie which bound all together was personal not local, kinship with a tribal god, kinship more or less real with fellow-tribesmen, kinship in status and rights. We meet with this tribal organisation everywhere in Indo-European history. It made movement from country to country possible. It made conquest possible. Celt and Teuton did not conquer in families any more than Greek or Hindu did. They conquered in tribes, and it was because of the strength of the tribal organisation during the period, first of migration and wandering and then of conquest, that the settlement after conquest was possible and was so strong. Everywhere we find these people conquerors and settlers. In India, in Iran, in Greece and Rome, in Scandinavia, in Celtic and Teutonic Europe, in Slavic Europe, they are moving tribes of conquerors come to settle and rule the people they conquer.[430] When Dr. Ridgeway asks whence came the Acheans,[431] he answers the question much in the same fashion as that in which Dr. Duncker describes the settlement on the Ganges:—

"The ancient population of the new states on the Ganges was not entirely extirpated, expelled, or enslaved. Life and freedom were allowed to those who submitted and conformed to the law of the conqueror; they might pass their lives as servants on the farms of the Aryas (Manu, i. 91). But though the remnant of this population was spared, the whole body of the immigrants looked down on them with the pride of conquerors—of superiority in arms, blood, and character—and in contrast to them they called themselves Vaiçyas, i.e. tribesmen, comrades, in other words those who belong to the community or body of rulers. Whether the Vaiçya belonged to

234

the order of the nobles, the minstrels and priests or peasants, was a matter of indifference, he regarded the old inhabitants as an inferior species of mankind.... In the new states on the Ganges therefore the population was separated into two sharply divided masses. How could the conquerors mix with the conquered? How could their pride stoop to any union with the despised servants?"[432]

These two divided masses thus so clearly described were, in fact, tribesmen and non-tribesmen, just that distinction which we meet with in Celtic and Teutonic law, and described in the same terms which Bishop Stubbs was obliged to use when he set forth the facts of the Teutonic invasion of Britain.

The terms are indeed necessary terms. Tribesmen capable of retaining the tribal organisation during the period of migration and conquest did not lightly lose that organisation when they settled. In Sir Alfred Lyall's pure genealogic clan of Central India[433] I recognise the unbroken tribal formation before the family group has arisen as a political unit. In Mr. Tupper's argument against the conclusions of Sir Henry Maine I recognise the Hindu evidence that the tribe was the earliest social group, breaking up, as later influences arose, into village communities and joint families.[434] In Bishop Stubbs's masterly analysis of English constitutional history the tribe appears at the outset—"the invaders," he says, "came in families and kindreds and in the full organisation of their tribes ... the tribe was as complete when it had removed to Kent as when it stayed in Jutland; the magistrate was the ruler of the tribe not of the soil; the divisions were those of the folk and the host not of the land; the laws were the usage of the nation not of the territory."[435] And so I agree with Mr. Skene as to the Celtic tribe that "the tuath or tribe preceded the fine or clan,"[436] and with the editors of the Irish law tracts that "the tribe existed before the family came into being and continued to exist after the latter had been dissolved "[437]

We need not go beyond this evidence. The tribe is the common form into which the early Indo-European peoples grouped themselves for the purpose of conquest and settlement. It was their primal unit. It may have been numerically large or small. It may have been the result of a combination of many smaller tribes into one great tribe. But in any case and under any conditions there stands out the tribal organisation, that great institutional force from which spring all later institutions. Its roots go back into the remotest past of Indo-European history; its active force caused the Indo-European people to become the mightiest in human history; its lasting results have scarcely yet ceased to shape the aspirations of political society and to affect the destinies of nations. The whole life of the early period was governed by tribal conditions—the political, social, legal, and even religious conceptions were tribal in form and expression.

The tribal institution of the Aryan-speaking peoples includes a life outside the tribe. That was an outlaw's life, a kinless outcast, whom no tribesman would look upon or assist, whom every tribesman considered as an enemy until he had reduced him to the position of helot or slave, but for whom every tribe had a place in its organisation and a legal status in its constitution. But it was the legal status imposed by the master over the servant, and the kinless included not only the outcast from the tribe, but the conquered aboriginal who had never been within the tribe. It is important to notice this, for it to some extent measures the strength of the tribal organisation. It not only allowed for a special position for all tribesmen, but it allowed for that position to have a definite relationship to persons who were not tribesmen, and it is in the combined forces of tribesmen and non-tribesmen that the tribal organisation which swept over part of Asia and over all Europe obtains its greatest power. There are tribal systems outside the Semitic and the Indo-European, but these do not have the distinctive features that the tribal systems of these two great civilising peoples possess. Like the Semitic and Aryan tribal systems, savage tribes are fashioned for conquest, but, unlike them, they are not fashioned for settlement and resettlement, and perhaps again and again conquest and resettlement. They spent all their power, or most of their power, in their one great effort of conquest, and whether we turn to the American Indian tribes, to the African tribes, or to the Asiatic tribes we find the same facts of frequent dissipation of power after sudden and complete conquest of it. The tribal system which led to civilisation has a different history. It has, too, a different constitution in that to the strength of tribesmen was added the subordination—politically, industrially, and economically—of non-tribesmen. They were the people who, in the terms of the northern poem,

"Laid fences, Enriched the plough lands, Tended swine, Herded goats, Dug peat."[438]

Unfortunately the institution of the tribe has never been properly studied by the great authorities in history, and students are left without guidance in this important matter. And yet in any attempt to get back to the earliest period of history in lands governed by an Aryan-speaking people we must proceed, can only proceed, on the basis of the tribe, and it is the failure to understand this which has made so much early history unsatisfactory and inconclusive and compels us to the conclusion that the master-hand is still needed to rewrite in terms of tribal history all that has been written in terms merely of political history.

If, however, history from the written records is thus at fault, so too is history from the traditional records. No systematic effort has been made to treat the traditional story or the traditional custom and belief as part of the tribal history of our race, and yet in the few cases where it has been so treated the results are obviously satisfactory. I can illustrate the value of this point of view by an example drawn from the period which witnessed the earliest struggles of our race. I think with Mr. Keary that in those German stories "which delight above all things in that portrait of the youngest son of the house—he is the youngest of three—who is left behind despised and neglected when his brothers go forth to seek their fortunes," we have traces of a veritable fact, of an historical condition where the elder sons actually went forth to conquest and to settlement and the youngest son remained in the original home as the hearth-child.[439] The position of hearth-child, surviving as it does in our law of Borough English, is of great significance, and that we can by the aid of tradition reach a state of society which gave birth to it is a point of the greatest importance, even if we could go no further. But there is a stage beyond it. The majority of these youngest-son stories relate to events not to be identified with any particular tribe or people, but which belong to all the tribes and peoples whose course of conquest and settlement took the common form. But if apart from these all-world stories there exist stories, or if there be but one story which has become identified with an episode, a person, or a place belonging to a particular people, we may claim it as part of the history of that particular people. It may be that the general story has become specialised in this one case, or it may be that an entirely new story has sprung out of the special case. But whichever be the origin of such a story attached to a particular people, it must tell us something of that people at a period when its history was being made rather than recorded. What it tells may be very little, may not lead up to anything very great or definite, so far as later history is concerned; but that for the period to which it belongs it relates to an episode worthy to have been kept in the memories of the descendants of the chief actors in the events is the point to bear in mind.

There is one such story which belongs to English history. One of the most famous of these youngest-son stories is that of Childe Rowland, and Mr. Jacobs, on examining its incidents and details, suggests that "our story may have a certain amount of historic basis and give a record which history fails to give of the very earliest conflict of races in these isles."[440] Mr. Jacobs gives good grounds for this conclusion, and shows up a picture of earliest English history which is certainly not contained elsewhere, and we are able by this means to pass from that large group of youngest-son stories, which have brought with them living testimony of an ancient institution of our race in its oldest home, to the narrower but more direct example which comes to us from events which happened just at the dawn of history in our own land. It is not necessary to emphasise the importance of this service to history at the instance of tradition, for it will be obvious to every student that many a struggle must have remained unrecorded and many a hero must have died unnamed in the events which belong to the period of tribal conquest and settlement. And to have still with us the far-off echo of these events is no slight encouragement to an inquiry which has for its object the reconstruction of the conditions under which such events took place.

This would be all the better understood if we could get a concrete case for illustration, and, fortunately, this is possible by turning to the evidence of India. "What we know of the manner in which the states of Upper India were founded," says Sir Alfred Lyall,

"gives a very fair sample of the movements and changes of the primitive world. When the dominant Rajput families lost their dominion in the rich Gangetic plains one part of their clan seems to have remained in the conquered country, having submitted to the foreigner, cultivating in strong communities of villages and federations of villages and paying such land tax as the ruler could extract. Another part of the clan, probably the near

238

kinsmen of the defeated chief, followed his family into exile, and helped him to carve out another, but a much poorer, dominion. Here the chief built himself a fort upon the hill; his clansmen slew or subdued the tribes they found in possession of the soil, and the lands were all parcelled off among the chief's kinsfolk, the indigenous proprietors being subjected to payment of a land tax, but not otherwise degraded. When the land grew too strait for the support of the chief's family or of the sept—that is, when there were no vacant allotments, a landless son of the chief would assemble a band, and set forth to make room for himself elsewhere."[441]

The evidence from India is fact, the evidence from England is tradition, and yet I do not think any student will deny that both fact and tradition are part and parcel of the same conditions of society, the same forces operating upon the same material. The conditions of society in both cases are tribal conditions, and the common factor having thus been discovered, it is possible to determine not only the inter-relationship between fact and tradition, but the means by which we may estimate the value of both.

We cannot, however, stop here. I carry on the same argument from the traditional legend to the traditional custom and belief, and affirm that it is only by their position as part of the tribal system that custom and belief in survival must be tested. If they have descended from early Celtic or Teutonic custom and belief, they have descended from tribal custom and belief, and somewhere in the stages of descent will be found the link which connects them definitely with the tribe. That not all custom and belief has so descended is due to the fact that much of it belongs to the pre-Celtic period, which was not tribal; some of it, no doubt, to comparatively modern times, when, as we have already seen, superstition had taken the place of thought, while some phases of early belief belong to conditions which transcend the division between pre-Aryan and Aryan folk. On this I will say something by way of explanation presently. In the meantime it is an extremely important task to classify survivals into tribal and non-tribal groups. Those which belong to Celtic or Teutonic origins must show their tribal origin, for they could not have come into existence apart from the tribe, and apart from the tribe they could not have survived after the break-up of the tribe consequent upon the development of national and political life. Custom and belief which do not fit into the ancient tribal system, therefore, cannot be recognised as ancient Celtic or ancient Teutonic custom and belief, and contrariwise when it is seen that they naturally fall into this system it may be argued that there we must search for their origin. Our Anglo-Saxon forefathers have left a curious testimony to this view of the question in their word "holy" or wholesome. What is wholesome is so for the whole group. The Anglo-Saxon idea of holiness implies as its chief element relation to the tribal life.[442]

The classification of survivals in folklore into tribal and non-tribal items is a lengthy and intricate process. Some years ago I made a start in a study of fire worship which I presented to the British Association,[443] and I hope shortly to be ready with a volume on *Tribal Custom*, which will embody a fuller study of fire worship and its accompanying beliefs, together with a complete study of all the remains of traditional custom, rite, and belief, which only as the detritus of the ancient tribal organisation receive adequate explanation of their presence in the midst of modern political and religious institutions. If I leave this part of my subject without further illustration in this present volume, I must add one important note upon the persistence of survivals of both kinless and kinship societies. I have shown that the tribal system of the advanced races included provision for non-tribesmen, provision which kept non-tribesmen outside the tribal bond, and at the same time kept them tied to the tribe by using them as the necessary dependent adjunct of the tribe, using them as bondmen and serfs in point of fact. This extremely important factor in the history of the tribal organisation, which has not been properly noticed by the few authorities who have investigated tribal institutions, receives additional importance when viewed from the standpoint of folklore, for it allows for the preservation of non-tribal cults side by side with tribal cults. Non-tribesmen preserved their custom, belief, and rite simply because they were not admitted to the custom, belief, and rite of the tribe, and this is the explanation of the existence, in survival, of folklore which goes back to pre-Celtic times. Some of this pre-Celtic folklore we have already had before us, and some of it I have studied in my *Ethnology in Folklore*. Later on I shall have something more to say on the subject. Here it is only necessary to emphasise the importance of having ascertained why it is that the Celtic conquerors of Britain and the earliest tribal conquerors of the Indo-European world generally permitted to live in their midst what in a sense was opposed to all that they believed, to all that they practised, to all that governed them in thought and action.

I think this is a strong position upon which to conduct folklore research. It includes the whole of the historical position; it takes due count of historical facts instead of ignoring them. It is based upon a scientific conception of the meaning of a survival of culture. A survival is that which has been left stranded amidst the development that is going on around. Its future life is not one of development but of decay. We are not dealing with the evolution of society, but with the decaying fragments of a social system which has passed away. We have to trace out its line of decay from the point where it almost vanishes as the mere superstition or practice of a peasant or an outcast, back to phases where it exists in more strenuous fashion, and finally back to its original position as part and parcel of a living social fabric. Moreover, the strength of our position is based upon a scientific conception of the development of the nation or people among whom survivals exist. It is not all parts of the nation which develop at the same rate, at the same time, and for the same period. There are social strata in every country, and it is the observance of these strata which has made it possible for the inquirer of to-day to use the evidence they afford for historical purposes.

FOOTNOTES:

[427] *Religion of the Semites*, 30. It is worth while quoting here Merivale's note in his Boyle lectures, *Conversion of the Northern Nations*, 122. "Pagan temples were always the public works of nations and communities. They were national buildings dedicated to national purposes. The mediæval churches, on the other hand, were the erection of individuals, monuments of personal piety, tokens of the hope of a personal reward." *Cf.* Stanley, *Hist. Westminster Abbey*, 12.

[428] Mr. Granger has a very instructive passage on this point in his *Worship of the Romans*, 210-214; *cf.* Robertson-Smith, *Religion of the Semites*, lec. ii.; Mr. MacDonald, *Africana*, i. 64, notes, too, that "the natives worship not so much individually as in villages or communities." Prof. Sayce, studying early religion, says in its outward form it "was made up of rites and ceremonies which could only be performed collectively."—*Science of Language*, ii. 290.

[429] Clarke's *Survey of the Lakes*, 36.

[430] Pritchard's *Researches into the Physical Hist. of Mankind*, vol. iii., may still be consulted for an account of the tribal movements in Europe.

[431] *Early Age of Greece*, i. cap. iv.

[432] *History of Antiquity*, iv. 116-17.

[433] *Asiatic Studies*, i. 173.

[434] *Punjab Customary Law*, ii. 3-59. *Cf.* Baden-Powell's *Indian Vill. Com.*, 230; Duncker, *Hist. Antiq.*, iv. 115-17.

[435] Stubbs's *Const. Hist.*, i. 64. *Cf. Essays in Anglo-Saxon Law*, 12.

[436] *Celtic Scotland*, iii. 137, note 4.

[437] *Anc. Laws of Ireland*, iv. p. 77. *Cf.* also Mr. Andrews' *Old English Manor*, p. 20, and Meyer, *Geschichte der Alterthums*, 2-3.

[438] Du Chaillu, *The Viking Age*, i. 488.

[439] Keary, *Origin of Primitive Belief*, 464-5. Mr. MacCulloch, *Childhood of Fiction*, devotes a chapter to the clever-youngest-son group of tales (cap. xiii.), which should be consulted.

[440] *Folklore*, ii. 194.

[441] Sir A. Lyall, *Asiatic Studies*, 184, and compare pp. 198, 208, 211.

[442] *Cf.* Granger, *Worship of the Romans*, 211. Mr. Granger uses terms which I do not quite accept, though his suggestion is entirely good in principle.

[443] *Report of British Association* (Liverpool Meeting).

Chapter VI

EUROPEAN CONDITIONS

There are obviously conditions attaching to European culture history which do not apply elsewhere, and as obviously the most important, perhaps the only important one, which it is necessary to consider in connection with the problems of folklore is that resulting from the introduction of a non-European religion and the adoption of this religion as part of the state machinery in the several countries. This religion is, of course, Christianity. It came into the home of a decaying, corrupt, and impossible state religion wherever the Roman Empire was established and into the homes of purer and sterner faiths, faiths that had belonged to the people through all the years of conquest and settlement, migration and resettlement, wherever the empire of Rome had not become established.

Until the advent of Christianity into Britain the Celtic peoples possessed their own customs, their own religious beliefs, their own usages. Until the Anglo-Saxons came into contact with Christianity in their new settlements in England, they also possessed their own customs, usages, and beliefs. So far as Celt and Teuton were responsible for continuing or allowing to continue the still older faiths, the faiths of savagery as we have accustomed ourselves to term them, they brought these faiths also into contact with Christianity, and Christianity dealt with the problem thus presented exactly as it dealt with the Celtic and Teutonic faiths, namely, by treating all alike as pagan, all equally to be set aside or used in any fashion that circumstances might demand. Let it be particularly noted that Christianity did not distinguish between the various shades of paganism. All that was not Christian was pagan.

Christianity was both antagonistic to and tolerant of pagan custom and belief. In principle and purpose it was antagonistic. In practice it was tolerant where it could tolerate safely. At the centre it aimed at purity of Christian doctrine, locally it permitted pagan practices to be continued under Christian auspices. In the earliest days it set itself against all forms of idolatry

243

and non-Christian practices; in later days, after the fifth century, says Gibbon,[444] it accepted both pagan practice and pagan ritual.

The relationship of Christianity to paganism is, therefore, a very complex subject, and it would not be possible in this place to work out one tithe of it. Nor is it needed. The two cardinal facts with which we are now concerned are the principle of antagonism and the practice of toleration. As to the former there need not be any discussion on the fact. Everywhere throughout Europe its effect is to be seen. It formed the most solid and systematic arresting force against the natural development of pagan belief and practice, and it is this fact of arrested development in pagan belief and practice which is of great importance. We can ascertain the point of stoppage, note the stage of arrested development, and trace out the subsequent history of a custom, belief, or rite so arrested. As a survival in a state of arrested development, a custom or belief is observable throughout its later history. All it does is to decay, and decay slowly, and each stage of decay may oftentimes be discovered. On the other hand, if no arrest of development had taken place there would have been no survival and no decay. The custom or belief which is not arrested by an opposing culture becomes a part of the religion or of the institutions of the nation, and the history of its development becomes, as a rule, lost in the general advance of religion and politics—custom develops into law, belief develops into religion, rite develops into ceremonial, and tradition ceases to be the force which keeps them alive. The two classes of custom and belief thus contrasted are of different value to the student. The one is important because it contains the germs and goes back to the origin of existing institutions. The other is important because, having been arrested by a strong opposing force, unable to destroy it altogether, it remains as evidence of custom and belief at the time of its arrestment. It will be seen at once how far this evidence may take us. It stretches back into the remotest past. It survives in the stage at which it was arrested, not of course in the form in which it then appeared, but in the decayed form which years of existence beneath the ever-opposing forces of the established civilisation must have brought about.

These opposing forces can be detected in working order. What can be more indicative of a dual system of belief than the cry of an old Scottish peasant when he came to worship at the sacred well?—"O Lord, Thou

244

knowest that well would it be for me this day an I had stoopit my knees and my heart before Thee in spirit and in truth as often as I have stoopit them afore this well. But we maun keep the customs of our fathers." It appears over and over again in the lives of early Christian saints who were only just parting from a living pagan faith. Thus St. Bega was the patroness of St. Bees in Cumberland, where she left a holy bracelet which was long an object of profound veneration; and in a prefatory statement by the compiler of a small collection of her miracles, written in the twelfth century, we learn among other things that whosoever forswore himself upon her bracelet swiftly incurred the heaviest punishment of perjury or a speedy death. It is to be observed that Beagas, the French Bague, is the Anglo-Saxon denomination for rings, and Dr. William Bell suggests that holy St. Bega was but a personification of one of the holy rings which, having gained great hold upon the minds of the heathen Cumbrians, it was not politic in their first Christian missionaries wholly to subvert.[445] These rings are, of course, the doom rings of the Scandinavian temples which are so often referred to in the Sagas.[446]

Baptism, an essentially Christian ceremony, might off-hand be supposed to contain nothing but evidence for Christianity. It might at most be expected that the details of the ceremony would contain relics of adapted pagan rites, and this we know is the case. But we can go beyond even this, and discover in the popular conception of the rite very clear indications of the early antagonism between Christianity and paganism—an antagonism which is certainly some eighteen hundred years old in this country, and though so old is still contained in the evidence of folklore.

An analysis of baptismal folklore shows us that its most important section is contained under the group which deals with the effect of non-baptism. In England we have it prevailing in the border counties, in Cornwall, Devonshire, Durham, Lancashire, Middlesex, Northumberland, and Yorkshire, and in North-East Scotland, that children joined the ranks of the fairies if they died unchristened, or that their souls wandered about in the air, restless and unhappy, until Judgment Day. Various penalties attended the condition of non-baptism, but perhaps the most significant is the Northumberland custom of burying an unbaptised babe at the feet of an adult Christian corpse—surely a relic of the old sacrifice at a burial which is indicated so frequently in the graves of prehistoric times, particularly of the long-barrow period. In Ireland we have the effect of non-baptism in a still more grim form. In the sixteenth century the rude Irish used to leave the right arms of their male children unchristened, to the intent that they might give a more ungracious and deadly blow.[447]

Rite of baptism on the font at Darenth, Kent (from Romilly Allen's "Early Christian Symbolism") **RITE OF BAPTISM, ON FONT AT DARENTH, KENT**

These, and their allied and variant customs, are relics, not so much of the absorption by Christian baptism of rites belonging to early paganism as of the struggle between Christianity and paganism for the mastery, of the anathemas of Christians against pagans, and of the terrible answer of the pagan. And what are we to say to it? Is it that the struggle itself has lasted all these centuries, or only its memory? My belief is that the struggle itself has lasted in reality though not in name.

But if we have been able to look through the very portals of Christianity to the regions of paganism behind, can we not boldly pass through altogether and recover from folklore much of the lost evidence of our prehistoric ancestors? I put the question in this way purposely, because it is the way which is indicated by the methods and data of folklore, and it is a question which has much to do with the different views held of the province of folklore.

I will answer by referring to the pre-baptismal rites of washing. In Northumberland we meet with the analogue of the sixteenth-century Irish practice, for there the child's right hand is left unwashed that it may gather riches better[448]—the golden coin taking the place of the ancient weapon in this as in other phases of civilisation. Not only is the water used for this purpose heated in the old-fashioned way by placing red-hot irons in it (*i.e.* the modern equivalent for stone-boiling), but in Yorkshire we have the custom that the newborn infant must be placed in the arms of a maiden before any

246

one else touches it, two practices represented exactly in the customs of the Canary Islanders, who were in the stone age of culture and are considered to be the last remnants of a race which once included Britain among its lands of occupation.[449]

The Rev. C. O'Connor, in his third letter of Columbanus, gives a very interesting statement of Irish well-worship in a letter addressed to his brother, the late Owen O'Connor Don, and which shows the living antagonism between Christian and pagan belief. He says:—

"I have often enquired of your tenants what they themselves thought of their pilgrimage to their wells of Kill Orcht, Tobbar-Brighde, Tobbar-Muire, near Elphin, and Moore, near Castlereagh, where multitudes assemble annually to celebrate what they, in broken English, termed Patterns; and when I pressed a very old man—Owen Hester—to state what possible advantage he expected to derive from the singular custom of frequenting in particular such wells as were contiguous to an old blasted oak, or an upright unhewn stone, and what the meaning was of the yet more singular custom of sticking rags in the branches of such trees and spitting on them, his answer, and the answer of the oldest men, was that their ancestors always did it; that it was a preservative against Geasa-Dravideacht, *i.e.* the sorceries of Druids; that their cattle was preserved by it from infectious disorders; that the davini maithe, *i.e.* the fairies, were kept in good humour by it; and so thoroughly persuaded were they of the sanctity of these pagan practices that they would travel bareheaded and barefooted from ten to twenty miles for the purpose of crawling on their knees round these wells and upright stones and oak trees westward as the sun travels, some three times, some six, some nine, and so on, in uneven numbers until their voluntary penances were completely fulfilled. The waters of Logh-Con were deemed so sacred from ancient usage that they would throw into the lake whole rolls of butter as a preservation for the milk of their cows against Geasa-Dravideacht."[450]

Scarcely less important than the effect of the antagonism of the Church in the production of arrested development is the effect of the toleration of the Church for pagan custom and belief. This toleration took the shape either of allowing the continuation of pagan custom and belief as a matter not affecting Christian doctrine or of actual absorption into Church practice and ritual. The story told to the full is a long and interesting one.

And it still awaits the telling. Gibbon, in a few sentences, has told us the outline.[451] Other authorities have told us small episodes. I am, of course, not concerned here with anything more than to adduce sufficient evidence to establish the fact that Christian tolerance of paganism has been one of the assistant causes for the long continuance of pagan survivals.

I shall not hesitate to begin by quoting at length a luminous passage from Grimm's great work. In the preface to his second edition he writes as follows:—

"Oftentimes the Church prudently permitted, or could not prevent, that heathen and Christian things should here and there run into one another; the clergy themselves would not always succeed in marking off the bounds of the two religions: their private leanings might let some things pass which they found firmly rooted in the multitude. In the language, together with a stock of newly-imported Greek and Latin terms, there still remained, even for ecclesiastical use, a number of Teutonic words previously employed in heathen services, just as the names of gods stood ineradicable in the days of the week; to such words old customs would still cling silent and unnoticed and take a new lease of life. The festivals of the people present a tough material: they are so closely bound up with its habits of life that they will put up with foreign additions if only to save a fragment of festivities long loved and tried. In this way Scandinavia, probably the Goths also for a time, and the Anglo-Saxons down to a late period, retained the heathenish Yule as all Teutonic Christians did the sanctity of Easter-tide; and from these two the Yule-boar and Yule-bread, the Easter pancake, Easter-sword, Easter-fire, and Easter-dance could not be separated. As faithfully were perpetuated the name and in many cases the observances of Midsummer. New Christian feasts, especially of saints, seem purposely, as well as accidentally, to have been made to fall on heathen holidays. Churches often rose precisely where a heathen god or his sacred tree had been pulled down, and the people trod their old paths to the accustomed site; sometimes the very walls of the heathen temple became those of the church, and cases occur in which idol images still found a place in a wall of the porch, or were set up outside the door, as at Bamberg Cathedral there lie Slavic heathen figures of animals inscribed with runes. Sacred hills and fountains were rechristened after saints, to whom their sanctity was transferred; sacred woods were handed over to the newly-founded convent or the king, and even under private ownership did not lose their long-accustomed homage. Law usages, particularly the ordeals and oath-takings, but also the beating of bounds, consecrations, image processions, spells and formulas, while retaining their heathen character, were simply clothed in Christian forms. In some customs there was little to change: the heathen practice of sprinkling a newborn babe with water closely resembled Christian baptism; the sign of the hammer, that of the cross; and the erection of tree crosses the irmensûls and world trees of paganism."[452]

This passage, written in 1844, has been abundantly illustrated by the research of specialists since that date, and, of course, Mr. Frazer's monumental work will occur to every reader. But, after all, the chief authority for the action of the Church towards paganism in this country is the famous letter of Pope Gregory to the Abbot Mellitus in A.D. 601, as preserved by the historian Beda. It is worth while quoting this once again, for it is an English historical document of priceless value. "We have been much concerned," writes the good St. Gregory,

"since the departure of our congregation that is with you, because we have received no account of the success of your journey. When, therefore, Almighty God shall bring you to the most reverend Bishop Augustine our brother, tell him what I have, upon mature deliberation on the affair of the English, determined upon, namely, that the temples of the idols [fana idolorum] in that nation [gente] ought not to be destroyed; but let the idols that are in them be destroyed; let holy water be made and sprinkled upon the said temples, let altars be erected and relics placed. For if these temples be well built, it is requisite that they be converted from the worship of devils [dæmonum] to the worship of the true God; that the nation seeing that their temples are not destroyed may remove error from their hearts, and knowing and adoring the true God may the more familiarly resort to the places to which they have been accustomed. And because they have been used to slaughter many oxen in the sacrifices to devils some solemnity must be exchanged for them on this account, so that on the day of the dedication, or the nativities of the holy martyrs whose relics are there deposited, they may build themselves huts of the boughs of trees, about those churches which have been turned to that use from temples and celebrate the solemnity with religious feasting and no more offer beasts to the devil [diabolo], but kill cattle to the praise of God in their eating, and return thanks to the giver of all things for their sustenance."[453]

The church of St. Pancras at Canterbury is claimed to be one of the temples so preserved,[454] and there have survived down to our own times examples of the animal sacrifice which in early Christian days may well have been preserved by this famous edict.[455] But beyond these illustrations of the two stated objects of Pope Gregory's letter there are innumerable additional results from such a policy,[456] results which prove that British pagandom was not stamped out by edict or by sword, but was rather gradually borne down before the strength of the new religion—borne down and pushed into the background out of sight of the Church and the State, relegated to the cottage homes, the cattle-sheds and the cornfields, the countryside and the denizens thereof.[457]

This is where we must search for it, and I think this important element in our studies will be better understood if we turn for one moment to the results of Christian contact with earlier belief in the one country where Christianity has set up its strongest political force, namely, Italy. Dr. Middleton wrote a series of remarkable letters which tell us much on this point, but before referring to this, I wish first to quote a hitherto buried record by an impartial observer[458] in the year 1704. It is a letter written from Venice to Sir Thomas Frankland, describing the travels and observations of a journey into Italy. The traveller writes:—

"I cannot leave Italy without making some general observations upon the country in general, and first as to their religion; it differs in name only now from what it was in the time of the ancient heathen Romans. I know this will sound very oddly with some sort of people, but compare them together and then let any reasonable man judge of the difference. The heathen Itallians had their gods for peace and for war, for plenty and poverty, for health and sickness, riches and poverty, to whom they addressed themselves and their wants; and the Christian Itallians have their patron saints for each of these things, to whom they also address according to their wants. The heathen sacrificed bulls and other beasts, and the Christian ones after the same manner a piece of bread, which a picture in the garden of Aldobrandina at Rome, painted in the time of Titus Vespasian, shews by the altar and the priests' vestments to have been the same as used now. The Pantheon at Rome was dedicated by the ancients to all the gods, and by the moderns to all the saints; the temple of Castor and Pollux at Rome is now dedicated to Cosmo and Damian, also twin brothers. The respect they pay to the Virgin Mary is far greater than what they pay to the Son, and whatever English Roman Catholics may be made to believe by their priests or impose upon us, it is certain that the devotion to the Madonnas in Italy is something more than a bare representation of the Virgin Mary when they desire her intercession. Miracles they pretend not only to be wrought by the Madonnas themselves, but there is far greater respect paid to a Madonna in one place than another, whereas if this statue were only a bare representation of the Virgin to keep them in mind of her, the respect would be equal. I visited all the famous ones, and it would fill a volume to tell you the fopperies that's said of them. That of Loretto, being what they say is the very house where the Virgin lived, is not to be described, the riches are so great, nor the devotion that's paid to the statue.... The Lady of Saronna is another famous one and very rich; she is much handsomer than she of Loretto and a whole church-full of the legend of the miracles she hath wrought. She is in great reputation, and it's thought will at last outtop the Lady of Loretto; there is another near Leghorne that I also visited called *La Madonna della Silva Nera*, to whom all Itallian ships that enter that port make a present of thanks for their happy voyage, and salute her with their cannon, and most ships going out give her something for her protection during their voyage. I could tire you with she at the Annunciata at Florence, she within a mile of Bollognia, for whom the magistracy have piazza'd the road all the way from her station to the city, that she may not be encumbered with sun or rain when she makes them a visit, and hundreds more that would fill a volume of fopperies that I had the curiosity to see, but it would be imposing too much upon your patience."[459]

This only confirms Dr. Middleton's conclusions, which received the approval of Gibbon, and those of later writers. 'As I descended from the Alps," writes the Rev. W. H. Blunt in 1823,

"I was admonished of my entrance into Italy by a little chapel to the Madonna, built upon a rock by the roadside, and from that time till I repassed this chain of mountains I received almost hourly proof that I was wandering amongst the descendants of that people which is described by Cicero to have been the most religious of mankind. Though the mixture of religion with all the common events of life is anything but an error, yet I could not avoid regretting that, like their heathen ancestors, the modern Italians had supplied the place of our great master mover by a countless host of inferior agents."[460]

Mr. Blunt goes on to give interesting details of the close connection between the modern religious festival, ceremony, or service, and those of classical times, and the conclusion is obvious. In modern days Dr. Mommsen has lent the sanction of his great authority to the identification of the birthday of Christ with that of Mithra,[461] and Mr. Leland has given such numerous identifications not only of the cults of pagan and Christian Italy, but of the god-names of ancient Rome with the saint-names or witch-names of modern times,[462] that it seems impossible to deny a place for this evidence. "It was," says Gibbon,

"the universal sentiment both of the Church and of heretics that the dæmons were the authors, the patrons, and the objects of idolatry; those rebellious spirits who had been degraded from the rank of angels were still permitted to roam upon earth, to torment the bodies and to seduce the minds of sinful men. It was confessed, or at least it was imagined, that they had distributed among themselves the most important characters of Polytheism, one dæmon assuming the name of Jupiter, another of Æsculapius, a third of Venus, and a fourth perhaps of Apollo."[463]

This, then, is recognition and adoption of pagan beliefs, not the uprooting of them. If the Roman Jupiter was a Christian dæmon, his existence at all events was recognised. But even this negative way of adopting the old beliefs gave way as the Church spread further. The tribe of dæmons soon included the popular fairy, elf, and goblin. And then came the positive adoption of pagan customs. Gibbon describes how the early Christians refused to decorate their doors with garlands and lamps, and to take part in the ceremonial of lifting the bride over the threshold of the house.[464] Both these customs have survived in popular folklore, in spite of the recorded action of the early Church, and it would be curious to ascertain whether they have survived by the help of the Church. We cannot answer that question of historical evidence just now, but it is a question which, in its wider aspect, as including many other items of folklore, ought to be examined into. There is no doubt, however, that by analogy it can be answered, because we have ample evidence, if the writings of reformers may be taken as historical facts and not polemical imaginations, that many very important customs, among the richest as well as the poorest treasures of folklore, have been, so to speak, Christianised by the Church, and that the Church has taken part in and adopted non-Christian customs, the survivors of olden-time life in Europe.[465]

Now it is clear from these considerations, and from the vast mass of information which is gradually being accumulated on the subject, that not only the arresting force of Christianity but also its toleration has assisted in the preservation of pre-Christian belief and custom. But the preservation has been in fragments only. The system which supported the older faith and might, if it had been allowed a natural growth, have produced a newer religion of its own, was completely shattered. It left no preservative force except that of tradition, the traditional instinct to do what has always been done, to believe what has always been believed. Pre-Christian belief and custom has thus become isolated beliefs and customs in survival. It has been broken up into innumerable fragments of unequal character, and containing unequal elements. It has been forced back into secret action wherever Christianity was wholly antagonistic, and hence primitive public worship has tended to become local worship, or household worship, or even personal worship, while all such worship which is not the authorised Church worship has tended to become superstition. Where Christianity was not wholly antagonistic, it absorbed rites, customs, and even beliefs, and these primitive survivals have taken their place in the evolution of Christian doctrine, and thus become lost to the students of Celtic and Teutonic antiquities. But even so, there are discoverable points where the dividing line between non-Christian and Christian belief has not been obliterated by the process of absorption. In all cases it is the duty of the student to note the stage of arrested development in the primitive rite, custom, or belief, whether it be caused by antagonism or by absorption. It is at this point, indeed, that the history of the survival begins. It is here that we have to turn from the polity, the religion, or cultus of a people to the belief, practices, or superstition of that portion of our nation which has not shared its progress from tribesmen

253

to citizens, from paganism to Christianity, from vain imaginings to science and philosophy. It is from this point we have to turn from the dignity of courts, the doings of armies, and the results of commerce, to the doings, sayings, and ideas of the peasantry who cannot read, and who have depended upon tradition for all, or almost all, they know outside the formalities of law and Church.

FOOTNOTES:

[444] *Decline and Fall of the Roman Empire* (Bury), iii. 214-15.

[445] *Royal Irish Academy*, viii. 258; *Brit. Arch. Assoc.* (Gloucester volume), 62.

[446] "The Story of the Ere Dwellers," Morris, *Saga Library*, ii. 8.

[447] Camden, *Britannia*, s.v. "Ireland."

[448] Henderson, *Folklore of Northern Counties*, 16.

[449] Glas, *Canary Islands*, 148.

[450] Betham, *Gael and Cymbri*, pp. 236-8.

[451] *Decline and Fall*, iii. p. 214 (edit. Bury).

[452] Grimm, *Teutonic Mythology*, by Stallybrass, iii. pp. 35, 36. A passage from Hakon's Saga, quoted by Du Chaillu in his *Viking Age*, i. p. 464, shows that the northern peoples adopted the same measures.

[453] Beda, lib. i. cap. 30; and consult Mr. Plummer's learned notes on this (vol. ii. 57-61).

[454] Stanley, *Memorials of Canterbury*, 37-38.

[455] *Cf.* my *Ethnology in Folklore*, 30-36, 136-140. Compare St. Patrick's dedication of pagan sacred stones to Christian purposes.—*Tripartite Life of St. Patrick*, i. 107.

[456] Thus Henry of Huntingdon records that Redwald, King of the East Angles, after his conversion to Christianity, "set up altars to Christ and the devil in the same chapel" (lib. iii.).

[457] *Cf.* Kemble, *Saxons in England*, i. 330-335. Dr. Hearn writes: "Even as the good Pope Gregory the Great permitted the newly converted English to retain their old temples and accustomed rites, attaching, however, to them another purpose and a new meaning, so his successors found means to utilize the simple beliefs of early animism. Long and vainly the Church struggled against this irresistible sentiment. Fifteen centuries ago it was charged against the Christians of that day that they appeased the shades of the dead with feasts like the Gentiles. In the Penitentials we find the prohibition of burning grains where a man had died. In the *Indiculus superstitionum et Paganiarum* among the Saxons complaint is made of the too ready canonisation of the dead; and the Church seems to have been much

255

troubled to keep within reasonable bounds this tendency to indiscriminate apotheosis. At length a compromise was effected, and the Feast of All Souls converted to pious uses that wealth of sentiment which previously was lavished on the dead" (*The Aryan Household*, p. 60). And, to close this short note upon an important subject, Mr. Metcalfe, speaking of the old poetic literature of the pagan English, says: "It was kidnapped, and its features so altered and disguised as not to be recognisable. It was supplanted by Christian poetical legends and Bible lays produced in rivalry of the popular lays of their heathen predecessors. Finding that the people would listen to nothing but these old lays, the missionaries affected their spirit and language, and borrowed the words and phrases of heathenism" (Metcalfe's *Englishman and Scandinavian*, p. 155).

[458] For some reason not apparent in the document itself, Mrs. S. C. Lomas, the editor of this report, says this interesting letter gives "a curious and evidently prejudiced description of the religious houses and observances." See preface to *Hist. MSS. Com. Report on the MSS. of Chequers Court, Bucks*, p. x.

[459] *Hist. MSS. Com., Chequers Court Papers*, pp. 171-2.

[460] *Vestiges of Ancient Manners and Customs in Italy*, p. 1.

[461] *Corpus insc. Lat.*, i. 409; and *cf.* Cumont's *Mysteries of Mithra* (1903).

[462] Leland, *Etruscan Roman Remains* (1892).

[463] *Decline and Fall of the Roman Empire* (Bury), ii. 15.

[464] *Decline and Fall*, ii. 17.

[465] Evidence is scattered far and wide in most of the reliable studies in folklore. Two special books may be mentioned. A great storehouse of examples is to be found in *The Popish Kingdoms*, by Thomas Naogeorgus, Englyshed by Barnabe Googe, 1570, a new edition of which was published by Mr. R. C. Hope in 1880; and Mr. H. M. Bower has exhaustively examined one important Italian ceremony in his *The Elevation and Procession of the Ceri at Gubbio*, published by the Folklore Society in 1897.

Chapter VII

ETHNOLOGICAL CONDITIONS

Already I have had to point out that an appeal to ethnological evidence is the means of avoiding the wholesale rejection of custom and belief recorded of early Britain, because it has been rejected as appertaining to the historic Celt. I will now proceed with the definite proposition that the survivals in folklore may be allocated and explained by their ethnological bearing.

Some years ago I advanced this proposition in my little book entitled *Ethnology in Folklore*. Only haltingly have my conclusions been accepted, but I nowhere find them disproved,[466] while here and there I find good authorities appealing to the ethnological element in folklore to help them in their views. Mr. MacCulloch, for instance, prefers to go for the basis of the Osiris and Dionysius myths to an earlier custom than that favoured by Mr. Frazer and Mr. Grant Allen, namely, to the practices of the neolithic folk, in Egypt and over a wide tract of country which includes Britain, of dismembering the dead body previous to its burial.[467] Mr. Lang, Mr. Frazer, Mr. Hartland, and others are strangely reticent on this subject. That Mr. Lang should be content to trace a story from the Vedas, in which Urvasi tells Pururavas that he must never let her see him naked, to "a traditional Aryan law of nuptial etiquette,"[468] seems to be using the heaviest machinery for the smallest purposes, while for other and greater purposes he fails to find in ethnological distinctions, explanations which escape his research.[469] That Mr. Frazer should have been able to examine in so remarkable a manner the agricultural rites of European peoples, and only to have touched upon their ethnological bearings in one or two isolated cases, seems to me to be neglecting one of the obvious means of arriving at the solution of the problem he starts out to solve.[470]

I do not want to discount these fragmentary appeals to the ethnological element in folklore. I accept them as evidence that the appeal has to be made. I would only urge that it may be done on more thorough lines, after due consideration of all the elements of the proposition and of all that it means to the study of folklore. We cannot surrender to the palæontologist all that folklore contains in tradition and in custom as to pygmy peoples, or to the Egyptologist all that it contains as to dismemberment burial rites, without at the same time realising that if it is correct to refer these two groups of folklore respectively to the earliest ages of man's existence as man and to the neolithic stage of culture, they must be withdrawn from all other classification. We cannot use the same items of folklore in two totally different ways. The results of withdrawal are as important as the results of allocation, and the necessity for the correct docketing of all groups of folklore is thus at once illustrated.

The first point in the argument for ethnological data being discoverable in folklore is that a survey of the survivals of custom, belief, and rites in any given country shows one marked feature, which results in a dividing line being drawn as between two distinct classes. This feature is the antagonism which is discoverable in these classes. On one side of the dividing line is a set of customs, beliefs, and rites which may be grouped together because they are consistent with each other, and on the other side is another set of customs, beliefs, and rites which may be grouped together on the same ground. But between these two sets of survivals there is no agreement. They are the negations of each other. They show absolutely different conceptions of all the phases of life and thought which they represent, and it is impossible to consider that they have both come from the same culture source. I have applied the test of ethnology to such cases in Britain, and this appears to answer the difficulty which their antagonism presents. It appears too to be the only answer.

The subjects which show this antagonism are all of vital importance. They include friendly and inimical relations with the dead; marriage as a sacred tribal rite and marriage as a rule of polyandrous society; birth ceremonies which tell of admittance into a sacred circle of kinsmen, and birth ceremonies which breathe of revenge and hostility; the reverential treatment of the aged folk and the killing of them off; the preservation of human life as part of the tribal blood, and human sacrifice as a certain cure for all personal evils; the worship of waters as a strongly localised cult, preserved because it is local by whatsoever race or people are in occupation and in successive occupation of the locality; totemic beliefs connected with animals and plants contrasted with ideas entirely unconnected with totemism—all this, and much more which has yet to be collected and classified, reveals two distinct streams of thought which cannot by any process be taken back to one original source.

This fact of definite antagonism between different sets of surviving beliefs existing together in one country leads to several very important conclusions. This is the case with the Irish Sids. These beings are said to be scattered over Ireland, and around them assembled for worship the family or clan of the deified patron. While there were thus a number of topical deities, each in a particular spot where he was to be invoked, the deities themselves with the rest of their non-deified but blessed brother spirits had as their special abode "Lands of the Living," the happy island or islands somewhere far away in the ocean. Now this Sid worship, we are told by Irish scholars, "had nothing to do with Druidism—in fact, was quite opposed to it," the Sids and the Druids being "frequently found at variance with each other in respect to mortals."[471]

This is the commencing point of the evidence which proves Druidism to have belonged to the pre-Celtic people, though finding an adopted home among them. This is so important a subject and has been so strangely and inconsistently dealt with by most authorities that it will be well to indicate where we have to search for the non-Celtic, and therefore pre-Celtic, origin of Druidism. The Druidism revealed by classical authorities is, for the most part, the Druidism of continental peoples and not of Britain, and I hesitate to accept off-hand that it is proper to transfer the continental system to Britain and say that the two systems were one and the same. There is certainly no evidence from the British side which would justify such a course, and I think there is sufficient argument against it to suspend judgment until the whole subject is before us. If Professor Rhys is right in concluding that Druidism is at its roots a non-Celtic religion,[472] we must add to this that it was undoubtedly a non-Teutonic religion. Celts and Teutons were sufficiently near in all the elements of their civilisation for this want of parallel in their relationship to Druidism to be an additional argument against the Celts having originated this cult. And then the explanation of the differences between continental and British Druidism becomes comparatively easy to understand. The continental Celts, mixing more thoroughly with the pre-Celtic aborigines than did the British Celts, would have absorbed more of the pre-Celtic religion than the British Celts, and hence all the details which classical authorities have left us of continental Druidism appear as part of the Celtic religion, while in Britain these details are for the most part absent. But this is not all. There are certain rites in Britain noted by the early authorities which are not attached to any particular cult. They are not Druidic; they are not Celtic. They are, as a matter of fact, special examples of rites practised in only one locality, and accordingly referred to as something extraordinary and not general. From this it is clearly correct to argue that the British Celts had in their midst a cult which, if they did not destroy, they certainly did not absorb, and that therefore this cult being non-Celtic must have been pre-Celtic.

I do not wish to argue this point out further than is necessary to explain the position which, it appears to me, Druidism occupies, and I will therefore only add a note as to the authorities for the statements I have advanced. The differences between continental and British Druidism are definite and pronounced,[473] the mixture of the continental Celts with the Iberic people, which they displaced, is attested, by ancient authority and modern anthropology,[474] while the only evidence of such a mixture in Britain is the prominently recorded instance of the Picts intermarrying with the Gael,[475] and this has to be set against the close distinction between tribesmen and non-tribesmen, which is such a remarkable feature of Celtic law;[476] the existence of local cults in early Britain having all the characteristics of a ruder and more savage origin, and not identified with Celticism, is a point derived from our early authorities.[477] These are the main facts of the case, and the subject has to be worked out in considerable detail before it can be settled.

There is one other primary subject which bears upon the question of race distinctions in folklore. With the fact of conquest to reckon with, the relationship of the conqueror to the conquered is a matter to consider. In the European tribal system it was a definite relationship, so definite that the conquered, as we have seen, formed an essential part of the tribal organisation—the kinless slaves beneath the tribal kindred. There was a place for the kinless in the tribal economy and in the tribal laws. There was also a

260

place for them in the tribal system of belief, and the mythic influence of the conquered is a subject that needs very careful consideration.

It is an influence which appears in all parts of the world. Thus, to give a few instances, in New Guinea they have no idols, and apparently no idea of a supreme being or a good spirit. Their only religious ideas consist in a belief in evil spirits. They live a life of slavish fear to these, but seem to have no idea of propitiating them by sacrifice or prayer. They believe in the deathlessness of the soul. A death in the village is the occasion of bringing plenty of ghosts to escort their new companion, and perhaps fetch some one else. All night the friends of the deceased sit up and keep the drums going to drive away the spirits; they strike the fences and posts of houses all through the village with sticks. This is done to drive back the spirits to their own quarters on the adjacent mountain tops. But it is the spirits of the inland tribes, the aborigines of the country, that the coast tribes most fear. They believe, when the natives are in the neighbourhood, that the whole plain is full of spirits who come with them. All calamities are attributed to the power and malice of these evil spirits. Drought, famine, storm and flood, disease and death are all supposed to be brought by Vata and his hosts, so that the people are an easy prey to any designing individuals who claim power over these. Some disease charmers and rain-makers levy heavy toll on the people.[478]

It appears that the native population of New Zealand was originally composed of two different races, which have retained some of their characteristic features, although in course of time they have in all other respects become mixed, and a number of intermediate varieties have thence resulted. From the existence of two races in New Zealand the conclusion might be drawn that the darker were the original proprietors of the soil anterior to the arrival of a stock of true Polynesian origin, that they were conquered by the latter and nearly exterminated There is a district in the northern island, situated between Taupo and Hawke's Bay, called Urewera, consisting of steep and barren hills. The scattered inhabitants of this region have the renown of being the greatest witches in the country. They are very much feared, and have little connection with the neighbouring tribes, who avoid them if possible. If they come to the coast the natives there scarcely venture to refuse them anything for fear of incurring their displeasure. They are said to use the saliva of the people whom they intend to bewitch, and visitors carefully conceal their spittle to give them no opportunity of working their evil. Like our witches and sorcerers of old, they appear to be a very harmless people, and but little mixed up with the quarrels of their neighbours.[479] The Australians, according to Oldfield, ascribe spirit powers to those residing north of themselves and hold them in great dread.[480]

In Asia the same idea prevails among the native races. Thus Colquhoun says,

"it was amusing to find the dread in which the Lawas [a hill tribe] are held by both Burmese and Siamese. This is due to a fear of being bitten by them and dying of the bite. They are called by their Burmese neighbours the 'man-bears.' A singular custom obtains amongst these people which may perhaps partly account for this superstition. On a certain night in the year the youths and maidens meet together for the purpose of pairing. Unacceptable youths are said to be bitten severely if they make advances to the ladies."[481]

The Semang pygmy people, afraid to approach the Malays even for purposes of barter, "learnt to work upon the superstition of the Malays by presenting them with medicines which they pretended to derive from particular shrubs and trees in the woods."[482] That this is a real superstition of the conquerors for the conquered is proved from other sources to which I have referred elsewhere.[483]

In Africa it appears as a living force, and we are told that the stories current in the country of the Ukerewé, "about the witchcraft practised by the people of Ukara island, prove that those islanders have been at pains to spread abroad a good repute for themselves; that they are cunning, and aware that superstition is a weakness of human nature have sought to thrive upon it."[484]

It appears in more definite form with the Hindus. The Kathkuri, or Katodi, have a belief that they are descended from the monkeys and bears which Adi Narayun in his tenth incarnation of Rama, took with him for the destruction of Rawun, King of Lanka, and he promised his allies that in the fourth age they should become human beings. They practise incantation, and encourage the awe with which the Hindu regards their imprecations, for a Hindu believes that a Katodi can transform himself into a tiger.[485]

To this day the Aryans settled in Chota-Nagpore and Singbhoom firmly believe that the Moondahs have powers as wizards and witches, and can transform themselves into tigers and other beasts of prey with the view of devouring their enemies, and that they can witch away the lives of man and beast. They were in all probability one of the tribes that were most persistent in their hostility to the Aryan invaders.[486] In Ceylon the remnants of the aborigines are found in the forests and on the mountains, and are universally looked upon and feared as demons, the beliefs engendered therefrom being exactly parallel to the witch beliefs of our own country.[487]

There is similar evidence among European peoples. Formerly in Sweden the name of Lapp seems to have been almost synonymous with that of sorcerer, and the same was the case with Finn. The inhabitants of the southern provinces of Sweden believed their countrymen in the north to have great experience in magic.[488] The famous Gundhild, of Saga renown, was believed to be a sorceress brought up among the Finns,[489] and even in respect of classical remains Mr. Warde Fowler "prefers to think of the Fauni as arising from the contact of the first clearers and cultivators of Italian soil with a wild aboriginal race of the hills and woods."[490]

These facts are sufficient to show that the mythic influence of a conquered race is a factor which may assist in the discussion of the ethnological conditions of folklore, and it is obvious that they reveal a very powerful influence for the continuance of ancient ideas as well as for the creation of fresh examples of ancient ideas applied to new experiences. It is well in this connection to remember certain historical facts connected with the settlement of the English in Britain.

From Freeman's *Old English History* it appears that at the beginning of the seventh century "the tract of country which the English then ruled over south of the Humber, coincided almost exactly with the boundary of the Gaulish portion of Britain," as distinct from non-Aryan Britain. This apparent recognition of Celtic landmarks, says Professor Rhys, by the later invaders, "is a fact, the historical and political significance of which I leave to be weighed by others,"[491] and I venture to suggest that one important result is to show Britain to have contained an Aryan culture-ground and a non-Aryan culture-ground. If we try to step from one to the other we quickly discover the mythic relationship of conqueror to the conquered.

A scene from the Anglo-Saxon life of St. Guthlac by Felix of Crowland, depicting the attack of the demons **SCENE FROM THE LIFE OF ST. GUTHLAC SHOWING THE ATTACKS OF THE DÆMONES**

Thus in the Anglo-Saxon life of St. Guthlac we have an interesting glimpse into the conditions of the country and the attitude of the two hostile races, Celts and Teutons, to each other.

"There is in Britain a fen of immense size which begins from the river Granta, not far from the city, which is named Grantchester ... a man named Tatwine said that he knew an island especially obscure, which ofttimes many men had attempted to inhabit, but no man could do it on account of manifold horrors and fears, and the loneliness of the wild wilderness.... No man ever could inhabit it before the holy man Guthlac came thither on account of the dwelling of the accursed spirits there.... There was on the island a great mound raised upon the earth, which same of yore men had dug and broken up in hopes of treasure.... Then in the stillness of the night it happened suddenly that there came great hosts of the accursed spirits, and they filled the house with their coming, and they poured in on every side from above and beneath and everywhere. They were in countenance horrible, and they had great heads and a long neck and lean visage; they were filthy and squalid in their beards, and they had rough ears and distorted face, and fierce eyes and foul mouths: and their teeth were like horses' tusks, and their throats were filled with flame, and they were grating in their voice: they had crooked shanks and knees, big and great behind, and distorted toes, and shrieked hoarsely with their voices, and they came with such immoderate noises and immense horror that it seemed to him that all between heaven and earth resounded with their dreadful cries. Without delay, when they were come into the house, they soon bound the holy man in all his limbs, and they pulled and led him out of the cottage and brought him to the black fen and threw and sunk him in the muddy waters. After that they brought him to the wild places of the wilderness, among the dense thickets of brambles that all his body was

264

torn. After they had a long time thus tormented him in darkness they let him abide and stand awhile, then commanded him to depart from the wilderness, or if he would not do so they would torment and try him with greater plagues."[492]

These doings are not sufficiently remote from sober fact for us to be unable to detect human enemies in the supposed beings of the spirit world, and this conclusion is confirmed by a later passage in the same narrative describing Guthlac awakened from his sleep and hearing "a great host of the accursed spirits speaking in British [bryttisc] and he knew and understood their words because he had been erewhile in exile among them."[493] Guthlac in England is only experiencing what other saints experienced elsewhere,[494] and we cannot doubt we have in these reminiscences of saintly experience that mixture of fact with traditional belief which would follow the priests of the new religions from their native homes to the cell.

It is necessary to consider another great element in human life with reference to its ethnological value, for folklore has always been intimately associated with it, and recently, owing to Mr. Frazer's brilliant researches, this branch of folklore has been almost unduly accentuated. I mean, of course, agriculture. Mr. Frazer has ignored the ethnological side of agriculture, and it has been appropriated by the student of economics as a purely historical institution. This has caused a special position to be given to agricultural rites and customs almost without question and certainly without examination, and it will be necessary to go rather closely into the subject in order to clear up the difficulties which present neglect has produced. I shall once again draw my illustrations from the British Isles.

A scene from the Anglo-Saxon life of St. Guthlac by Felix of Crowland, depicting the attack of the demons **SCENE FROM THE LIFE OF ST. GUTHLAC SHOWING THE ATTACKS OF THE DÆMONES**

I put my facts in this way: (1) In all parts of Great Britain there exist rites, customs, and usages connected with agriculture which are obviously and admittedly not of legislative or political origin, and which present details exactly similar to each other in *character*, but differing from each other in *status*; (2) that the difference in status is to be accounted for by the effects of successive conquests; (3) that the identity in character is not to be accounted for by reference to manorial history, because the area of manorial institutions is not coincident with the area of these rites, customs, and usages; (4) that exact parallels to them exist in India as integral portions of village institutions; (5) that the Indian parallels carry the subject a step further than the European examples because they are stamped with the mark of difference in race-origin, one portion belonging to the Aryan people and the other to the non-Aryan.

I shall now pick out some examples, and explain from them the evidence which seems to me to prove that race-distinction is the key for the origin of these agricultural rites and usages in Europe as in India. I have dealt with these examples at some length in my book on the village community, and I shall only use such details as I require for my immediate purpose.

My first point is that to get at the survivals of the village community in Britain it is not necessary to approach it through the medium of manorial history. Extremely ancient as I am inclined to think manorial history is, it is unquestionably loaded with an artificial terminology and with the chains so deftly forged by lawyers. An analysis of the chief features in the types of the English village community shows that the manorial element is by no means a common factor in the series. These types mark the transition from the tribal form to the village form. In Harris Island we have the chief with his free tribesmen around him, connected by blood kinship, living in scattered homesteads, just like the German tribes described by Tacitus. Under this tribal community is the embryo of the village community, consisting of smaller tenantry and cottar serfs, who live together in minute villages, holding their land in common and yearly distributing the holdings by lot. In this type the tribal constitution is the real factor, and the village constitution the subordinated factor as yet wholly undeveloped, scarcely indeed discernible except by very close scrutiny.

At Kilmorie the tribal community is represented merely by the scattered homesteads. These are occupied by a joint farm-tenantry, who hold their lands upon the system of the village community. Here the village

266

constitution has gradually entered into, so to speak, the tribal constitution, and has almost absorbed it.

At Heisgier and Lauder the tribal community is represented by the last link under the process of dissolution, namely, the free council of the community by which the village rights are governed, while the village community has developed to a considerable extent.

At Aston and at Malmesbury the old tribal constitution is still kept alive in a remarkable manner, and I will venture to quote from my book the account of the evolution at Aston of a tenantry from the older tribal constitution, because in this case we are actually dealing with a manor, and the evidence is unique so far as England is concerned.

The first point is that the village organisation, the rights of assembly, the free open-air meetings, and the corporate action incident to the manor of Aston and Cote, attach themselves to the land divisions of sixteen hides, because although these hides had grown in 1657 into a considerable tenancy, fortunately as a tenancy they kept their original unity in full force and so obstinately clung to their old system of government as to keep up by *representation* the once undivided holding of the hide. If the organisation of the hide had itself disappeared, it still formed the basis of the village government, the sixteen hides sending up their sixteen *elected* representatives. How the tenancy grew out of the original sixteen homesteads may perhaps be conjecturally set forth. In the first place the owners of the yard-lands succeeded to the place originally occupied by the owners of the sixteen hides. Instead of the original sixteen group-owners we have therefore sixty-four individual owners, each yard-land having remained in possession of an owner. And then at succeeding stages of this dissolution we find the yard-lands broken up until, in 1848, "some farmers of Aston have only half or even a quarter of a yard-land, while some have as many as ten or eleven yard-lands in their single occupation." Then disintegration proceeded to the other proprietary rights, which, originally appendant to the homestead only, became appendant to the person and not to the residence, and are consequently "bought and sold as separate property, by which means it results that persons resident at Bampton, or even at great distance, have rights on Aston and Cote Common." And finally we lose all trace of the system, as described by Mr. Horde and as depicted by the representative character of the Sixteens, and in its place find that "there are some tenants who have rights in the common field and not in the pasture, and *vice versâ* several occupiers have the right of pasture who do not possess any portion of arable land in the common field," so that both yard-lands and hides have now disappeared, and absolute ownership of land has taken their place. Mr. Horde's MS. enables us to proceed back from modern tenancy-holding to the holding by yard-lands; the rights of election in the yard-lands enable us to proceed back to the original holding of the sixteen hides.

At Hitchin, which is Mr. Seebohm's famous example, we meet with the manorial type. But its features are in no way peculiar. There is nothing which has not its counterpart, in more or less well-defined degree, in the other types which are not manorial. In short, the manorial framework within which it is enclosed does little more than fix the details into an immovable setting, accentuating some at the expense of others, legalising everything so as to bring it all under the iron sovereignty which was inaugurated by the Angevin kings.

My suggestion is that these examples are but varying types of one original. The Teutonic people, and their Celtic predecessors, came to Britain with a tribal, not an agricultural, constitution. In the outlying parts of the land this tribal constitution settled down, and was only slightly affected by the economical conditions of the people they found there; in the more thickly populated parts this tribal constitution was superimposed upon an already existing village constitution in full vigour. We, therefore, find the tribal constitution everywhere—in almost perfect condition in the north, in Wales, and in Ireland; in less perfect condition in England. We also find the village constitution everywhere—in almost embryo form in the north, Wales, and in Ireland; in full vigour and force in England, especially in that area which, as already noted, has been identified as the constant occupation-ground of all the races who have settled in Britain.

Now the factor which is most apparent in all these cases is the singular dual constitution which I have called tribal and village. It is only when we get to such cases as Rothwell and Hitchin that almost all traces of the tribal element are lost, the village element only remaining. But inasmuch as this village element is identical in *kind*, if not in degree, with the village element in the other types, and inasmuch as topographically they are closely connected, we are, I contend, justified in concluding that it is derived from the same original—an original which was composed of a tribal community with a village community in serfdom under it.

This dual element should, I think, be translated into terms of ethnology by appealing to the parallel evidence of India. There the types of the village community are not, as was thought by Sir Henry Maine and others, homogeneous. There the dual element appears, the tribal community at the top of the system, the village community at the bottom of the system. But in India a new factor is introduced by the equation of the two elements with two different races—the tribal element being Aryan, and the village element non-Aryan. Race-origins are there still kept up and rigidly adhered to. They have not been crushed out, as in Europe, by political or economical activity.

But if crushed out of prominent recognition in Europe, are we, therefore, to conclude that their relics do not exist in peasant custom? My argument is that we cannot have such close parallels in India and in England without seeing that they virtually tell the same story in both countries. It would require a great deal to prove that customs, which in India belong now to non-Aryan aborigines and are rejected by the Aryans, are in Europe the heritage of the Aryan race.

The objections to my theory have been formulated by Mr. Ashley, who follows Mr. Seebohm and M. Fustel de Coulanges as an adherent of the chronological method of studying institutions. Like the old school of antiquaries, this new school of investigators into the history of institutions gets back to the period of Roman history, and there stops. Mr. Ashley suggests that because Cæsar describes the Celtic Britons as pastoral, therefore agriculture in Britain must be post-Celtic. I will not stop to raise the question as to who were the tribes from which Cæsar obtained his evidence. But it will suffice to point out that if Cæsar is speaking of the Aryan Celts of Britain—and this much seems certain—he only proves of them what Tacitus proves of the Aryan Teutons, what the sagas prove of the Aryan Scandinavians, what the vedas prove of the Aryan Indians, what philology, in short, proves of the primitive Aryans generally, namely, that they were distinctly hunters and warriors, and hated and despised the tillers of the soil.

It does not, in point of fact, then, help the question as to the origin of agricultural rites and usages to turn to Aryan history at all. In this emergency Roman history is appealed to. But this is just one of those cases where a small portion of the facts are squeezed in to do duty for the whole.

Both M. Fustel de Coulanges and Mr. Seebohm think that if a Roman origin can be *primâ facie* shown for the economical side of agricultural institutions, there is nothing more to be said. But they leave out of consideration a whole set of connected institutions. Readers of Mr. Frazer's *Golden Bough* are now in possession of facts which it would take a very long time to explain. They see that side by side with agricultural economics is agricultural religion, of great rudeness and barbarity, of considerable complexity, and bearing the stamp of immense antiquity. The same villagers who were the observers of those rules of economics which are thought to be due to Roman origin were also observers of ritual and usages which are known to be savage in theory and practice. Must we, then, say that all this ritual and usage are Roman? or must we go on ignoring them as elements in the argument as to the origin of agricultural institutions? One or the other of these alternatives must, I contend, be accepted by the inquirer.

Because the State has chosen or been compelled for political reasons to lift up peasant economics into manorial legal rules, thus forcibly divorcing this portion of peasant life from its natural associations, there is no reason why students should fix upon this arbitrary proceeding as the point at which to begin their examination into the origin of village agriculture. Manorial tenants pay their dues to the lord, lot out their lands in intermixed strips, cultivate in common, and perform generally all those interesting functions of village life with which Mr. Seebohm has made us familiar. But, in close and intimate connection with these selfsame agricultural economical proceedings, it is the same body of manorial tenants who perform irrational and rude customs, who carry the last sheaf of corn represented in human or animal form, who sacrifice animals to their earth deities, who carry fire round fields and crops, who, in a scarcely disguised ritual, still worship deities which there is little difficulty in recognising as the counterparts of those religious goddesses of India who are worshipped and venerated by non-Aryan votaries. Christianity has not followed the lead of politics, and lifted all this portion of peasant agricultural life into something that is religious and definite. And because it remains sanctioned by tradition, we must, in considering origins, take it into account in conjunction with those economic practices which have been unduly emphasised in the history of village institutions. In India primitive economics and religion go hand in hand as part of the village life of the people; in England primitive economics and *survivals* of old religions, which we call folklore, go hand in hand as part of the village life of the people. And it is not in the province of students to separate one from the other when they are considering the question of origin.

This is practically the whole of my argument from the folklore point of view. But it is not the whole of the argument against the theory of the Roman origin of the village community. I cannot on this occasion re-state what this argument is, as it is set forth at some length in my book. But I should like to point out that it is in reality supported by arguments to be drawn from ethnological facts. Mr. Ashley surrenders to my view of the question the important point that ethnological data, derived from craniological investigation, fit in "very readily with the supposition that under the Celtic, and therefore under the Roman rule, the cultivating class was largely composed of the pre-Celtic race; and allows us to believe that the agricultural population was but little disturbed." Economically it was certainly not disturbed by the Romans. If the agricultural implements known to and used by the Romans were never used in Britain after their departure; if the old methods of land-surveying under the agrimensores is not to be traced in Britain as a continuing system; if wattle and daub, rude, uncarpentered trees turned root upwards to form roofs, were the leading principles of house-architecture, it cannot be alleged that the Romans left behind any permanent marks of their economical standard upon the "little disturbed agricultural population." Why, then, should they be credited with the introduction of a system of lordship and serf-bound tenants, when both lordship and serfdom are to be traced in lands where Roman power has never penetrated, under conditions almost exactly similar to the feudal elements in Europe? If it be accepted that the early agricultural population of Britain was non-Aryan; if we find non-Aryan agricultural rites and festivals surviving as folklore among the peasants of to-day; why should it be necessary, why should it be accepted as a reasonable hypothesis, to go to the imperial and advanced economics of Rome to account for those other elements in the composition of the village community which, equally with the rites and festivals, are to be found paralleled among the non-Aryan population living under an Aryan lordship in India? The only argument for such a process is one of convenience. It does so happen that the Roman theory *may* account for some of the English phenomena. But, then, the Celtic and Teutonic, or Aryan theory also accounts for the same English phenomena, and, what is more, it accounts for other phenomena not reckoned by the Roman theory. My proposition is that the history of the village community in Britain is the history of the economical condition of the non-Aryan aborigines; that the history of the tribal community is the history of the Aryan conquerors, who appear as overlords; and that the Romans, except as another wave of Aryan conquerors at an advanced stage of civilisation, had very little to do with shaping the village institutions of Britain.[495]

It is necessary before leaving this subject to take note of a point which may lead, and in fact has led to misconception of the argument. I have stated that all custom, rite, and belief which is Aryan custom, rite, and belief, as distinct from that which is pre-Aryan—pre-Celtic in our own country—must have a position in the tribal system, and I have said that custom, rite, and belief which cannot be traced back to the tribal system may be safely pronounced to be pre-tribal in origin and therefore pre-Celtic, to have survived, that is, from the people whom the Celts found in occupation of the country when first they landed on its shores. I did not interrupt my statement of the case to point out one important modification of it, because this modification has nothing to do with the great mass of custom and belief now surviving as folklore, but I will deal with this modification now so that I may clear up any misconception. We have already ascertained that over and above the custom and belief, which may be traced back to their tribal origins, there are both customs and beliefs which owe their origin to psychological conditions, and there are myths surviving as folk-tales or legends which owe their origin to the primitive philosophy of earliest man. Neither of these departments of folklore enters into the question of race development. The first may be called post-ethnologic because they arise in a political society of modern civilisation which transcends the boundaries of race; the second may be called pre-ethnologic, because they arise in a savage society before the great races had begun their distinctive evolution. The point about this class of

272

belief is that it has never been called upon to do duty for social improvement and organisation, has never been specialised by the Celt or Teuton in Europe, nor by other branches of the same race. The myth alone of these two groups of folklore could have had an ethnological influence, and this must have been very slight. It remained in the mind of Aryan man, but has never descended to the arena of his practical life. It has influenced his practical life indirectly of course, but it has never become a brick in the building up of his practical life. This distinction between custom and belief which are tribal and custom and belief which are not tribal, is of vast importance. It has been urged against the classification of custom, rite, and belief into ethnological groups that it does not allow for the presence of a great mass of belief, primitive in character and undoubtedly Aryan, if not in origin at all events in fact. The objection is not valid. The custom, rite, and belief which can be classified as distinctively Aryan is that portion of the whole corpus of primitive custom, rite, and belief, which was used by the Aryan-speaking folk in the building up of their tribal organisation. They divorced it by this use from the general primitive conceptions, and developed it along special lines. It is in its special characteristics that this belief belongs to the tribal system of the Aryans, not in its general characteristics. Not every custom, rite, and belief was so used and developed. The specialisation caused the deliberate rejection or neglect of much custom, rite, and belief which was opposed to the new order of things, and did not affect the practical doings of Aryan life.

There are thus three elements to consider: (1) the custom, rite, and belief specialised by the Aryan-speaking people in the formation and development of their tribal system; (2) the custom, rite, and belief rejected or neglected by the Aryan tribesmen; and (3) the belief which was not affected by or used for the tribal development, but which, not being directly antagonistic to it, remained with the primitive Aryan folk as survivals of their science and philosophy.

For ethnological purposes we have only to do with the first group. It is definite, and it is capable of definite recognition within the tribe. When once it was brought into the tribal system it ceased to exist in the form in which it was known to general savage belief; it developed highly specialised forms, took its part in the formation of a great social force, a great fighting and conquering force, a great migratory force. In accomplishing this task it grew into a solid system, each part in touch with all other parts, each part an essential factor in the ever-active forces which it helped to fashion and control.

It is in this wise that we must study its survivals wherever they are to be found, and the study must be concentrated within certain definite ethnographic areas. If I were to pursue the subject and choose for my study the folklore of Britain, I should have to object to the treatment accorded to British custom, rite, and belief by even so great an authority as Mr. Frazer, because they are used not as parts of a tribal system but as mere detritus of a primitive system of science, or philosophy. According to my views they had long since become separated from any such system and it is placing them in a wrong perspective, giving them a false value, associating them with elements to which they have no affinity to divorce them from their tribal connection. The custom, rite, and belief which were tribal, when they were brought to their present ethnographic area, cannot be considered in the varied forms of their survival except by restoration to the tribal organisation from which they were torn when they began their life as survivals.

What I have endeavoured to explain in this way are the principles which should govern folklore research in relation to ethnological conditions. The differing races which made up the peoples of Europe before the era of political history must have left their distinctive remains in folklore, if folklore is rightly considered as the traditional survivals of the prehistory period. To get at and classify these remains we must be clear as to the problems which surround inquiry into them. The solution of these problems will place us in possession of a mass of survivals in folklore which are naturally associated with each other, and which stand apart from other survivals also naturally associated with each other. In these two masses we may detect the main influences of the great tribal races and the non-tribal races. We cannot, I think, get much beyond this. We may, perhaps, here and there, detect smaller race divisions—Celtic, Teutonic, Scandinavian or other distinctions, according to the area of investigation—but these will be less apparent, less determinable, and will not be so valuable to historical science as the larger division. To this we shall by proper investigation be indebted for the solution of many doubtful points of the prehistoric period, and it is in this respect that it will appeal to the student of folklore.

FOOTNOTES:

[466] Mr. Nutt's presidential address to the Folklore Society in 1899 does not, I think, disprove my theory. It ignores it, and confines the problem to legend and folk-tale. Mr. Nutt's powerful, but not conclusive, study is to be found in *Folklore*, x. 71-86, and my reply and correspondence resulting therefrom are to be found at pp. 129-149.

[467] MacCulloch, *Childhood of Fiction*, 90-101; Greenwell, *British Barrows*, 17, 18.

[468] *Custom and Myth*, 76.

[469] *Myth, Ritual and Religion*, ii. 215, compared with Gomme, *Ethnology in Folklore*, 16.

[470] I have discussed this point at greater length in *Folklore*, xii. 222-225.

[471] Mr. J. O'Beirne Crowe in *Journ. Arch. and Hist. Assoc. of Ireland*, 3rd ser., i. 321.

[472] Rhys, *Lectures on Welsh Philology*, 32; *Celtic Heathendom*, 216; *Celtic Britain*, 67-75; Rhys and Brynmôr-Jones, *Welsh People*, 83.

[473] The continental evidence has been collected together in convenient shape by modern scholars: thus Mr. Stock, in his work on *Cæsar de bello Gallico*, notes and compares the evidence of Cæsar, Strabo, Diodorus Siculus, Ammianus Marcellinus, Mela, Lucan, and Pliny as it has been interpreted by modern scholars (see pp. 107-113), and he is followed by Mr. T. Rice Holmes in his study of *Cæsar's Conquest of Gaul*, pp. 532-536. The Druidic cult of belief in immortality, metempsychosis, ritual of the grove, augury, human sacrifice, is all set out and discussed. These are the continental Druidic beliefs and practices, and they may be compared with the Druidic Irish beliefs and practices in Eugene O'Curry's *Manners and Customs of the Ancient Irish*, lect. ix. and x. vol. ii. pp. 179-228, and Dr. Joyce's *Social History of Ancient Ireland*, i. 219-248, where "the points of agreement and difference between Irish and Gaulish Druids" are discussed. Mr. Elton notices the difference between the continental and the British Druids, but ascribes it to unequal development (*Origins of Eng. Hist.*, 267-268). Cæsar's well-known account of the wickerwork sacrifice is very circumstantial. It is not repeated

by either Diodorus or Strabo, who both refer to individual human sacrifice. Pliny introduces the mistletoe, oak, and serpent cults, and the other three authorities are apparently dependent upon their predecessors.

[474] The mixture of Celt and Iberian is very ably dealt with by Mr. Holmes in his *Cæsar's Conquest of Gaul*, pp. 245-322, and by Ripley, *Races of Europe*, 461, 467, together with cap. vii. and xii.; see also Sergi, *Mediterranean Race*, cap. xii.

[475] The intermarrying of the Picts with the Celts of the district they conquered is mentioned in all the chronicles as an important and significant rite, which determined the succession to the Pictish throne through the female side (Skene's *Chron. of the Picts and Scots*, 40, 45, 126, 319, 328, 329). Beda, i. cap. i., mentions female succession. Skene discusses this point in *Celtic Scotland*, i. 232-235, and McLennan includes it in his evidence from anthropological data (*Studies in Anc. Hist.*, 99).

[476] Mr. Seebohm is the best authority for the importance of the non-tribesman in Celtic law (*Tribal System in Wales*, 54-60).

[477] The local cults in Great Britain which are not Celtic in form, and do not seem to be connected with Celtic religion on any analogy, are those relating to Cromm Cruaich, referred to in the *Tripartite Life of St. Patrick* (see Whitley Stokes in *Revue Celtique*, i. 260, xvi. 35-36; O'Curry, *MS. Materials of Anc. Irish History*, 538-9; Joyce, *Social History of Ancient Ireland*, i. 275-276; Rhys, *Celtic Heathendom*, 200-201). I do not follow Rhys in his identification of this cult as a part of the ceremonies on mounds, and suggest that Mr. Bury in his *Life of St. Patrick*, 123-125, gives the clue to the purely local character of this idol worship which I claim for it. Similarly the overthrow of the temple at Goodmanham, Godmundingham, described by Beda, ii. cap. 13, with its priest who was not allowed to carry arms, or to ride on any but a mare, is the destruction of a successful local cult, not of a national or tribal religion. I confess that Dr. Greenwell's observations in connection with his barrow discoveries (*British Barrows*, 286-331) are in favour of an early Anglican cultus, but I think his facts may be otherwise interpreted, and in any case they confirm my view of the special localisation of this cult.

[478] Rev. W. G. Lawes in *Journ. Royal Geographical Soc.*, new series, iii. 615. *Cf.* Romilly, *From my Verandah*, 249; *Journ. Indian Archipelago* vi. 310, 329.

[479] Dieffenbach, *Travels in New Zealand*, ii. 7, 10, 59.

[480] *Trans. Ethnol. Soc.*, new series, iii. 235.

[481] Colquhoun's *Amongst the Shans*, 52; Bastian, *Oestl. Asien*, i. 119.

[482] Skeat and Blagden, *Pagan Races of the Malay Peninsula*, i. 228; and compare Rev. P. Favre, *Account of Wild Tribes of the Malayan Peninsula* (Paris, 1865), p. 95.

[483] *Ethnology in Folklore*, 45; and see Tylor, *Primitive Culture*, i. 112-113.

[484] Stanley, *Through the Dark Continent*, i. 253. *Cf.* Burrows, *Land of the Pigmies*, 180, for the state of fear which the pygmies cause to their neighbours.

[485] Latham, *Descriptive Ethnology*, ii. 457.

[486] *Journ. As. Soc. Bengal*, 1866, ii. 158; see also Geiger, *Civilisation of Eastern Iranians*, i. 20-21.

[487] *Journ. Ceylon As. Soc.*, 1865-1866, p. 3. *Journ. Ind. Archipelago*, i. 328; Tennant, *Ceylon*, i. 331; J. F. Campbell, *My Circular Notes*, 155-157.

[488] Landtman, *Origin of Priesthood*, p. 82, quoting the original authorities.

[489] Vigfusson and Powell, *Corpus Boreale*, ii. 38; and see i. 408.

[490] *Roman Festivals*, 264.

[491] Rhys, *Lectures on Welsh Philology*, 196.

[492] *Life of St. Guthlac*, by Felix of Crowland, edit. C. W. Goodwin, pp. 21, 23, 27, 35.

[493] *Life of St. Guthlac*, p. 43.

[494] Wright, *Essays on Popular Superstitions of the Middle Ages*, ii. 4-10.

[495] The substance of this part of my subject, with more elaboration in detail, is taken from a paper I contributed to the *Transactions of the Folklore Congress*, 1891.